Monkee Music: Second Edition

Andrew Hickey

BY THE SAME AUTHOR:

Non-Fiction

- Sci-Ence! Justice Leak!

- The Beatles In Mono

- The Beach Boys On CD: vol 1 - 1961-1969

- The Beach Boys On CD: vol 2 - 1970-1984

- The Beach Boys On CD: vol 3 - 1985-2015

- An Incomprehensible Condition:An Unauthorised Guide To Grant Morrison's Seven Soldiers

- Preservation: The Kinks' Music 1964-1974

- California Dreaming: The LA Pop Music Scene and the 1960s

- The Black Archive: The Mind Robber

- Welcome to the Multiverse: An Unauthorised Guide to Grant Morrison's Multiversity (ebook only)

- Fifty Stories for Fifty Years: An Unauthorised Look at Doctor Who

Fiction

- Ideas and Entities (short stories)

- Faction Paradox: Head of State

- Doctor Watson Investigates: The Curse of the Scarlet Neckerchief (ebook only)

- Destroyer: A Black Magic Story

- The Basilisk Murders: A Sarah Turner Mystery

- The Glam Rock Murders: A Sarah Turner Mystery

4

For Holly

Contents

Introduction

Why would anyone write a book on the Monkees' music? Everyone knows they didn't even play their own instruments.[1] As *The Simpsons* put it so memorably, "That's not even Mike Nesmith's real hat!"

Except that's not the whole story, not by a long way.

The Monkees didn't start as a band; rather they started as a TV show about a band, and as Micky Dolenz often points out, in those early years criticising them for not being a real band was much like criticising Leonard Nimoy for not really being able to pilot a starship.

But very quickly, they took control of their music and, Pinocchio-like, became a real band. Contrary to myth, many of the Monkees' most famous hits, including "Daydream Believer", "Pleasant Valley Sunday" and "Randy Scouse Git", feature the band themselves, playing as well as singing.

---

[1]"And by the way, what do you mean, or does anybody mean for that matter, 'play their own instruments'? Whose instruments do you suggest we play? Or is this just a parroted phrase, whose garbled meaning only bothers serious writers?" - Michael Nesmith, posting to alt.music.monkees, 1996

And a remarkable thing resulted. The four Monkees hadn't been chosen for their musical compatibility, and all four had very different ideas about what music they should make once they had the ability to take control of their own musical direction. Michael Nesmith wanted to make straightforward country music and oblique psychedelic rock. Davy Jones wanted to do good old-fashioned tunes his dad could hum. Micky Dolenz wanted to be James Brown, when he wasn't busy doing experimental electronic noises. And Peter Tork wanted to be a folk banjo player.

Of course, these four strong forces all pulling in different directions couldn't last long. It was barely two years between the band's first single, "Last Train to Clarksville", and Peter Tork's departure, which marked the beginning of the end for the band. But in that time, the band released six albums, at least four of which are qualified masterpieces, as good as anything by any of their more critically-acclaimed contemporaries.

This book, then, deals with the music - not the TV and film appearances, not the infighting or the personalities, except insofar as those impact the music the band made. In it I examine every song released by the Monkees throughout their career.

As many of these songs were recorded on multiple occasions and in multiple versions, and have been released on multiple CDs, I have had to find some way to sensibly deal with this. My rule is - if a song appears on a studio album, I deal with all recordings of it in the entry for that album. If it doesn't appear on a studio album, I deal with all versions of it on the first album for which it is available as a bonus track, and if it only appears on a live album I deal with it on the live album. Unless otherwise stated, I'm using the "deluxe editions" of the albums, when those are available. In the case of *The Monkees* and *More of the Monkees*, I'm using the "super deluxe" editions – those albums were released as two-CD deluxe versions, but then more recently released as three-CD versions like the deluxe versions of the post-*Pisces* albums. There is one exception to this, which is the song "Propinquity", which appears on the deluxe edition of *The Monkees,* but *not* on the "super deluxe" version – this has still been dealt with in the entry for *The Monkees*.

A note on the ordering of the bonus tracks – I have dealt with songs on albums in the order in which they appear on the albums, but as there is no "canonical" ordering for the bonus tracks, they are dealt with in orders that seem sensible to me given issues such as page layout and wanting to avoid dealing with too many similar songs in a row (though the latter is sometimes unavoidable). If the location of a song isn't immediately apparent, the song index at the back of the print version should provide the information you need. (Ebook readers can, of course, locate it by text search).

Sometimes I may appear harsh about some of this music. That's because some of it is, frankly, awful. But given that the Monkees recorded over two hundred separate songs (many in multiple versions) between 1966 and 1970, while also touring the world, appearing in a feature film, making fifty-eight episodes of a TV show plus a TV special, and in that time also trying to do all the normal young-adult things like get married and have children, what's amazing is that most of it *isn't*.

Likewise, I may seem harder on some band members' output than on others, but that doesn't mean I have anything less than the greatest respect for their achievements. This is a band that deliberately gave up on commercial success in order to create the music they wanted to - and which yet still managed to have some of their greatest commercial successes after doing just that.

This second edition of the book has been revised heavily. A lot has happened in the six years since I initially wrote this book – Davy Jones' tragic death, Michael Nesmith coming out of retirement, a new Monkees album, and more – and this is reflected in the text. A lot of the text is updated to reflect new information, and new perspectives on the band, but the basic thrust of the book – that the Monkees were and are a band who should be taken seriously as musicians – remains the same.

I saw three of the Monkees perform live, in May 2011 (and since then I have seen them in other combinations, and solo, on several occasions). They played over forty songs, almost every one a classic piece of pop, and did so while entertaining for every second a crowd that had come only to hear the hits. They're some of the hardest-working entertainers I've ever seen, and even if they hadn't been able to play a note, that wouldn't have made a difference.

But during the show, Peter Tork played keyboard, guitar, banjo, french horn and bass, Micky Dolenz played guitar, drums and tympani, and Davy Jones played guitar and percussion. Of course I've no idea if they were 'their own' instruments, or if they were rented. But that doesn't matter.

Like the songs, they made them their own.

The Bubblegum Period (October 1966 - January 1967)

The Monkees

The Monkees' first album was put together very quickly, in anticipation of the band's TV debut. For the pilot of the TV show, several songs by Screen Gems[2] writers Tommy Boyce and Bobby Hart had been recorded by Hart's band the Candy Store Prophets, as the four band members hadn't yet been cast. As a reward for their work on the pilot, after sessions with legendary producer Snuff Garrett, who wanted Davy Jones to be sole lead vocalist, had broken down, Boyce and Hart were allowed to supervise the initial batch of sessions for the show and the first album (albeit with assistance from the more experienced Jack Keller on early sessions).

In fact, so much material was needed for the show that songs originally recorded during these sessions, but put aside or only used on the TV, would turn up on records (sometimes in rerecorded form) for the rest of the band's career. Sometimes

---

[2]The television division of Columbia Pictures, responsible for the Monkees' TV show. Screen Gems had bought out Don Kirshner's music publishing company Aldon in 1963, and this company published the songs the Monkees performed. Screen Gems was also co-owner, with RCA Records, of ColGems, the label the Monkees' albums were released on, and owned ColPix, a label to which both Nesmith and Jones had been signed prior to forming the Monkees.

15

two sessions would be going on at once, with Michael Nesmith (who was allowed to write and produce two tracks on the album) running one session in one part of town while Boyce and Hart were running another elsewhere.

Surprisingly enough, the finished product is a rather good album of its type. While nowhere near as musically interesting as the results once the band took control of their own career, there's still some great pop music mixed in with the filler.

(Theme From) The Monkees

Writers: Tommy Boyce and Bobby Hart

Lead vocalist: Micky Dolenz

Other Monkees present: None

Producers: Tommy Boyce, Bobby Hart and Jack Keller

Or "Hey hey, we're the Candy Store Prophets", as with the exception of Dolenz's vocals this track, like much of *The Monkees*, was performed by Boyce and Hart's band (Gerry McGee on guitar, Larry Taylor on bass and Billy Lewis on drums), with augmentation from a couple of session musicians - percussionist Gene Estes (a talented jazz vibraphone player, here reduced to hitting a tambourine on the off-beat, though he may also provide the finger-snaps) and guitarists Wayne Erwin and Louie Shelton. This group of musicians (with Hart on occasional keyboards and Boyce on backing vocals) would provide almost all the backing for the album.

While harmonically simple (staying for the most part in the key of Am in the verses apart from one V-of-V chord, and staying entirely in C for the choruses, and not using any chord more complex than a 7th), like most Boyce and Hart songs, the track is full of musical ideas. Starting with the famous 'falling' drum sound, the verse then combines Larry Taylor's strutting bassline with fingersnapping and hi-hat to create an impressive air of swaggering cool, before going into the famous chorus.

The track is very blatantly "inspired" by the Dave Clark Five's "Catch Us if You Can", down to starting with a single throbbing bass note and "Here [we/they] come..." but is far more meticulously constructed, and a much more memorable record.

The one weak spot of the track is the way it shifts gears out of the chorus into the second verse, which doesn't quite come off, but then the track really kicks off in the second chorus, with the key change up a tone for "We're just trying to be friendly..."

The guitar solo - surprisingly late in the track, after the third chorus - is a pastiche of George Harrison's Chet Atkins imitations, and the whole thing then builds to a powerful climax with a repeat of the second chorus with its key change.

Lyrically, the song is a perfect introduction to TV show for which it was the theme, though I'm not too keen on the line "we're the young generation and we've got something to say", which seems slightly patronising - especially since at the time the band members were prevented from saying anything even slightly controversial.

Saturday's Child

Writer: David Gates

Lead vocalist: Micky Dolenz

Other Monkees present: None

Producers: Tommy Boyce, Bobby Hart and Jack Keller

Astonishingly for something written by the man who would go on to form Bread, one of the softest of all AOR bands, "Saturday's Child" is close to heavy metal, especially in the mono mix (which is a much more powerful track than the comparatively weak stereo version). The lumbering bottom-string guitar riff and throbbing bass part could almost be Deep Purple or early Black Sabbath, though Dolenz's soft, faintly sinister vocal is as far from that style as you can get - Dolenz at his best being one of the most controlled vocalists in the business, and heavy metal vocals being all about (perceived) loss of control.

This track was originally recorded with Peter Tork on lead vocals, and while he's officially not on the finished track, one of the double-tracked backing vocal parts singing the chorus countermelody does sound an awful lot like him.

I Wanna Be Free

Writers: Tommy Boyce and Bobby Hart

Lead vocalist: Davy Jones

Other Monkees present: None

Producers: Tommy Boyce and Bobby Hart

And from "Saturday's Child" we go to "Sunday Morning"... this track in its finished version bears quite an astonishing resemblance to the later Velvet Underground song, both harmonically and in the general shape of its melody and its feel.

Which makes it all the more surprising that while the finished version is a gentle ballad based around some lovely, sparse acoustic guitars, harpsichord and a string quartet, earlier that day the same song had been recorded in a totally different arrangement owing far more to Dylan's "Like a Rolling Stone", with Dolenz and Jones singing the verses in unison and Dolenz, rather than Jones, taking the middle eight. (This faster version is available on various compilations and as a bonus track on the Deluxe Edition of *The Monkees*, as well as being featured in the TV show).

Truth be told, the fast, Hammond-led version that was originally attempted suited the lyrics far better than the version finally released on the album, because the lyrics are anything but romantic. The protagonist of the song is quite possibly one of the most unpleasant in any song, insisting on utter devotion from his girlfriend ("say you'll always be my friend, babe/We can make it to the end, babe"), but on freedom from all commitments himself ("doing all those things without any strings to tie me down"). His girlfriend is not even allowed to say that she loves him - just that she likes him - but is to give him total freedom.

That said, this unpleasant - frankly almost psychopathic - lyric is backed by one of the most beautiful arrangements on any Monkees record, nicely understated rather than over-lush, and Jones' wistful vocal almost sells the song.

Tomorrow's Gonna Be Another Day

Writers: Tommy Boyce and Steve Venet

Lead vocalist: Micky Dolenz

Other Monkees present: None

Producers: Tommy Boyce and Bobby Hart

A quick knock-off track that probably took about as long to write as it does to listen to, this seems to have been written with the rough aim of trying to write something that sounded like the Beatles' more country-flavoured songs like "Another Girl", though the harmonica part and "hey hey hey hey" vocal line sound more reminiscent of the Rolling Stones.

The vaguely train-like rhythm (and "I'm gonna catch me the fastest train" lyric) suggest that this was essentially a failed attempt at writing "Last Train to Clarksville", although this song was originally written in 1965 and released by Sir Raleigh and the Cupons, a band fronted by future Buffalo Springfield drummer Dewey Martin. However, on its own merits this is a perfectly pleasant country-blues number.

Papa Gene's Blues

Writer: Michael Nesmith

Lead vocalist: Michael Nesmith

Other Monkees present: Micky Dolenz (backing vocals), Peter Tork (guitar), Davy Jones (vocals)[3]

Producer: Michael Nesmith

If this sounds very different from the rest of the album up to this point, it's because rather than being a Boyce/Hart production with an augmented Candy Store Prophets, this is a Nesmith production with members of the Wrecking Crew[4], who would play on most of Nesmith's productions from this time. It's also the closest thing to a group performance on the album, with Tork one of the several acoustic guitar players (as well as possibly providing some backing vocals on a rejected mix) and Dolenz harmonising with Nesmith throughout.

Already, Nesmith was pushing for the band to have creative involvement in their own records, and so this track more than any others on this album points the way forward to the music the band would be making from their third album onwards.

---

[3] Jones is not clearly audible on the finished track, but examination of the isolated backing track shows leakage from Jones singing the lead vocal. That leakage is presumably also on the finished version, and Jones may be in the backing vocal stack.

[4] A term for the group of session musicians who played on most L.A.-based hit records in the 1960s, including drummers Hal Blaine and Jim Gordon, guitarist Glen Campbell and others. Note that Carol Kaye, a bass player who was often part of the Wrecking Crew, has claimed to have played on many Monkees hits. However, Ms Kaye's claims are, at best, unreliable, and she is only known to have played on two Monkees songs released during the 60s, both album tracks on *More of the Monkees*.

A Latin-infused country song, with tons of percussion, this is musically not much more sophisticated than Boyce and Hart's tracks, though much fuller sounding (and with some wonderful guitar work, presumably by James Burton). But lyrically, while still being a basic love song, there's an awareness of language that is mostly absent from the Boyce/Hart material.

Nesmith's lyrics are often slightly archaic in their choice of words, and the tumbling Dylanesque phrases here ("So take my hand, I'll start my journey, free from all the helpless worry, that besets a man when he's alone") are a joy. And the combination of Nesmith and Dolenz's vocals, while all too rare, is by far the best vocal blend the band had.

Easily the highlight of the album.

Take a Giant Step

Writers: Gerry Goffin and Carole King

Lead vocalist: Micky Dolenz

Other Monkees present: None

Producers: Tommy Boyce and Bobby Hart

The first of Goffin and King's many attempts at cod-psychedelia for the Monkees (although the song wasn't written specifically for them – it had earlier been recorded by the Rising Sons, a blues-rock band featuring Ry Cooder and Taj Mahal, though their version wasn't released until the 1990s), this works about as well as you'd expect two Brill Building songwriters attempting to be down with the kids by inviting you to "take a giant step outside your mind" to work.

That said, there are points of interest - there's some nice pseudo-Indian oboe playing (by Bob Cooper), and the melody is as strong as all King's work, especially the "It's time you learned to live again at last" over descending chords, which is reminiscent of much of her best work.

But the whole thing sounds like it was written and recorded by people who'd heard about psychedelia and not understood it, but thought "well, if this is what the kids are listening to..."

Last Train to Clarksville

Writers: Tommy Boyce and Bobby Hart

Lead vocalist: Micky Dolenz

Other Monkees present: None

Producers: Tommy Boyce and Bobby Hart

Recorded toward the end of the sessions for this album, this became the Monkees' first single and first number one. Based roughly around the structure of the Beatles' "Paperback Writer", which like this stays on G7 for the whole verse before switching briefly to C7 in the chorus, this was inspired by hearing only the tag of that song and thinking that McCartney was singing "take the last train".

The almost-moronic guitar riff (based around an open G chord) was inspired by "Day Tripper", but when combined with the train rhythm and the obsession on a single chord sounds almost like "Smokestack Lightning", if "Smokestack Lightning" had been recorded by L.A. pop musicians rather than Chicago blues ones.

Of all the Boyce/Hart tracks on this album, this one is far and away the best thought out, both lyrically (actually having a story to it, with a very mildly anti-war sentiment) and musically - it's simplistic, but in all the right ways, the product of people who've been listening to every record on the radio and stripped all of them down to their most basic essentials, then rebuilt them into a pop masterpiece.

I may occasionally seem a little harsh on Boyce and Hart in this book, and it's true that some of their work was sub-par, but that's because they were producing such a lot of music in such a small amount of time. When they were on form, as they were here, they were as good as anyone.

This Just Doesn't Seem to Be My Day

Writers: Tommy Boyce and Bobby Hart

Lead vocalist: Davy Jones

Other Monkees present: None

Producers: Tommy Boyce, Bobby Hart and Jack Keller

Three decent musical ideas (a rewrite of "I've Just Seen a Face", a pesudo-Indian instrumental break, and a cello-led baroque middle eight) jammed together with no real thought as to how they'd work together. Combined with a poor, sloppily double-tracked vocal from Jones, the end result is less than the sum of its parts.

Let's Dance On

Writers: Tommy Boyce and Bobby Hart

Lead vocalist: Micky Dolenz

Other Monkees present: None

Producers: Tommy Boyce, Bobby Hart, and Jack Keller

A simple dance track based on the "Twist and Shout" riff, but also taking elements from two other songs that used the same chord sequence, "Hang on Sloopy" and "Little Latin Lupe Lou", this is generic garage band filler of the sort that was being churned out by the ton in 1965 and 66.

I'll Be True to You

Writers: Gerry Goffin and Russ Titelman

Lead vocalist: Davy Jones

Other Monkees present: None

Producers: Tommy Boyce, Bobby Hart and Jack Keller

A cover of a vapid ballad that had been a British hit for the Hollies the year earlier under the name "Yes I Will", presumably chosen because Jones, like the Hollies, was from Manchester, this is a terrible song performed terribly. Jones sings the song consistently flat, and in a weird stage-school accent with strangely mangled vowels.

The lowest point is when Jones recites the lyrics of one verse, rather than singing them, letting you - yes *you*, teenage American girl in your bedroom - know that he will be true to you and only you. Horrible.

Sweet Young Thing

Writers: Michael Nesmith, Gerry Goffin and Carole King

Lead vocalist: Michael Nesmith

Other Monkees present: Micky Dolenz (backing vocals), Peter Tork (guitar and backing vocals)

Producer: Michael Nesmith

A bizarre and rather brilliantly eccentric production, the distorted guitar and country fiddle combination here is eerily premonitory of the similar sound the Velvet Underground would get with John Cale's viola a few months later. Almost exhausting to listen to, with the bass and drums pummelling the listener into submission, and Nesmith sounding audibly out of breath by the end of the track, this is another highlight from Nesmith.

This was apparently written at Don Kirshner's insistence, Kirshner arguing that if Nesmith was going to insist on writing he should try to collaborate with more commercial songwriters. Nesmith apparently disliked the experience of collaborating with Goffin and King intensely, and the result is almost wilfully uncommercial.

But no matter how much Nesmith disliked working with Goffin and King, the results speak for themselves – this is one of the best things Nesmith did on these early Monkees albums, and shows that however frustrated Nesmith was with the process of making these records, that frustration could lead to truly exceptional music.

Gonna Buy Me a Dog

Writers: Tommy Boyce and Bobby Hart

Lead vocalist: Davy Jones and Micky Dolenz

Other Monkees present: None

Producers: Tommy Boyce and Bobby Hart

A terrible song made into a terrible "comedy" track, as an attempt to create a Ringo-style song for the album. Absolutely no redeeming features at all.

Strangely, Nesmith also produced a backing track for this song with his normal Wrecking Crew musicians (available as a bonus track on *The Monkees*) which has a slightly more bluesy feel. It still wouldn't set the musical world alight, though.

Bonus Tracks

I Don't Think You Know Me

Writers: Gerry Goffin and Carole King

Lead vocalist: Michael Nesmith/Micky Dolenz

Other Monkees present: none

Producer: Michael Nesmith

A song that the band tried recording on several occasions, this rather preachy Goffin/King song ("If you think my goals could be so trivial and small/I don't think you know me at all") has been released in three versions. The deluxe edition of *The Monkees* contains versions with Nesmith and Dolenz taking lead, singing over the same backing track, while *More of the Monkees* has a version with Tork on lead as a bonus. (In the revised "Super Deluxe" versions of these albums, the version with Nesmith on lead has been moved to *More of the Monkees*).

While it was never released at the time, this has become a staple of Monkees reunion tours, with Tork singing lead. It has some nice moments (the "Nowhere Man"-esque 'la la la' break) but has neither the power of Nesmith's songs nor the catchiness of the better Boyce/Hart tracks.

So Goes Love

Writers: Gerry Goffin and Carole King

Lead vocalist: Davy Jones

Other Monkees present: Peter Tork (guitar)

Producer: Michael Nesmith

A vaguely Latin-infused track with a lovely, jazzy arrangement, this has been released in two versions (on *Missing Links* and on *The Monkees* deluxe edition) which sound like the same performance but run at different speeds/keys. The faster version (on *Missing Links*) is definitely preferable.

Jones does a very creditable job on the verses, where he's comfortably within his range, but on the middle eight he's audibly straining at points.

All the King's Horses

Writer: Michael Nesmith

Lead vocalist: Michael Nesmith

Other Monkees present: Micky Dolenz, Peter Tork and Davy Jones (backing vocals)

Producer: Michael Nesmith

An early Nesmith song, originally recorded with his pre-Monkees trio, the imaginatively-named Mike, John, and Bill, this shows little sign of his later songwriting talent, but is still catchy enough that it's surprising it was not placed on the album, especially since it's apparently the only track on the entire CD to feature all four Monkees (though Jones is inaudible).

Propinquity (I've Just Begun to Care)

Writer: Michael Nesmith

Lead vocalist: Michael Nesmith

Other Monkees present: None

Producer: Michael Nesmith

And here we have Nesmith's first ever songwriting masterpiece. A gentle, beautiful country song, with the chorus line "I've known you for a long time but I've just begun to care", Nesmith would record this three times. The version released on the deluxe edition of *The Monkees* (but oddly *not* on the more recent three-CD "Super Deluxe" version – this is the only performance not available in some form on the most recent expanded editions of the albums) is a demo, with John London

(Nesmith's former bandmate in Mike, John, and Bill and his stand-in for the TV show) on bass and Nesmith on guitar.

Nesmith would re-record this with a full band in 1969 (that version is on *Missing Links vol 3* and the *Instant Replay* deluxe edition) and then again with the First National Band on his third solo album, *Nevada Fighter*. All these versions are wonderful, but this early version is possibly the best. The line "I've seen you make a look of love from just an icy stare" is still possibly the best line in any Monkees song.

Of You

Writers: Bill and John Chadwick

Lead vocalist: Michael Nesmith

Other Monkees present: Micky Dolenz (backing vocals)

Producers: Michael Nesmith

Written by two of Nesmith's friends (Bill Chadwick had been in folk band the Survivors with him, and had actually auditioned to be in the Monkees as well), this was recorded at the same session that produced "Mary, Mary" for *More of the Monkees*, and is quite a pleasant country song, with some nice guitar picking from James Burton and Glen Campbell, but it's easy to see why it didn't make the quota of two Nesmith productions for the album.

Nesmith obviously liked the song - he tried rerecording his vocal in 1969 (that version is on the deluxe edition of *The Monkees Present*) but while it's infinitely better than some of the throwaways Boyce and Hart submitted for inclusion on *More of the*

Monkees, it's not up to the quality of Nesmith's own better work.

Kellogg's Jingle

Writers: Unknown (Tommy Boyce and Bobby Hart?)

Lead vocalist: Micky Dolenz

Other Monkees present: None

Producers: Unknown (Tommy Boyce and Bobby Hart ?)

A tiny snippet, presumably a Boyce and Hart production, used to introduce the TV show. Apparently Kellogg's cereals are "K-E-double-L-O-double-good Kellogg's best for you!"
So now you know.

Jokes (mono backing track)

Writers: Tommy Boyce and Bobby Hart

Monkees present: None

Producers: Tommy Boyce and Bobby Hart

A country-flavoured track with some fun fast picking from Louie Shelton, Gerry McGee, and Wayne Erwin, this bears a quite striking resemblance to some of Nesmith's work, most notably "Papa Gene's Blues" and "Down the Highway", but really much of his 1968 and 69 recordings. Melodically, it seems to be a slight variation, at least in the verse, on "When the Saints Go Marchin' In", although it's hard to tell how this would have sounded with vocals.

It's a shame that this was never taken any further at the time, as it would have perhaps provided a bit of a stylistic bridge between Nesmith's tracks on the album and the Boyce/Hart material, and thus given the album a little more of a sense of cohesion.

(I Prithee) Do Not Ask For Love

Writer: Michael Murphey

Lead vocalist: Davy Jones/Micky Dolenz

Other Monkees present: Peter Tork (guitar)

Producer: Michael Nesmith

Another song that was attempted by the band multiple times, this was recorded with Davy on lead over a harpsichord-based backing track (the version on *The Monkees* deluxe edition), with Micky on lead over the same backing track (available as a bonus track on *More of the Monkees*), with Peter over slow, heavily-reverbed electric guitar (on *The Birds, the Bees and the Monkees* deluxe edition) and finally with Peter over a sitar-based track (on the *33 1/3 Revolutions Per Monkee* TV special – the backing track for this version, but only the backing track, is on the *Instant Replay* deluxe edition).

My own favourite version is the reverbed version with Tork on vocals, but every version of this pseudo-Elizabethean ballad by Nesmith's friend Michael Martin Murphey is simply stunning.

More of the Monkees

With the huge success of *The Monkees* and "Last Train to Clarksville", the Monkees' music became a battleground. The Monkees (or at least Nesmith and Tork) wanted more control over their own music, but Don Kirshner wanted them to have less. He also wanted to move their music away from Boyce and Hart , who he regarded as second-rate, and away from California, to his New York base.

Boyce and Hart seemed, at first, to be unaware of this, and so recorded more than another album's worth of material, much of which would be released on subsequent albums, as well as a lot of...experimental...material that seemed to be mostly for their own amusement[5]. Meanwhile Kirshner had given primary responsibility for the Monkees' music to Jeff Barry, who produced tracks with the Wrecking Crew in L.A. and with other session musicians in New York.

On top of this, various of Kirshner's other writers were producing their own tracks for the Monkees, using L.A. musicians, and Nesmith was still producing tracks.

---

[5] Much of this material is available as bonus tracks on the deluxe and super deluxe editions of *More of the Monkees*, but as most of the songs were later released on other albums, they will be dealt with there.

The result is a much less focused album than the previous collection, with no sort of coherent artistic vision, not even the sort that comes from just having a single journeyman team produce the bulk of the material. The only vision here is Kirshner's rigid plan for what he believed an album needed to include - a hit single, a comedy track, a song with a girl's name in the title and so on.

The Monkees themselves had no input into the final song choices, the cover (featuring them modelling J.C. Penney clothes in a marketing tie-in) or the liner notes (by Kirshner, almost an autohagiography), and weren't impressed with the final result, which they famously had to buy from a shop, having not been properly informed of its release - Nesmith actually described it in an interview at the time as "probably the worst record in the history of the world".

This is unfair. The album is clearly packed with filler, but at least six of the twelve tracks are excellent by any standard (though as Nesmith had no taste for pop music he would possibly disagree about some of them). It doesn't match the more inventive, experimental music that was being made by other bands at the same time - this is no *Pet Sounds, Revolver* or *Freak Out!* - but as a collection of pop music, intended to be ephemeral and disposable, this stands up rather well.

Even so, it's the next four albums, rather than this one, that their artistic reputation rests on, even as this marks their commercial peak.

She

Writers: Tommy Boyce and Bobby Hart

Lead vocalist: Micky Dolenz

Other Monkees present: None

Producers: Tommy Boyce and Bobby Hart

After dominating the previous album, Boyce and Hart this time only get to provide two tracks for *More of the Monkees*, but both are far above the weak average of their work on the previous album. "She" is a stomping garage rocker with a two-chord verse (with a single passing chord), which becomes more interesting harmonically as it goes along, by adding an augmented chord in the bridge and having a *Pet Sounds*-esque minor third key change to the middle eight.

Despite this, however, "She" remains fundamentally a garage rock track, driven by fuzz guitar and Hart's Hammond organ stabbing out chords. While Boyce and Hart may have been journeyman songwriters who would turn their hand to anything, they were definitely at their best with this kind of proto-punk, and Dolenz manages to get across the adolescent lust and frustration of the lyrics perfectly.

Inspired by bands like Love and the Leaves (to whom Boyce and Hart gave "Words" when the Monkees' release of that track was put on hold), the sneery punk feel of this song would easily have fit on Love's first, eponymous album, with lines like "And now I know just why she keeps me hanging round/she needs someone to walk on, so her feet don't touch the ground."

I have been critical of Boyce and Hart's work at several points in this book, but when they were good they were extremely good, and here they were excellent.

When Love Comes Knockin' (At Your Door)

Writers: Neil Sedaka and Carole Bayer

Lead vocalist: Davy Jones

Other Monkees present: None

Producers: Neil Sedaka and Carole Bayer

One of several songs on this album recorded in New York, rather than in Los Angeles, this track by Neil Sedaka (then in a post-Beatles career slump that would see him able to write hits for others but not to have any himself) and lyricist Carole Bayer (later known as Carole Bayer Sager) is a typically jaunty Sedaka piece of fluff.

Harmonically more sophisticated than much of the more simplistic music on these early albums, it, rather unusually, changes key down a tone for the coda, and repeats the trick Sedaka used in his own hit "Breaking Up is Hard to Do" by having Jones sing two separate counter-melodies, with different lyrics, over the second half of the song.

Lyrically, though, it's a little more disturbing, with Jones urging an unnamed girl who's afraid of loving him to stop fighting and "open up and let him in"...

A precursor to the "Broadway rock" style Jones would use on several later albums, this is inventive enough, and at 1:46 short enough, not to outstay its welcome, but is still a comparatively weak track.

Mary, Mary

Writer: Michael Nesmith

Lead vocalist: Micky Dolenz

Other Monkees present: Peter Tork (guitar), Davy Jones (backing vocal)

Producer: Michael Nesmith

The Monkees were having to produce so much material for their TV show that this track was actually recorded at the same time as "Last Train to Clarksville", in a different studio - Nesmith using his usual Wrecking Crew members while the Candy Store Prophets were recording with Boyce and Hart.

This Nesmith track seems to have been written in an attempt at compromise with Don Kirshner, whose set formula for albums included as many songs as possible with girls' names in the title (so the girls with that name would buy them). Based around simplistic two-chord riffs (I-IV in the verses and IV-V in the bridges), this was intended as a bluesier track than it became, as Glen Campbell's attempts at playing the distinctive riff came out more country than blues. Nesmith had previously given the song to the Paul Butterfield Blues Band, and claims their rougher version is closer to his intention.

Nonetheless, of the non-single tracks on the album, this is definitely the one that most deserved more exposure. Of all Nesmith's songs this is probably the closest to the Monkees formula, with a Dolenz lead vocal, a simple hook, and simplistic, easily-learnable lyrics (though lines like "this one thing I will vow ya" and "I've done more now than a clear-thinking man would do" are still distinctively Nesmith), as well as being another one with vaguely creepy sexual politics ("Where you go

I will follow/Til I win your heart again/I'll walk beside you, but until then...").

Hold on Girl

Writers: Ben Raleigh, Billy Carr and Jack Keller

Lead vocalist: Davy Jones

Other Monkees present: Micky Dolenz (backing vocals)

Producers: Jeff Barry and Jack Keller

After having been an experienced studio hand helping Boyce and Hart with their early Monkees sessions, Jack Keller was granted two songs on *More of the Monkees* on condition that he co-produce with Jeff Barry, who had been put in charge of the hit-making portion of the Monkees juggernaut by Kirshner. The first, and better, of the two Keller tracks is this baroque-flavoured pop song with Davy on lead.

A very pleasant, but rather generic, pop song livened up by a nicely inventive keyboard break, and driven by what sounds like a sped-up electric piano, this is a decent piece of album filler that would never even have been considered as a single.

An earlier, slower take of the song, available as a bonus track and originally released on *Missing Links vol 2*, was produced by Boyce and Hart . That version had a harpsichord (played by Wrecking Crew member Michael Rubini) playing the keyboard part and a more authentically baroque arrangement, including oboe. There's not much to choose between the two tracks, but I find the Boyce/Hart version mildly more interesting.

Your Auntie Grizelda

Writers: Jack Keller and Diane Hildebrand

Lead vocalist: Peter Tork

Other Monkees present: None

Producers: Jeff Barry and Jack Keller

The second of Keller's tracks, this time co-written with Diane Hildebrand, who would go on to collaborate on several further Monkees tracks, was this three-chord song modelled very closely on the Rolling Stones' "19th Nervous Breakdown".

However, while the music was a fair approximation of that track, lyrically Keller and Hildebrand were aiming at a "protest song" and missed completely.

As a result, Tork, who was completely contemptuous of the song even though it was his first solo lead vocal (and one of only two he would get released during the Monkees' original career), and Barry decided to play it for laughs. Tork did a single take of the vocal, and spent most of the instrumental break making a variety of funny noises, squawks, screeches and clicks.

This saved the song, which was now given the "I'm Gonna Buy Me a Dog" Ringo-style novelty song place in Kirshner's album formula, and it's at least more imaginative than that track.

As Tork sang very few leads in the studio, this became a regular in the Monkees' set during their 60s shows, and has also made an appearance on every reunion show in which Tork has taken part, usually giving Tork a chance to clown around and engage in a bit of self-mockery about how few lead vocals he took.

(I'm Not Your) Steppin' Stone

Writers: Tommy Boyce and Bobby Hart

Lead vocalist: Micky Dolenz

Other Monkees present: None

Producers: Tommy Boyce and Bobby Hart

Originally given to Paul Revere and the Raiders, this became the B-side to "I'm a Believer" and charted separately at number 20 in the US.

Another proto-punk number like "She", and again driven by Hart's organ playing, this is if anything even simpler, being just a four-chord riff, all major chords, repeated over and over, except for the double-time bridge/coda, which reduces the number of chords to three.

One of the catchiest of the Monkees' early records, as well as one of the best-sounding, this shows that Boyce and Hart - and the Candy Store Prophets - were at their best as garage rockers. This especially goes for Larry Taylor whose simple, prowling bass-line drives this song, and who would later go on to play with Canned Heat and Tom Waits.

The simplicity and aggression of this song also made it a favourite for garage-band and punk cover versions, and it was later famously covered by the Sex Pistols, among many others. The Monkees' bubblegum image means that their music gets remembered as lighter and more frothy than it is, but in fact the Candy Store Prophets' music was heavily influenced by L.A. garage-punk musicians like Love, and tracks like this have a real kick to them.

Look Out (Here Comes Tomorrow)

Writer: Neil Diamond

Lead vocalist: Davy Jones

Other Monkees present: Micky Dolenz and Peter Tork (backing vocals)

Producer: Jeff Barry

Neil Diamond had already had two hit singles, "Solitary Man" and "Cherry, Cherry", when he was asked by Kirshner if he had any songs which could be used for the Monkees. One of the songs he provided, "I'm a Believer", became the band's second number one single, but this one was destined to be just an album track.

A simple four-chord song, based on a variant of the three-chord trick substituting ii for IV in the verses, with a key change to IV in the chorus, this bears some slight musical resemblance to Diamond's later hit "Cracklin' Rosie". Its simple melody, with very little range, also suits Jones' voice; a natural baritone, Jones was always made to sing in the tenor range to suit his light and youthful image, causing pitching problems for him on anything rangey, but here he does a sterling job.

On the choruses, especially, Jones lets rip in a way that he very rarely managed, and this is his most convincing rock and roll performance by some way, nicely contrasted to his more mannered, actorly performance on the verses.

Lyrically, the song is as nakedly commercial as it gets - Jones is having to choose between two women, both of whom he loves, which gives him a chance to say both "Mary, I love you" and "Sandra, I love you". Chalk one more name up for Kirshner's plan. Possibly there was some inspiration here from the song

"Did You Ever Have to Make up Your Mind?" by the Lovin' Spoonful, who had been one of the bands used as inspiration for the original Monkees idea.

But for all its simplicity and brazenness, this is still one of the highlights of the album, and probably the best track with a Jones lead vocal until "Daydream Believer" three albums later.

One oddity that was released as a bonus track is an alternate version of this with Tork "narrating" - "Ladies and gentlemen, you are listening to the instrumental... thank you, we hope you enjoyed it, and now back to the song" and so forth. This was apparently done in order to give Tork slightly more involvement with the album than he would otherwise have had, but was wisely dropped.

The Kind of Girl I Could Love

Writers: Michael Nesmith and Roger Atkins

Lead vocalist: Michael Nesmith

Other Monkees present: Micky Dolenz, Davy Jones and Peter Tork(backing vocals)

Producer: Michael Nesmith

This Latin-flavoured Nesmith song, which bears a slight resemblance in melody, chord sequence and arrangement to Mickey and Sylvia's recent hit version of "Love is Strange", is the first track to be released to feature all four Monkees, as well as being the first to feature an instrumental contribution from Nesmith, who plays the rather hesitant steel guitar part.

Like "Sweet Young Thing", this was a collaboration between Nesmith and a co-writer forced on him by Kirshner, this time

Roger Atkins, who had recently written "It's My Life" for the Animals.

Driven by a wonderful dual-drum part played by Hal Blaine and Jim Gordon, this is Nesmith at his poppiest, while still retaining his unique blend of Latin and country influences. Probably the closest thing to this in the charts at the time (other than the Mickey and Sylvia track) was the Sir Douglas Quintet, whose blend of Tex-Mex and *ersatz* Merseybeat landed them in a very similar musical place to this. But other than that, there was really nothing like this being made in pop music at the time.

The Day we Fall in Love

Writers: Sandy Linzner and Denny Randell

Lead vocalist: Davy Jones

Other Monkees present: None

Producer: Jeff Barry

Over a gentle instrumental backing, Davy whispers a "poem" about what it'll be like when your favourite Monkee falls in love with you, yes YOU teenage girl listening to this record.

As well as being the most calculated, cynical thing ever, this is also just offensively bad on an aesthetic level. Tracks like this are, one presumes, what led Nesmith to his infamously low opinions of *More of the Monkees*. Had all the album been as bad as this, one could see his point.

Happily, this is easily the worst thing on the album, and the only track on the album that fully justifies the album's relatively low reputation.

Incidentally, this is one of the two tracks that Carol Kaye, who claims to have played on most of the Monkees' hits, actually did play on. . .

Sometime in the Morning

Writers: Gerry Goffin and Carole King

Lead vocalist: Micky Dolenz

Other Monkees present: Davy Jones and Peter Tork (backing vocals)

Producers: Jeff Barry, Gerry Goffin and Carole King

To all intents and purposes this is a Carole King record by another name. Goffin and King recorded the backing track in New York, and along with it King recorded a three-part-harmony vocal demo whose arrangement and phrasing the Monkees replicated precisely under Jeff Barry's supervision.

A pleasant, simple ballad with a slightly confused lyric[6], Dolenz sings this winsomely enough over a folk-rockish backing of jangly guitars and organ, but it's somewhat inconsequential. The main musical point of note is the way the vocal line continues over the change between verse and bridge ("You will realise how much you never knew before") - this is a trick that Paul McCartney used to great effect later in "The Fool on the Hill".

---

[6]The lyric is mostly addressed to a second person, who will in turn discover the love of a third (female) person - except that sometimes the second person appears to be the (female) lover of the protagonist, so either the protagonist of the song is a lesbian or bisexual woman who refers to herself in the third person or the writers got confused somewhere.

Laugh

Writers: Philip Margo, Mitchell Margo, Henry Medress, and Jay Siegel

Lead vocalist: Davy Jones

Other Monkees present: None

Producer: Jeff Barry

A dreadful, dreadful track, with Jones and the Wrecking Crew plodding through an appalling piece of drivel that stays on two chords for the most part (with a third poking in briefly in the middle eight). Apparently intended as a comedy track, the lyrics ("laugh/'cos the music is funny/yeah the bass sounds off-beat/ain't that neat?") might even have worked had the music in fact been funny, or if the bass had been even slightly off-beat.

As it is, this is (along with "The Day we Fall In Love") definitely the low-point of the album.

I'm a Believer

Writer: Neil Diamond

Lead vocalist: Micky Dolenz

Other Monkees present: Peter Tork and Davy Jones (backing vocals)

Producer: Jeff Barry

The Monkees' second single - and second number one - was this Neil Diamond track. A simple, catchy, four-chord pop track with a slight country feel, Jeff Barry originally asked Nesmith to sing this (rather embarrassingly for him, Nesmith said "I'm a producer too, and that ain't no hit") before eventually getting Dolenz to sing it.

Originally intended as a track for Diamond's own second album, this was rightly a massive hit, though the fact that it sold a million copies before anyone had even heard it says more about the promotional juggernaut that was the Monkees phenomenon than it does about the record's quality.

This is an almost-perfect pop track, from the adolescent misery of the verses ("what's the use in trying/all you get is pain/when I needed sunshine I got rain") to the joy of the chorus, while the simplistic organ riff is a precursor to the later Barry hit "Sugar Sugar"[7]. Dolenz turns in one of his best vocals, while Jones is very audible in the backing vocals, making this seem more of a group performance than their previous hit.

Likewise the organ solo (which sounds to my ears inspired by the Surfaris' "Wipe Out") is exactly right - simple, but melodic, and adding a new element which works perfectly with the rest of the track. The one fly in the ointment, to my mind, is the bass line, which is far too busy and sounds improvised rather than properly thought out (though it again shows a certain "Wipe Out" influence).

But that's just nit-picking. This is a glorious, wonderful pop single. In general I take Nesmith's side in his dispute with Kirshner, but this time he was just wrong.

---

[7] Almost every book on the Monkees, including the first edition of this one, states that "Sugar Sugar" was itself offered to the Monkees to record, but this is a fallacy.

Bonus Tracks

Apples, Peaches, Bananas and Pears

Writers: Tommy Boyce and Bobby Hart

Lead vocalist: Micky Dolenz

Other Monkees present: None

Producers: Tommy Boyce and Bobby Hart

While Boyce and Hart turned in some of their best work for this album, almost everyone involved was agreed that they were writing and producing too many tracks for the Monkees, and that much of what they were doing was sub-par.

This is a perfect example - "to show how much I care/I'll bring you apples, peaches, bananas and pears". Dolenz does his best, but clearly nobody could care less, and this remained unreleased until the 1980s.

Kicking Stones

Writers: Lynne Castle and Wayne Erwin

Lead vocalist: Micky Dolenz

Other Monkees present: None

Producers: Tommy Boyce and Bobby Hart

A song about a 'teeny tiny gnome', with words by Boyce and Hart's hairdresser. According to the liner notes for the *More of the Monkees* deluxe edition, the TV show's producer Bert Schneider sent out a memo saying this track was 'of dubious value'. He was probably being over-generous.

To be fair to Boyce and Hart, they were producing a *lot* of material at this time, including many tracks that would become hits when released on future albums. But there was clearly no way that tracks like this could ever have been considered remotely releasable, and they must have known it.

I Love You Really

Writer: Stu Phillips

Lead vocalist: Davy Jones

Other Monkees present: None

Producer: None credited, presumably Phillips

This is just three different twelve-second takes of a sloppy run-through of a chorus for a generic song, recorded for the TV show. The "song", such as it is, was written by Stu Phillips, who composed the music for the TV show and was also responsible for the Hollyridge Strings easy-listening albums. Indeed, Phillips released a Hollyridge Strings-esque album of Monkees covers – *Stu Phillips Presents the Monkees Song Book Played by the Golden Gate Strings* – at the height of the show's success.

This isn't really something anyone would choose to listen to as music, but it's included in the super deluxe version of *More of the Monkees* in the spirit of getting absolutely everything released.

Undecided

Writers: Charlie Shavers, Sid Robin

Lead vocalists: Davy Jones, Kelly Jean Peters

Other Monkees present: None

Producer: None credited, presumably Stu Phillips

Another stumbling thirty-second run through for the TV series, this time of the 1938 jazz standard, with a female lead vocal.

Different Drum

Writer: Michael Nesmith

Lead vocalist: Michael Nesmith

Lead vocalist: Michael Nesmith

Producer: None credited

Another track recorded for use in the TV series, this is thirty-nine seconds of Nesmith comically stumbling through his own song, unmusically, hesitantly, and too fast. It works in the context of the comedy bit in the TV show, but it's absolutely not a proper performance of the song, which would have to wait for a Nesmith-sung version until his solo album *And the Hits Just Keep on Comin'*, although the Stone Poneys' version was a major hit in late 1967.

It's a shame, because the song itself is rightly considered a minor classic. Nesmith had written it before joining the Monkees, and it had been recorded by the Greenbriar Boys, who had heard Nesmith perform it in a solo club show and included · it on their 1966 album *Better Late Than Never*. The Stone

Poneys' version, actually only featuring Linda Ronstadt and Wrecking Crew members, became a top twenty hit and is still fondly remembered today. It would have been nice to have a proper Monkees version of Nesmith's most famous song.

She's So Far Out She's In

Writer: Thomas Knight

Lead vocalist: Michael Nesmith

Other Monkees present: Peter Tork (bass), Micky Dolenz (drums), Davy Jones (tambourine)

The super deluxe version of *More of the Monkees* finishes with ten tracks from a live show in Arizona from 1967. These are even rougher and rawer-sounding than the similar recordings heard on *Summer 1967: The Complete U.S. Concert Recordings*, and it's easy to see why they were never released at the time — much of the time the band is inaudible over the sound of screaming.

Nevertheless, there's some interesting material there, not least this song, which was attempted during the *Headquarters* sessions, but for which a vocal was never recorded. The original of this was recorded by teen band Dino, Desi, and Billy (who consisted of Dino Martin, son of Dean Martin; Desi Arnaz Jr, son of Arnaz Sr and Lucille Ball; and lead vocalist Billy Hinsche, who later went on to play for many decades with the Beach Boys).

The Monkees' cover version sticks closely to Dino, Desi, and Billy's version, but this makes sense — like much of Nesmith's own songwriting at this point, it's essentially a slightly country-blues inflected take on The Beatles' "She's a Woman" or the Sir

Douglas Quintet's "She's About a Mover", and it bears more than a little resemblance to "Sunny Girlfriend".

Cripple Creek

Writer: Trad. arr. Tork

Lead vocalist: Peter Tork

Other Monkees present: none

At each show, as well as performing as a band, each band member would also perform a solo song. For this tour, Jones, Dolenz, and Nesmith were all backed by the Candy Store Prophets for their solos, but Tork here performs "Cripple Creek" absolutely solo, accompanied by himself on the banjo.

"Cripple Creek" is an old Appalachian folk song, which is performed by almost every bluegrass musician to this day. Tork's performance allows him to show off his banjo playing (which is really very good by any standards), while the song's melody has a limited enough range that it doesn't stretch his vocals past their breaking point.

No producers were credited on any of these live tracks.

You Can't Judge a Book By the Cover

Writer: Willie Dixon

Lead vocalist: Michael Nesmith

Other Monkees present: none

Nesmith's solo song in the 1967 tours was a cover version of a Bo Diddley classic, although unlike many of Diddley's other hits this was written not by Diddley but by the great blues song-writer Willie Dixon (who wrote the bulk of the great Chicago blues songbook). As with his earlier solo cover of Diddley's "Who Do You Love?" (see the appendices for more details on this) Nesmith does a more than acceptable job of this song, and shows that he could easily have been a successful R&B vocalist had he chosen to go in that direction.

Gonna Build a Mountain

Writers: Anthony Newley and Leslie Bricusse

Lead vocalist: Davy Jones

Other Monkees present: none

And where Tork shows his folk roots and Nesmith his love of the blues, Jones shows that he was, above all else, a song and dance man. This song was originally written by Anthony Newley (a British actor and pop star, who was coincidentally around this time influencing a British namesake of Jones who had just changed his name to Bowie) and his songwriting partner Leslie Bricusse (with whom Newley wrote, among many other songs, "Feelin' Good" and "Goldfinger") for their musical *Stop the World I Want to Get Off*, which Newley had starred in. On Broadway, Newley's role, Littlechap, had been played by Sammy Davis Jr, and Davis had had a big hit with "What Kind of Fool Am I?" from the same show.

"Gonna Build A Mountain" had, since the show's 1961 debut, become something of a standard, recorded by Dusty Springfield and Matt Monro among others. With its gospel melody, and its religious lines about "the good Lord's grace" in its last verse, it has also become a popular song for choirs.

Jones, whose vocal style was quite similar to Newley's in many respects and who came from a similar musical theatre background, was more comfortable with this kind of material than with much of the rock music that was charting at the time, and it's rather a shame that there was never a studio version of this, rather than the much less interesting examples of "Broadway rock" Jones would later inflict on albums.

I Got A Woman

Writer: Ray Charles

Lead vocalist: Micky Dolenz

Other Monkees present: none

And Dolenz's solo spot is, unfortunately, the weakest of the four. This isn't down to any particular weakness in Dolenz or the Candy Store Prophets, it's just that while Dolenz is a fine singer, he's not Ray Charles, and no-one covering a Ray Charles song can do themselves any favours by the comparison. Dolenz lacks Charles' subtlety and humour, and the song – which was never much of a song in itself, as much as an excuse for Charles' vocals – isn't really helped by the six-minute length to which it's extended here and in the other live performances of the song (found on *Summer 1967*). Dolenz does as good a job as one could imagine him doing, and it must have been a lot of fun to watch live, but it's not really especially worthwhile as a recorded performance.

Self-Control (January 1967 to November 1968)

Headquarters

After *More of the Monkees* was a huge commercial success but (in the opinion of at least some of the Monkees, most vocally Nesmith) an artistic failure, the working relationship between the band (other than Davy Jones) and Don Kirshner, Screen Gems' music supervisor, reached breaking point.

The band were growing increasingly embarrassed by attacks on them for not playing the instruments on their records (attacks which ignored the fact that this was true for the majority of successful American bands of the time) and Nesmith intensely disliked the bubblegum music the band had been producing up until this point. Tork, meanwhile, had auditioned for the TV show because he wanted to be in a proper rock band, and wanted the four of them to play together, while Dolenz wanted to show solidarity with his colleagues.

The resulting rows, with Kirshner wanting the band to shut up and take the money and do as they were told, and the Monkees insisting on making their own music, led to Kirshner losing his job with Screen Gems and the Monkees being allowed to record as a band (see the entry for "A Little Bit Me, a Little Bit You" for more on Kirshner's ousting).

Headquarters was the first - and as it turned out, the only - album the band produced as a band. With producer Chip Douglas (who had never produced before, having previously been bass player in the Turtles), the band cut the basic tracks live, with Tork and Nesmith handling all guitars and keyboards (with a little help from Dolenz), Dolenz on drums, and Jones on hand percussion.

The only parts of the rhythm tracks that were performed by other musicians were the bass parts, which were mostly handled by Douglas but with Jerry Yester (a well-known LA musician who'd previously been in the Modern Folk Quartet with Douglas and would later be in the Lovin' Spoonful, as well as working with Tim Buckley, the Association and others) and Nesmith's friend John London sometimes stepping in.

The band also, for the first time, provided all their own backing vocals on an album – on the first two albums, while they'd performed many of the backing vocal parts, members of the Candy Store Prophets had contributed some.

The result was a huge success. While commercially the album did less well than its predecessors - it 'only' went to number one for one week, though it stayed at number two for the rest of the summer after being knocked down by *Sgt. Pepper* - artistically it's a fascinating work. It's patchy, but the highs are higher than anything the band had previously released, while the lows are at least of the 'interesting experiment' type, rather than being nakedly manipulative. This was the start of a run of four albums that's up there with the great runs of albums of the 60s, and the next two years would see the Monkees go artistically from strength to strength, even as their commercial career began its inevitable downward slide.

Unless otherwise noted, all tracks on this album feature all the Monkees, so the "Other Monkees present" credit will be left off for this album. Likewise, Chip Douglas produced every track, so the "producer" credit is absent. The generic credits are:

Michael Nesmith: vocals, pedal steel guitar, 6-string guitar, organ

Davy Jones: vocals, percussion

Micky Dolenz: vocals, drums, guitar)

Peter Tork: vocals, keyboards, twelve-string guitar, bass, banjo

Chip Douglas: bass

Produced by: Chip Douglas

You Told Me

Writer: Michael Nesmith

Lead vocalist: Michael Nesmith

The first song we hear to feature all the Monkees instrumentally (though as on many songs on this album Jones' instrumental contribution is limited to some token bits of hand percussion, buried in a bass-heavy mix) shows that Kirshner's worries about them as instrumentalists were unfounded.

Dolenz is clearly the most limited of the bunch as a musician (unlike Tork and Nesmith, he was an actor first, a singer second and a musician a distant third) but even so his drumming here is perfectly competent. He's a tad stiff at moments, and the tempo varies a little (only a very small amount, mostly due to getting excited at the good bits, so it ends up having a more organic feel anyway), so he's clearly not up to the standards of Hal Blaine or Jim Gordon, but he's playing with genuine energy, and his zither playing is an interesting addition.

Nesmith, on twelve-string guitar, turns in a good performance, but truth be told this would be a hard song to mess up on guitar, being just four major chords.

But Tork's banjo playing is an absolute revelation, and the start of a brief period where Tork is truly allowed to shine as a musician. The song itself is a clear attempt to sound as much like George Harrison as possible - the bass-line is from "Taxman" (which is nodded to in the intro, parodying its "one, two, three, four" intro), while the melody line is a slightly more rangey version of the melody to Harrison's "I Need You", but Tork's double-time bluegrass picking adds an incongruous, but perfect, element. (In fact Tork would shortly add banjo to a Harrison recording, the *Wonderwall* film soundtrack).

Other than a few production tricks (what sounds like backwards reverb on the backing vocals) and minimal overdubs, this is the sound of a very good Beatles-inspired garage band with an excellent vocalist, who've somehow managed to get a virtuoso banjo player to play along with them.

It's a world away from the sound of the first two albums, but still an excellent piece of country pop music.

I'll Spend My Life With You

Writers: Tommy Boyce and Bobby Hart

Lead vocalist: Micky Dolenz

And this track shows that the Monkees (or at least Tork, who appears to have done much of the heavy lifting with the arrangements on this album) were also better arrangers than the professionals they'd been working with.

A pleasant Boyce and Hart mid-tempo ballad, this had originally been recorded with its writers producing during the *More of the Monkees* sessions (and that version is available as a bonus track on the *More of the Monkees* CD), but had, rightly, been turned down. That original version sounds like little more than a demo, with a badly double-tracked Dolenz backed by a couple of strummed acoustic guitars.

The version here, though, as well as having a much more sensitive performance from Dolenz, is much more subtly arranged. Rather than a drum kit, we have Dolenz providing Johnny Cash style boom-chicka-boom rhythm guitar and Jones adding tambourine. Nesmith adds subtle colouring on pedal steel, and Tork provides faint organ tones, a gentle celeste solo, and most importantly some technically quite demanding ragtime twelve-string guitar.

Tork's musicianship gets neglected when people discuss the Monkees' music - partly because he was allowed to display it so briefly - but his ability to play in a variety of folk and classical idioms added hugely to the band's stylistic range. And more importantly, in a band full of huge egos, he seems to have had no problem at all with playing subtle, difficult parts that get almost buried in the mix but which add enormously to the finished product.

When compared to the Boyce and Hart original, it becomes very clear that while the Monkees weren't necessarily good enough songwriters to hold together an entire album, they were definitely more than capable of playing and arranging their music themselves.

Forget That Girl

Writer: Douglas Farthing Hatlelid (Chip Douglas)

Lead vocalist: Davy Jones

Written by producer/bassist Chip Douglas, and originally in-tended to have a feel similar to "Rescue Me" by Fontella Bass, this ended up being the closest thing on the album to the sound of the first two albums, with a much softer, acoustic pop sound.

It's also a genuine group performance of the type the band would mime on the TV. Other than Douglas' bass, this is the band all playing the instruments they were known for – Dolenz on drums, Nesmith on guitar, Tork on electric piano and Jones singing and playing maracas.

A lightweight song, with some slightly jazzy chords, this is lifted above mediocrity by a truly exceptional vocal performance by Jones. Usually the weakest of the band's three main lead vocalists, here he turns in a light, almost whispered, vocal right at the top of his range, shading into falsetto at several points.

Band 6

Writers: David Jones, Micky Dolenz, Peter Tork and Michael Nesmith

Lead vocalist: instrumental

A forty-second snippet, edited together from several sections of in-studio messing about, this consists of about twenty-five seconds of Dolenz on drums and Nesmith on pedal steel playing totally unrelated parts, before coming together to play a brief burst of "Merrily We Roll Along" (the *Merrie Melodies* theme).

You Just May Be the One

Writer: Michael Nesmith

Lead vocalist: Michael Nesmith

Another full-group performance, this time with Tork on bass (double-tracked, with one bass sounding like a Danelectro bass - a trick Nesmith had used to give a country sound to several of his recordings over the previous year) this Nesmith song had originally been recorded with members of the Wrecking Crew and used in the TV show (that version is on the deluxe editions of *The Monkees*).

A catchy Beatlesque pop song, this is full of hooks, from the two extra beats dropped into the first line of the verses (which can be broken down into a bar of four, a bar of six and a bar of four), to the way the instruments drop out for the start of the title line, to the way the backing vocals all hold the same high note on the middle eight while the lead vocal descends down the scale. That backing vocal hook was something that had been in the song from the beginning – Douglas had seen Nesmith perform the song at the Troubadour with Bill Chadwick before the Monkees formed, and remembered that arrangement touch and asked if Dolenz could sing the same part on the record.

Had there not been a *de facto* ban by the record label on releasing singles with a lead vocal by anyone other than Dolenz or Jones, this would have been an obvious hit single. It manages perfectly to straddle the boundaries between country music and jangly powerpop in a way that few others could, pointing the way forward to bands like Big Star or mid-period R.E.M., but with a lighter touch. Sublime.

Shades of Gray

Writers: Barry Mann and Cynthia Weil

Lead vocalists: Davy Jones and Peter Tork

The only track on the album to feature instrumentalists other than the Monkees (plus a friend on bass), this has folk-rocker Jerry Yester providing bass, but also features cello and French horn parts performed by session musicians (but arranged by Nesmith and Tork).

A clear attempt at being this album's "I Wanna Be Free", like that song this is hugely popular among Monkees fans, and also like that song I dislike it intensely, although nowhere near as much as "I Wanna Be Free". Where I believe that song to be actively unpleasant, my problem with "Shades of Gray" is just that it's a fundamentally callow song, the kind of thing best left to teenage poetry, written by people who clearly think they were being terribly profound.

Tork does, however, get to share the lead vocals with Jones on this one, making it only his second lead to be released.

I Can't Get Her Off of My Mind

Writers: Tommy Boyce and Bobby Hart

Lead vocalist: Davy Jones

Another song that had been recorded and rejected in the band's early sessions (that version is available on the deluxe versions of *The Monkees*), this is a rather insipid old-fashioned song of the type Jones seemed to enjoy doing.

While in this version the song has a rinky-dink knees-up feel similar to some of the material Jones had done on his first solo album, it was originally intended to have a very different style. Boyce and Hart originally wrote it for the Dixie Cups, a girl group who'd had hits with songs like "Iko Iko" and "Chapel of Love", and when they turned it down it was first recorded by Sandra Gee in 1964 and then as a 1966 B-side for Dino, Desi, and Billy.

This track has very little to recommend it, other than that it's better than the original version, thanks to some nice barrelhouse piano from Tork. Jerry Yester again adds bass.

For Pete's Sake

Writers: Peter Tork and Joey Richards

Lead vocalist: Micky Dolenz

Tork's first attempt at songwriting, this later became the closing theme for series two of the Monkees' TV show. A simple, naive song of hippy hope ("in this generation, we will make the world a shine"), it's a very strong construction as a recording and arrangement, with a powerful vocal by Dolenz and some simplistic but effective Hammond from Nesmith (and some surprisingly dodgy guitar playing, that's buried quite far in the mix).

The combination of the great guitar hook at the beginning and the build from D to E to Fmaj7 on "we must be what we're going to be" mean the record ends up being quite effective, but it's still ultimately rather empty of content as a song.

This song has since become a staple of Monkees reunion tours, where Tork rather than Dolenz takes the lead vocal.

Mr. Webster

Writers: Tommy Boyce and Bobby Hart

Lead vocalist: Micky Dolenz

Another Boyce/Hart song, this had originally been recorded in a rather overwrought pseudo-baroque harpsichord-driven version (that version can be heard on the *More of the Monkees* deluxe edition). This version is recorded in the same style as "I'll Spend My Life With You", though with Chip Douglas rather than Yester on bass. Otherwise it's the same line-up - Tork on piano, Dolenz on rhythm guitar, Nesmith on pedal steel and Jones on tambourine.

One of Boyce and Hart's better songs, this was their attempt to write a song like "Eleanor Rigby", but in fact it sounds far more like some of Paul Simon's early efforts - "A Most Peculiar Man" or "Richard Corey". It tells the story of a bank employee (inspired by a security guard they saw at their local bank, but the employee's job is not mentioned), constantly passed over for raises even though he repeatedly stops bank robberies, who steals all the money in the bank on the day of his retirement.

Once again the Monkees and Douglas show themselves to be more effective arrangers than Boyce and Hart, with every element perfectly placed, and with a wonderful start-stop rhythm that works most effectively on the line "sorry STOP, cannot attend."

But either version of the track is well worth listening to, and an example of just how good Boyce and Hart could be as song-writers.

Sunny Girlfriend

Writer: Michael Nesmith

Lead vocalist: Michael Nesmith

A full-band performance with long-time Nesmith collaborator John London joining on bass, this simple Nesmith country-pop song is enlivened by some great bluegrass-esque harmonies from Dolenz from the second verse on, and some backwards-recorded cymbals on the intro. Tork provides the lead guitar.

It's a fun song, and one that rightly remained in the Monkees' setlist whenever Nesmith toured with them, but possibly let down by its similarity to "You Just May Be the One".

Zilch

Writers: Peter Tork, David Jones, Micky Dolenz, and Michael Nesmith

Lead vocalist: Peter Tork, David Jones, Micky Dolenz, and Michael Nesmith

A simple spoken round, with each band member repeating a single phrase over and over. In order we have Tork saying "Mr. Dobalina, Mr Bob Dobalina" (a phrase Dolenz had heard over an airport tannoy, later sampled by rapper Del Tha Funkee Homosapien for the song "Mistadobalina"), Jones saying "China Clipper calling Alameda" (a line from the Humphrey Bogart film *China Clipper*), Dolenz saying "Never mind the furthermore, the plea is self-defence" (a line from *Oklahoma!* - "It was self-defence, and furthermore..." "Never mind the furthermore. The plea is self-defence."), and Nesmith saying "It is of my opinion that the people are intending" (apparently from a political speech).

On the *Headquarters Sessions* box set, these spoken tracks can be heard isolated.

No Time

Writer: Hank Cicalo (Peter Tork, David Jones, Micky Dolenz, and Michael Nesmith)

Lead vocalist: Micky Dolenz

Built around a jam session variously reported as being on a Chuck Berry or Little Richard song (given that the piano break is a very sloppy attempt at the guitar part from Berry's "Johnny B Goode", that was probably the song they were attempting - the resemblance is closer on the early instrumental version that can be heard on the *Headquarters Sessions* set), this was given lyrics, mostly by Dolenz and Nesmith, referencing various counterculture-ish things (Andy Warhol, drug busts and so on), with the first verse being Bill Cosby nonsense words ("Hober reeber sabasoben/Hobaseeba snick/Seeberraber hobosoben/What did you expect?")

Almost all the point of this track comes from the energy of the performance - not just from Dolenz's screaming vocal but also from the backing vocals (Jones sounds permanently on the point of hysteria).

While the song evolved from a jam, the band decided to give the songwriting credit to engineer Hank Cicalo, in thanks for his work on the album. Cicalo made a considerable amount of money from the royalties from this song over the years, but it caused trouble with his bosses at RCA, who had to be persuaded that the credit was a gift from the band rather than him corruptly using his position to get them to record his own material.

Early Morning Blues and Greens

Writers: Diane Hildebrand and Jack Keller

Lead vocalist: Davy Jones

Strangely, after the Monkees disliked "Your Auntie Grizelda", they accepted another song by the same writers. Luckily, this is much, much better than that. A meditative piece detailing Hildebrand's impressions while drinking a cup of coffee, this actually bears a slight resemblance to Nesmith's contemporaneous "The Girl I Knew Somewhere".

And much like that track, much of the power of this comes from Tork's musicianship. The song is driven by his soft electric piano arpeggios and Hammond playing, with the rest of the instrumentation coming from some simple muted twelve-string guitar from Nesmith, a simple, repetitive bass riff from Chip Douglas and a percussion part which seems to consist just of hi-hat from Dolenz and maracas from Jones.

The most interesting feature of this is the crashing sound every two bars in the later part of the song. This is actually two different instrumental parts, sometimes playing together and sometimes separately - one of them is the organ part, the other sounds like *very* heavily reverbed guitar, possibly with the strings being hit with a drumstick.

And Jones, in one of only two solo lead performances on this album, his fewest on any Monkees album released in his lifetime, more than justifies his presence, providing some gorgeous harmonies with himself. Jones was generally a weaker vocalist than Nesmith or Dolenz, but on this album he rises to the occasion.

Hildebrand later used this song as the title track of her only solo album.

Alternate Title (aka "Randy Scouse Git")

Writer: Micky Dolenz

Lead vocalist: Micky Dolenz

Dolenz's first songwriting contribution to the band is also the highlight of the album, and maybe of the band's career. Based on a simple four-chord progression (a broken up version of the standard doo-wop I-vi-ii-V progression) in the sixteen-bar verses, with a one-chord eight-bar chorus, this track is proof, if proof be needed, that harmonic sophistication is not needed to create a complex, rewarding piece of pop music.

The structure of the song breaks down as follows:

Intro by Dolenz on tympani, playing a rhythm - roughly five quavers followed by a beat and a half of silence, repeated over and over, that will later be heard in the chorus (we'll call this the intro rhythm). The tympani then fades out.

Tork then repeats the intro rhythm on piano, twice, with Douglas adding comical single-note bass interjections in the silences, before playing a variation of the rhythm that leads into the first verse.

In the first verse we have just Dolenz on vocals, Tork playing syncopated piano chords, and Douglas adding a simple descending scalar bassline, leading to a ragtime feel.

In the second verse, Nesmith comes in, doubling the piano part on guitar, while Dolenz adds some woodblock percussion. Towards the end, the tympani becomes audible again, almost subliminally.

For the chorus, the piano all but drops out, and it turns into a guitar-led rave-up, with a full drum kit playing a fairly straight-forward rock part while the tympani play the intro rhythm. Douglas meanwhile is playing a country bass part (similar to that of, for example, "Rawhide"). Jones joins in on backing vocals here.

We get another verse, with the same instrumentation as the second verse, but with added cymbals in the second half and an altogether looser feeling, and another chorus.

We then get a verse, taken at the same fast tempo as the choruses and with the same guitar-led instrumental, but Dolenz scatting wildly over the top, in a manner that was possibly influenced by the band's friend Harry Nilsson (of whom much more later). We briefly get a tympani reprise of the intro rhythm before going into another, double length chorus.

This last chorus has a prominent organ holding the chord down, on top of the rest of the instrumentation, and has Dolenz the chorus while Jones simultaneously sings the verse (possibly inspired by the similar effect on "When Love Comes Knocking at Your Door"). We then get a repeat of the piano part of the intro, ending on a guitar discord and what sounds like drumsticks dropping to the floor, and then the tympani fades in, and back out again, playing the intro rhythm. (Oddly, an early mix of the song, available on the *Headquarters Sessions* box set, features instead of the tympani fade, a hard edit into Tork and Dolenz singing the folk song "I Was Born in East Virginia" to banjo accompaniment. The box set also features the full performance of that song).

The whole thing lasts just two minutes and thirty-five seconds, and remarkably manages to stand up well against the great experimental singles of the period, like "Good Vibrations" or "Strawberry Fields Forever", even though the Beatles and Beach Boys were moving towards greater use of studio musicians and trickery at precisely the point where the Monkees were, briefly, being a 'real rock band' (though *Headquarters* ended up being the only album on which all the Monkees performed on every track, and on which Dolenz was the only drummer).

Lyrically, the song is an elliptical description of Dolenz's experiences visiting England, with lyrics referencing Dolenz's first wife (the Mancunian Samantha Juste, then a TV host on BBC 1's *Top of the Pops*), the Beatles, and hotel doormen ("he reminds me of a penguin, with few and plaster hairs"). Unfortunately for Dolenz, the song's title, another reference to his British trip (an overheard line from the sitcom *Til Death Us Do Part*), was considered obscene in the UK at the time, and so the song was given the alternate title "Alternate Title" for its release as a single in those countries that speak British English.

Bonus Tracks

All of Your Toys

Writer: Bill Martin

Lead vocalist: Micky Dolenz

A bouncy, harpsichord-driven track written by a friend of Chip Douglas. A wonderful arrangement with a descending scalar bassline, harpsichord chords and twelve-string arpeggios, with Dolenz singing lead and answering vocals, and a wonderful vocal harmony break, this sounds like an attempt to do something similar to the work Brian Wilson was doing at the time, but actually comes out slightly closer to soft-pop classics like Jan and Dean's *Carnival of Sound* or the contemporaneous work by Curt Boettcher and Gary Usher.

Unfortunately, this was never released at the time because of contractual problems - Martin was signed to a publisher other than Screen Gems, and so this had to wait two decades for release.

The Girl I Knew Somewhere

Writer: Michael Nesmith

Lead vocalist: Michael Nesmith/Micky Dolenz

One of Nesmith's better pop songs, this story of a man who's been betrayed before and is wary of getting together with someone similar was intended for single release - to the extent that Nesmith's original vocal was replaced with one by Dolenz, because at this point only Dolenz or Jones vocals were considered for release on singles.

This was in most ways a shame - Nesmith's original vocal is a more mature, stronger performance than Dolenz's - but it did allow the wonderful touch in the last verse where Dolenz's lines are echoed by Nesmith.

With a wonderful harpsichord break by Tork and its Beatlesque backing vocals, this is a sophisticated, strong piece of music that should have been a huge hit single. As it was, it ended up as the B-side of "A Little Bit Me, a Little Bit You".

Peter Gunn's Gun

Writer: Henry Mancini

Lead vocalist: instrumental

A studio jam, based loosely round a rather incompetent rendition of the riff from Mancini's "Peter Gunn". This was never intended for release, and other than Tork's spoken interjection "What are you, kidding me? Psycho Jello!" probably should have stayed in the can. This sort of thing is how every band in the world lets off steam, and it's fun for the band, but not really for the listeners.

Jericho

Writer: trad.

Lead vocalist: Micky Dolenz and Peter Tork

A bit of studio chatter - Dolenz attempts to play the French horn, and this reminds him of Joshua and the battle of Jericho. Dolenz and Tork then break into an impromptu *a capella* rendition of the gospel song "Joshua Fit the Battle of Jericho". It's actually quite an extraordinary performance, and shows the musicality of both men, with Tork's folk sensibilities combining to great effect with Dolenz's James Brown-inspired gospel shrieking.

It's only studio tomfoolery, but is much better than the previous track, and manages to highlight one of the great strengths of the Monkees when they were working together as a group — they all had different musical tastes and instincts, which gave the band a much wider palette to draw from than most bands have.

Nine Times Blue

Writer: Michael Nesmith

Lead vocalist: Michael Nesmith

A contender for greatest song ever written, this has the simple, sparse, heartbreaking elegance of a "You Don't Know Me" or "I'm So Lonesome I Could Cry", and Nesmith here matches John Lennon or Brian Wilson in the portrayal of an angry, jealous man humbled by a woman who's clearly better than him but loves him anyway.

Nesmith clearly realised it was good. He attempted it multiple times - a bizarre instrumental version on the tax write-off solo album *The Wichita Train Whistle Sings*, versions with both himself and Jones on lead vocals during the sessions for *The Birds, the Bees and the Monkees*, and a version for a TV performance with Jones and Dolenz providing harmonies during the last days of the band's career - before finally releasing it on his solo album *Magnetic South*.

Still, though, I think the best version is the acoustic demo version here, partly because the simplicity of the arrangement (two guitars, what sounds like one twelve-string and one six-string, and vocals) works well for the song, but also because between this and the later versions he changed the line "the lessons I've learned here is worth it all" to "the lessons I've learned here *are* worth it all".

The latter is, of course, more grammatically correct, but the earlier version sounds more honest, like the product of a man who's too overcome emotionally to bother about grammar.

But in every version, this is one of the truly great songs, and deserves much wider recognition.

A Little Bit Me, a Little Bit You

Writer: Neil Diamond

Lead vocalist: Davy Jones

Other Monkees present: None

Producer: Jeff Barry

The Monkees' third single, this was cut in New York at the insistence of Don Kirshner, who had promised Neil Diamond the next Monkees single after the success of "I'm a Believer". Jones, who was the only Monkee still on speaking terms with Kirshner, cut several vocals on a trip to New York, of which this and its original B-Side "She Hangs Out" were two.

Unfortunately for Kirshner, he insisted on putting both tracks out on the same single, after the record company had agreed with the band that every single would have at least one track on which the Monkees themselves played, so the single was pulled, "She Hangs Out" replaced with "The Girl I Knew Somewhere", and Kirshner lost his job supervising the band's music.

The single, the first not to feature Dolenz on lead, sold 1.5 million copies before it came out, and went gold on the day of release.

Not up to the standard of the band's previous singles, this is still a pleasant, vaguely Latin-infused track, driven by acoustic guitars and handclaps. Jones' vocal is not one of his most convincing, though, and he fails to sell the "oh no, hey now girl..." supposed *ad lib* ending. Despite that, this is still a fondly-remembered song, and one of only two Jones leads (along with "Daydream Believer") to be so demanded by audiences that they are in Dolenz's solo sets.

You Can't Tie a Mustang Down

Writers: Jeff Barry, Jerry Leiber and Mike Stoller

Lead vocalist: Davy Jones

Other Monkees present: None

Producer: Jeff Barry

Another song from the same New York sessions, this is a rare misstep from Leiber and Stoller, who wrote some of the best songs of the 1950s and 60s. This song about being a young, powerful man who can't be tied down by women might possibly have passed muster for Elvis Presley, who could have infused it with a swaggering sexuality, and who had enough humour in his phrasing that he could even have sold the clunky last chorus line "You can't keep an ocean in a cup/You can't tie a mustang down. . . or up!"

Davy Jones, however, is far closer to a Shetland pony, or possibly a seaside donkey ride, than to a mustang. This song was wisely left unreleased until a cheap hits compilation in 1998.

If I Learned to Play the Violin

Writers: Joey Levine and Artie Resnick

Lead vocalist: Davy Jones

Other Monkees present: None

Producer: Jeff Barry

Yet another song from the New York session, this was clearly another attempt at an "I Wanna Be Free"-style ballad showcase for Davy, who does easily his best vocal of this bunch of tracks here, especially with his Everly Brothers-style harmony on the line "take up more discreet ways" in the middle eight (this harmony part is unaccountably mixed down on the version on the *Headquarters* deluxe edition, but can be heard on the original mix).

The main problem here is the lyric, from the point of view of a young, rebellious man offering to become respectable instead of a long-haired guitar-playing beatnik, so his girlfriend's parents will accept him. It's just, frankly, terrible - it's hard to know which to dislike more, the sentiment or the execution (with some appalling scansion, stresses falling all over the place but rarely where they naturally should). It's also, as mentioned above, quite difficult to imagine Davy Jones as a rebellious firebrand who needed taming.

The song, wisely, remained unreleased until it was sneaked out on a CD-ROM in 1996.

She'll Be There

Writers: Micky and Coco Dolenz

Lead vocalist: Micky and Coco Dolenz

Other Monkees present: None

One of several demos recorded early in the *Headquarters* sessions, this is Micky Dolenz and his sister Coco, backed by a single acoustic guitar, singing a close-harmony ballad very clearly modelled after those Felice and Boudleaux Bryant wrote for the Everly Brothers. A lovely, lovely performance of what is quite a slight song.

Headquarters Sessions

In 2003, Rhino Handmade released a 3-CD box set of out-takes from the *Headquarters* sessions, now out of print (though available on some streaming services). This was a strictly obsessives-only release, consisting of three-and-a-half hours of studio chatter, demos, instrumental backing tracks and other ephemera, as well as the original mono mix of the album in a different, rejected running order.

The box set is no longer available, and most of the interesting material from it has since ended up on the later two-CD deluxe edition of *Headquarters*, and is reviewed under that album, but a few tracks, mostly instrumental noodling, remain unavailable elsewhere. Those are covered here. As with the entries for *Headquarters*, all tracks feature all Monkees and are produced by Chip Douglas unless otherwise stated.

Seeger's Theme

Writer: Pete Seeger

Lead vocalist: instrumental (Peter Tork)

A brief piece by folk legend Pete Seeger, this was recorded three times by the Monkees, first during the *Headquarters* demo sessions (the version on the *Headquarters Sessions* box set) with Tork on very fast picked acoustic guitar while whistling the melody, then in two full band versions in the sessions for *The Birds, the Bees and the Monkees*, one guitar-driven and one banjo-driven.

None of these versions last more than eighty seconds or so, with the full band ones lasting a mere forty or fifty. But it's a pleasant, typically-Seeger, melody.

Where Has it All Gone?

Writer: Michael Nesmith

Lead vocalist: instrumental

A Nesmith song that was never finished, two versions of this were released on the *Headquarters Sessions* box set - the first an almost unlistenable mess, the second a fairly solid Hammond-driven swamp-rock track.

Memphis Tennessee

Writer: Chuck Berry

Lead vocalist: instrumental

A quick jam during the recording for "Where Has it All Gone?" Not worth listening to, unless you like listening to garage bands noodling semi-competently on Chuck Berry riffs.

Twelve-String Improvisation

Writers: Michael Nesmith, Peter Tork, Davy Jones, Micky Dolenz, John London

Lead vocalist: instrumental

More unnecessary jamming, this time around a variant of the "Day Tripper" riff.

Masking Tape

Writers: Barry Mann and Cynthia Weil?/Unknown [8]

Lead vocalist: instrumental

This song sounds like a Nesmith track, with Jerry Yester playing a very McCartney-esque bassline, and was apparently an actual song rather than a jam session, but the band never returned to it.

Blues

Writers: Michael Nesmith, Peter Tork, Davy Jones, Micky Dolenz

Lead vocalist: instrumental

A lazy blues jam session, in a vaguely Jerry Reed style, performed by Nesmith, Tork, Dolenz, Yester and session guitarists Keith Allison and Gerry McGee, this can be heard on the *Headquarters Sessions* box in two versions - a pleasant-but-overlong four minute excerpt and a mindbogglingly stultifyingly dull ten minute complete version.

---

[8] This is credited in at least one source as by Mann/Weil, but it appears to be a mistake, due to the song having been recorded during the same sessions as the Mann/Weil song "Shades of Gray".

Banjo Jam

Writers: Michael Nesmith, Peter Tork, Davy Jones, Micky Dolenz

Lead vocalist: instrumental

From the same session as the above, this is some noodling around with Tork on the banjo.

Six-String Improvisation

Writers: Michael Nesmith, Peter Tork, Davy Jones, Micky Dolenz

Lead vocalist: instrumental

Yet more aimless noodling, this time led by Nesmith on guitar.

The Story of Rock and Roll

Writer: Harry Nilsson

Lead vocalist: Instrumental

Two attempts at this Nilsson track are included on the *Headquarters Sessions* box, and they're by far the most interesting of the instrumental tracks that didn't go any further, showing the band tight and playing together well (with Chip Douglas on bass, and without Jones) on a relatively challenging piece.

The song is in Nilsson's early style, much like his songs for the Modern Folk Quartet (the band which Douglas and occasional bass player Jerry Yester had been in), and while the Monkees never recorded vocals for it, Douglas later produced a near-identical version for his old band the Turtles, which was a minor hit.

Two-Part Invention in F Major

Writer: J.S. Bach

Lead vocalist: instrumental (Peter Tork)

Tork playing through a Bach piece, very competently, though taking it at quite a slow pace (it was meant to be sped up for any final release). This is just a run-through, so it's not a perfect performance, but it on its own should show anyone who believed the Monkees incapable of playing their instruments that Tork, at least, was more than capable. This later became a regular feature for Tork in live shows, both solo and in Monkees reunions.

Don't Be Cruel

Writers: Otis Blackwell and Elvis Presley

Lead vocalist: instrumental (Peter Tork)

Forty-six seconds of the Elvis hit, played by Tork on piano and Dolenz on drums. Tork would later include this song in his solo live set.

Fever

Writers: Michael Nesmith, Peter Tork, Davy Jones, Micky Dolenz

Lead vocalist: instrumental

Aimless instrumental noodling again, but this time with interesting reverb on the piano part. No relation to the Little Willie John song of the same name.

I Was Born in East Virginia

Writer: Traditional (possibly A.P. Carter)

Lead vocalists: Peter Tork and Micky Dolenz

Dolenz and Tork here running through an old folk tune, singing close harmony over Tork's banjo playing. Quite a nice performance, part of which was edited on as the tag to an early mix of "Randy Scouse Git".

Summer 1967: The Complete U.S. Concert Recordings

Summer 1967: The Complete U.S. Concert Recordings is a collection of four live recordings, all recorded in August 1967. It has much the same kind of sound and sound quality as the concert recordings which were dealt with in the *More of the Monkees* deluxe edition.

Each show follows the exact same format, and has the same setlist – the band come out, and play nine songs as a band, emphasising songs written by Nesmith, and with every band member getting a turn at the lead vocals (Dolenz takes three, Nesmith three, Jones two, and Tork only "Your Auntie Grizelda").

After these opening nine songs, the band members each get a solo spot – Tork does a solo performance of "Cripple Creek", and then Nesmith, Jones, and Dolenz are each backed by the support act, the Sundowners, as they do their own solo songs. The band then get back together for a further three songs, all

Dolenz lead vocals – "I'm a Believer", "Randy Scouse Git", and "Steppin' Stone".

The performances are often sloppy, but no more so than might be expected at the time – given the screaming crowds and inadequate amplification, it was impossible for bands with audiences like the Monkees' to hear themselves when performing, and the Monkees are no worse here as musicians than, say, the Beatles in their Hollywood Bowl shows.

Tork, in particular, shows himself to have been a truly excellent bass player. It's rather a shame that in the band's various reunion lineups he has mostly played guitar, banjo, or keyboards – and indeed it's also a shame that Dolenz rarely plays drums live for more than a handful of songs. The combination of Tork's musicianship and Dolenz's untutored, idiosyncratic, drumming style makes for a much more interesting rhythm section than one would expect, and one which they never really explored on records (even when Dolenz played drums on the records, it was usually someone other than Tork playing bass). Indeed, the sound here is not far at all from bands like the Who, who similarly combined rudimentary guitar, a highly mobile bass part, and a drummer who made up in enthusiasm and imagination what he lacked in technical finesse.

The recording and mixing is also not the best – often some instrument will only be vaguely heard, as leakage into another mic, rather than being properly in the mix. Sometimes Jones' tambourine or maracas, for example, will overwhelm everything else for a few bars and then fade out, presumably as he moved away from the microphone. On the first show, during "Your Auntie Grizelda", for much of the track it may as well be an *a capella* mix, as Tork's vocal is the only audible thing other than the audience's screaming.

What is impressive about these shows, however, is the amount of effort the band were putting in at giving a good show. It was normal at the time for a headlining band to do fifteen minutes, or half an hour at most, at the top of a bill with half a dozen other acts on. That was starting to change, but not very quickly, and given the Monkees' teen fanbase and relative inexperience as live performers it would have been expected and acceptable for them to do twenty minutes. Instead, their performances had a single opening act, and they performed for just over an hour – the total running time of this set is four hours and thirty-eight minutes.

A compilation of these tracks, with one version of each song, was released as the single-CD *Live 1967*, and that is probably a better purchase for anyone who just wants a live album by the band in the sixties – the full set is probably only of interest as a historical record rather than as a listening experience, given the quality of the performances and recording. But taken in the proper historical context, and compared to similar live recordings by other bands from the mid sixties, these shows are remarkably impressive.

One point that should be made though is that some of the stage banter might cause offence now – in particular, at one point Jones, when doing the normal "clap your hands and stamp your feet" bit, also says "beat on your wife if she's here". It's a joke which can, perhaps, be forgiven given the time period and the band's youth, but which makes me cringe now, and may well cause a worse reaction than that in some, so be warned.

The four-CD set is currently out of print, but can be found on most streaming services.

The tracklist for all shows is:

- Last Train to Clarksville
- You Just May Be the One
- The Girl I Knew Somewhere
- I Wanna Be Free
- Sunny Girlfriend
- Your Auntie Grizelda
- Forget That Girl
- Sweet Young Thing
- Mary, Mary
- Cripple Creek (Peter Tork)
- You Can't Judge a Book By the Cover (Michael Nesmith with the Sundowners)
- Gonna Build a Mountain (Davy Jones with the Sundowners)
- I Got a Woman (Micky Dolenz with the Sundowners)
- I'm a Believer
- Randy Scouse Git
- (I'm Not Your) Steppin' Stone

Pisces, Aquarius, Capricorn & Jones Ltd

The second and last of the albums where the Monkees provided the bulk of the instrumentation is their absolute masterpiece. While Dolenz was no longer playing much on the records, the band were still working as a unit in the studio, albeit an augmented one, and all four members were contributing creatively.

The result is one of the great mid-60s albums, that easily stands up with *Revolver*, *Absolutely Free*, *Forever Changes*, *Smiley Smile* and so on as a serious piece of work. The fact that this was recorded by a band who were being dismissed as pre-teen pabulum (*and* who were having to work on a TV show full time at the same time) is nothing short of extraordinary.

If you want a sense of what was possible in popular music as 1967 drew to a close, you could do far, far worse than *Pisces, Aquarius, Capricorn & Jones, Ltd*, where influences as diverse as Frank Zappa, the Beatles, bluegrass, Mose Allison and Robert A. Heinlein collide, and the result is something unlike anything else in popular music.

All tracks produced by Chip Douglas.

Salesman

Writer: Craig Smith

Lead vocalist: Michael Nesmith

Other Monkees present: Micky Dolenz and Davy Jones (percussion and backing vocals), Peter Tork (possible guitar).

One can see from the very first song on *Pisces, Aquarius, Capricorn & Jones Ltd* that this is something very different from the earlier Monkees albums. For the first time ever on an album, Nesmith is taking a lead vocal on a song he didn't write. In fact, Nesmith dominates this album vocally – after previously having taken no more than three leads per album, here he takes five, of which he only wrote one.

This song was written by Nesmith's friend Craig Smith, of psych-pop band the Penny Arkade. Smith later changed his name to Satya Sai Maitreya Kali and recorded his own version of this, featuring Mike Love of the Beach Boys.

The recording is loosely modelled on "She's About a Mover" by the Sir Douglas Quintet (which was itself based on "She's a Woman" by the Beatles), which Nesmith liked for its "Tex-Mex oompah", and like both those earlier records is driven by a prominent bass-line with stabbing guitars on the off-beat.

This song caused some controversy for the drug references (more blatant in the extended mix, which features a monologue by Nesmith about different cigarette-rolling machines), with NBC not wishing to feature it on the TV show. Actually, the song is at least moderately anti-drug, or at least anti-dealer, with its portrayal of a salesman selling 'every pot' and 'sailing so high' but who has a 'short life span'.

On many of the band's other albums, this would have been a highlight, but on an album where nearly every song is a minor masterpiece, this is 'just' an album track.

While the Monkees were no longer playing together as a band in-studio, this album does feature a band of sorts, with Nesmith on guitar, Tork on guitar and keyboards, Chip Douglas on bass and Eddie Hoh on drums on almost every track. In this case it's unsure whether Tork played on the track, but this studio unit would feature on nine of the thirteen tracks on the album.

She Hangs Out

Writers: Jeff Barry and Ellie Greenwich

Lead vocalist: Davy Jones

Other Monkees present: Michael Nesmith (electric guitar), Peter Tork (organ), Micky Dolenz (backing vocals)

Pisces, Aquarius almost alternates between two very different types of song. The first type is either sung or written by Nesmith, and is a country-psych-pop track with oblique lyrics. "Salesman", the opening track, is an example of this type.

The other type features Jones on vocals and is at least mildly misogynist. This great pop track is an example of the second type. One could write an entire thesis on the attitude towards women displayed on Jones' tracks on this album, which is all the more bizarre when one considers that they were all written by different outside songwriters, and two of them were co-written by women.

Either way, this is one of the less offensive of these tracks, and the catchiest, being based around a warning - "How old you say your sister was? You know you'd better keep an eye on her" - about a young girl 'hanging out' with an older crowd, but its lascivious attitude ("I know you taught your sister to boogaloo...well, she could teach you a thing or two") makes for somewhat uncomfortable listening in context with the rest of the album.

This had originally been released as a quickly-withdrawn B-side to "A Little Bit Me, a Little Bit You", in a version featuring only Jones and produced by Jeff Barry. This version, re-recorded with the Nesmith/Tork/Douglas/Hoh backing band, keeps the best bits of that arrangement (the answering vocals and 'doo da ron day ron day's) while expanding the organ part (which in Barry's version had been very similar to those in "I'm a Believer" or his later hit "Sugar Sugar"), getting rid of the incongruous fuzz guitar and adding a horn section. The result is a great, and for the Monkees quite funky, dance record, with Jones' sleazy, strained vocals working perfectly in this context.

The Door Into Summer

Writers: Chip Douglas and Bill Martin

Lead vocalist: Michael Nesmith

Other Monkees present: Micky Dolenz (backing vocals, additional drums), Peter Tork (keyboards)

One of only two songs on this album to feature Dolenz on drums (he plays one of the two drum parts audible on the record, with Hoh playing the other), this song by the band's friend Bill Martin seems musically to have been inspired by some of Love's music at the time - the acoustic guitar intro sounding very like many of the acoustic parts on the *Forever Changes* and *Da Capo* albums.

Lyrically, the inspiration is more obvious - the title of the song comes from the Robert A. Heinlein novel of the same name. In the first half of the book, before it descends into the usual late-Heinlein sexual creepiness (though for a change it's paedophilia, not incest, that Heinlein advocates in this one), the protagonist makes a lot of money from sales of stock in a company he founded, before going into cryogenic suspension and waking up in the future.

Douglas and Martin seem to have taken elements of this basic idea and used them as a metaphor for a businessman giving up most of his life and constantly postponing doing what he wants to advance his career for no real reason.

Easily one of the best tracks the band ever did, everything on this track works well, from Dolenz and Nesmith's harmonies on the chorus, to the interplay between the banjo (played by Doug Dillard) and Tork's keyboard, to the wonderful pseudo-Indian melismatic wailing on the end (by Dolenz, possibly with Harry Nilsson adding some extra vocals) in imitation of the Beatles' "Rain".

Love is Only Sleeping

Writers: Barry Mann and Cynthia Weil

Lead vocalist: Michael Nesmith

Other Monkees present: Micky Dolenz (backing vocals), Davy Jones (percussion, backing vocals), Peter Tork (keyboards)

Another Nesmith-sung psych-pop track, this one seems to be modelled on some of John Lennon's songs on *Revolver*, with their odd time signatures (the verse for this is in $\frac{7}{4}$) and driving guitar riffs. One of the slighter actual songs here, this becomes a worthwhile track thanks to the production tricks, and to one of Nesmith's very best vocal performances.

Nesmith here really shows off his versatility, from the low, speak-sung, "once I loved but love was dead" to the near-falsetto 'sleeping' at the end of the middle eight, he sings in a number of different voices, each one chosen perfectly for the section of the song in question. Dolenz - rightly - gets a lot of acclaim for his actorly phrasing, but Nesmith is at least as sensitive a vocalist here.

Cuddly Toy

Writer: Harry Nilsson

Lead vocalist: Davy Jones

Other Monkees present: Micky Dolenz (drums and backing vocals), Peter Tork (piano), Michael Nesmith (guitar)

The last Monkees studio track to feature Dolenz on drums for nearly thirty years, this song was brought to them by their new 'discovery' Harry Nilsson.

Nilsson had been working as a bank clerk while submitting songs to various people for several years, writing songs like the Lovin' Spoonful rip-off "This Could Be the Night" for Phil Spector. (That song was given to the Modern Folk Quartet, who had featured both Chip Douglas and sometime Monkees studio bass player Jerry Yester).

But at a time when the Monkees were drifting apart musically as a band, Nilsson's astonishing talents were something they could all agree on, appealing as they did both to Nesmith's desire to expand his musical palette (both Nesmith and Nilsson were equally influenced by both pre-rock popular music and by the Beatles' contemporary work) and to Jones' desire to make 'Broadway rock' his father's generation could enjoy.

Not that Jones' father's generation would approve of the lyrics - or at least one would hope not. This song has been variously described as being about various sordid practices up to and including gang rape, but in fact seems pretty clearly to 'only' be someone callously dumping a girl after taking her virginity - "You're not the only cherry delight that was left in the night and gave up without a fight", "I never told you that I loved no other, you must have dreamed it in your sleep."

Not quite as callous a performance as Nilsson's own recording (which includes tossed-off 'sob sob' asides), this song still works because of the way the jaunty, upbeat, vaudeville style music, and Jones' cheerful performance (doubled almost all the way through by Dolenz) contrast with the vicious psychopathy of the lyrics.

Very, very far from a pleasant song, but still a great one.

Words

Writers: Tommy Boyce and Bobby Hart

Lead vocalist: Micky Dolenz and Peter Tork

Other Monkees present: Michael Nesmith (guitar), Davy Jones (percussion)

One of the few occasions on which Tork actually plays bass on record, this track, which closes side one, was originally recorded during the *More of the Monkees* sessions with Boyce and Hart producing and the Candy Store Prophets backing. That version had featured on the TV series before being remade during these sessions.

There are very few differences between the two performances - the original has some extra lead guitar, a small bit of backwards recording, and has a flute part rather than Tork's Hammond organ solo, but otherwise the two tracks are almost identical, even down to the chimes that can be heard faintly (going across the stereo spectrum in the stereo mix).

Starting with a verse that stays on one minor chord for the whole verse, Dolenz and Tork overlap vocal lines (Tork's only vocal leads on a Boyce and Hart song), in a moody downbeat manner, before Dolenz becomes sole lead vocalist for the bridge (which by the time this came out would have sounded like it was based on "Heroes and Villains" by the Beach Boys, having the same bass riff as that song, but which was probably, like the Beach Boys' track, inspired by the version of "Save the Last Dance for Me" that Phil Spector had recently produced for Tina Turner).

The chorus is one of Boyce and Hart's garage-psych classics - a two-chord riff played for four bars, then repeated a tone up, with a bassline that's playing a variation on a boogie line (going constantly up instead of up then down), and is just ridiculously exciting.

This became the B-side to "Pleasant Valley Sunday" and charted in its own right at number eleven. As the only example of Tork singing lead on a hit single, it has been a part of the setlist during all the reunion tours in which Tork has participated.

Hard to Believe

Writers: David Jones, Kim Capli, Eddie Brick and Charlie Rockett

Lead vocalist: Davy Jones

Other Monkees present: none

Side two of the album opens with the song that marks the end of the Monkees as a recording group. The first song Jones ever co-wrote with anyone outside the band, this was written with two members of the band's tour support band the Sundowners, plus Rockett, their roadie, while on tour.

A bossa nova-lite track that fits in with the 'Broadway rock' idea Jones had been discussing in interviews for a while, this is the only proper song on the album to feature no Monkee involvement other than the lead vocalist. Instead Kim Capli plays the whole rhythm track, building up from the (excellent) drum and percussion parts.

Actually quite a catchy song (and the heavy breathing in the tag sounds like it may have inspired the similar effect in "Time of the Season" by the Zombies), this could easily have been a hit for Tom Jones or Dusty Springfield at the time. But a faultline was appearing in popular music by this point, with Vegas-style singers like those on one side, and rock music on the other, and Jones was trying firmly to ensconce himself on one side of that line, while his bandmates were all on the other.

Possibly because it was the only song to feature none of the rest of the band, this is the only song from the album never to be featured in the TV show. But it points the way to the future of the band - by their next album they would be working independently of each other more often than not, and solo tracks like this would become the norm.

What Am I Doing Hangin' 'Round?

Writers: "Travis Lewis and Boomer Clark" (Michael Martin Murphey and Owens Castleman)

Lead vocalist: Michael Nesmith

Other Monkees present: Micky Dolenz and Davy Jones (backing vocals)

In its own way, this track also shows the way the band were falling apart as a recording unit. While the track features Nesmith on guitar, Douglas on bass and Hoh on drums, the standard rhythm section for this album, the banjo is supplied not by Tork (who had played the banjo on *Headquarters*) but by bluegrass legend Doug Dillard.

While it sounds like a fairly standard country song, this is far more harmonically sophisticated than was normal in country music at that time. Nesmith points out (in an interview quoted in Andrew Sandoval's liner notes to the deluxe edition of this album) the I7-vi7 change in the bridge as a particularly 'uncountry' element, but the song plays with key ambiguity quite a bit, not being able to decide whether it's in C or F (in a mirror of its protagonist's own self-questioning), and going to a D♭in the chorus (at the start of the line "I should be ridin' on that train to San Anton' ") which belongs to neither key.

Nesmith provides one of his very best vocals here, going from the resigned "boy I sure missed mine" to the almost howled last chorus.

While this has precursors in some of Nesmith's own earlier work, and on some tracks on the Beatles albums *Beatles For Sale* and *Help!*, this song was, at the time, probably the most successful ever example of country-rock, managing to combine the emotional sophistication and musicianship of the former genre with the energy of the latter without sacrificing either.

This song has become a recent highlight of the Monkees' reunion tours, where Tork has taken the lead vocal when Nesmith is not present. As has the next track...

Peter Percival Patterson's Pet Pig Porky

Writer: Peter Tork

Lead vocalist: Peter Tork

Other Monkees present: None

A tongue-twister credited to Tork as arranger, this twenty-seven second spoken word track is just a bit of fun, with Tork showing how much fun plosives can be.

Pleasant Valley Sunday

Writers: Gerry Goffin and Carole King

Lead vocalist: Micky Dolenz

Other Monkees present: Peter Tork (piano), Michael Nesmith (guitar and backing vocals), Davy Jones (backing vocals and percussion)

If ever proof were needed that the Monkees were capable of producing great pop records without the involvement of Don Kirshner, this is it. With an instrumental track by Tork, Nesmith, Douglas and Hoh (with additional acoustic guitar by Bill Chadwick and possibly Dolenz), this shows that the band could, when left to their own devices, create spectacular pop singles.

Every band member gets to shine here - Dolenz of course takes the lead vocal, and does his usual superb job, Nesmith plays the "Day Tripper"-esque guitar riff (composed by Chip Douglas) and adds harmonies (and the Dolenz/Nesmith harmony blend, while underutilised, is one of the band's most thrilling elements), Tork adds the piano part under the middle eight (which otherwise would have seemed woefully poor, having as it does only a single chord), and Jones gives the vocal performance of his life, on the nasal, sarcastic 'ta ta ta ta' section.

Given that the song itself is relatively weak, being just an example of the mid-60s tendency to cruelly mock people for daring to want a comfortable life (see for example much of George Harrison or Ray Davies' songwriting around this time), the power of the track must be attributed entirely to the performance, production and arrangement. And every element here is spot-on (as can be heard on the 'karaoke' version made available on a Japanese best-of CD, where every detail of the backing track can be heard).

It's not the song itself that made this a hit, but Douglas' riff and the understanding of dynamics. This track builds from a relatively sedate beginning towards an almost orgasmic peak, with the riff and Nesmith and Dolenz's wailing being lost in a wall of reverb that it turn gets fed back on itself. The ending wouldn't be out of place on a Led Zeppelin record, but because it's been contextualised as part of a piece of simple pop music, no-one blinked an eye.

Quite rightly, this is a favourite of the band members - Peter Tork recorded a truly odd remake of it with his band the New Monks in 1980, for example - because of all their classic singles, it's the only one which allowed them all to shine as a group.

Daily Nightly

Writer: Michael Nesmith

Lead vocalist: Micky Dolenz

Other Monkees present: Peter Tork (keyboards), Michael Nesmith (guitar)

Oddly, for an album so dominated vocally by Nesmith, his first songwriting contribution to the album is one of the handful of Dolenz lead vocals.

This song, in fact, shows the new songwriting style Nesmith would be trying out for the next few albums. While it's harmonically simple (only three chords), the lyrics, which it's claimed began life as an impressionistic poem about the Sunset Strip riots, but which are fairly blatantly about sex workers, give up on standard ideas of sense in order to play with language:

> Startled eyes that sometimes see phantasmagoric splendour
>
> Pirouette down palsied paths with pennies for the vendor
>
> Salvation's yours for just the time it takes to pay the dancer.

Meanwhile Dolenz turns in the performance of his life, not just on vocal, but on Moog. Dolenz had only bought the Moog (one of a handful in existence at the time) the previous weekend, and this was its first use on a pop record. Dolenz here just twiddles knobs and makes interesting sounds, but in so doing he manages to do pretty much everything worthwhile that there is to do with a Moog.

The whole thing has a dense, brooding feel, and is in a sonic world completely different from anything else on the album. Tork's Hammond organ and Douglas' bass are very much of their time - the basic backing track could be by Julie Driscoll, Brian Auger and the Trinity or Jefferson Airplane - but adding Dolenz's vocals and the Moog's siren-like wails makes this something very special.

Don't Call on Me

Writers: Michael Nesmith and John London

Lead vocalist: Michael Nesmith

Other Monkees present: Peter Tork (keyboards), Micky Dolenz and Davy Jones (intro chatter)

And from a pointer to Nesmith's songwriting future, we look to his past, with this song he'd written four years earlier.

This lounge-flavoured song was originally written as an exercise in learning how to use major 7ths (which are what give it its lush feeling), and an acoustic demo exists of it from the early 60s in an almost McCartney-esque style, but it probably came back to its composer's mind after hearing "America Drinks and Goes Home" by the Mothers of Invention.

Frank Zappa, the Mothers' leader, had become a big influence on the Monkees, especially Nesmith, and would appear in the second series of the TV show and make a cameo appearance in the band's film *Head*, and "America Drinks and Goes Home" is both harmonically and lyrically similar to this song, though Zappa plays it entirely for laughs, while Nesmith takes the song perfectly straight (though like the Mothers' record, the track opens and ends with fake-drunk audience chatter and lounge piano).

This is actually a lovely ballad, with Nesmith singing right at the top of his range, sounding utterly unlike his normal baritone, and would be a stand-out track were it not for the fact that nearly every track on this album is a stand-out track.

Star Collector

Writers: Gerry Goffin and Carole King

Lead vocalist: Davy Jones

Other Monkees present: Micky Dolenz (backing vocals), Peter Tork (keyboards), Michael Nesmith (guitar)

Well, we've not had any Jones misogyny for a little while, so why not close the album with it? This rather nasty Goffin/King song about groupies (last line of the chorus "how can I love her when I just don't respect her?") is catchy, but after some of the wonderful music we've had it's a shallow, heartless song to end on, although it's easy to see why it was chosen as the closer, having as it does an extended Moog jam to fade on which would be difficult to follow. (The Moog here is played by session player Paul Beaver, far less inventively than Dolenz's performance on "Daily Nightly").

On any other Monkees album this would be a decent slightly-below-average track with an interesting ending. Here it's easily the least interesting track except maybe "Hard to Believe".

But that is, of course, a relative judgement, and one that can only be made because the general quality of *Pisces, Aquarius, Capricorn & Jones Ltd* is so very high. It's the only Monkees album until *Good Times!* about which one can honestly say there are no truly bad tracks, and the only one in which all the band members are given opportunities to shine. It's a true masterpiece.

Bonus Tracks

Special Announcement

Writer: unknown

Lead vocalist: Peter Tork

Other Monkees present: None

This is a little spoken-word joke, with Tork imitating the voice of Robert Keith Morrison, who introduced the reference tones for Ampex alignment tapes (used by sound engineers to calibrate equipment), introducing tones at various levels, the last of which is inaudible - but we hear a dog barking instead. This was originally intended as the opening track of the album.

It's been suggested that this was a joke about the 'silent' track at the end of *Sgt. Pepper,* which could only be heard by dogs, but a few weeks prior to this recording, the album *Safe as Milk* by Captain Beefheart and his Magic Band had been released. The Magic Band and the Monkees were friendly, and Nesmith had on occasion loaned the Magic Band amplifiers when their own equipment had been unavailable.

Safe as Milk was recorded in the same RCA studio as this album, and with Hank Cicalo (the Monkees' regular engineer at this time) engineering, opened on side two with the track "Kandy Korn", which starts with producer Richard Perry doing a near-identical Morrison imitation. For that reason, The Captain

Beefheart Radar Station [9] (from which I got some of the details here) calls this track 'the first ever Beefheart cover version'.

Goin' Down

Writers: Diane Hildebrand, Peter Tork, Michael Nesmith, Micky Dolenz and David Jones

Lead vocalist: Micky Dolenz

Other Monkees present: Davy Jones (percussion), Peter Tork and Michael Nesmith (guitar)

This track developed from a jam on the Mose Allison classic "Parchman Farm" (which it resembles closely enough that it's amazing Allison didn't sue - it still has almost an identical melody). Nesmith liked the results, but didn't see why the band should pay Allison royalties when they could just put a new vocal line on top, and so Diane Hildebrand (co-writer of "Early Morning Blues and Greens" and "Your Auntie Grizelda") was asked to write a new lyric.

The result is stunning - Hildebrand's lyrics turns this into a patter song or talking blues, with lyrics and internal rhymes tumbling out of Dolenz's mouth in a flow that would shame most modern rappers. The lyrics themselves are hilarious - the thoughts of someone drunkenly attempting suicide by drowning in the Mississippi, regretting it, and eventually deciding to go with the flow, quite literally. Between Dolenz's frenetic performance and the squealing saxophone, this is as exciting a record as it gets, and was released as the B-side of "Daydream Believer".

---

[9] http://www.beefheart.com/zigzag/books/
barnescompanswers2.htm

Riu Chiu

Writer: traditional

Lead vocalist: all four Monkees

And we finish with a stunning piece of vocal harmony, with the four Monkees singing a traditional Spanish Christmas carol.

I've got friends who believe that because Boyce and Hart provided the backing vocals on many of the early hits, that the Monkees themselves couldn't sing in harmony. This track should prove them wrong - an *a capella* performance of a complicated arrangement that's every bit as good as any of the harmony work pulled off by the Beach Boys, the Zombies or the Beatles.

In fact, there's an even better version of this song on the *Missing Links vol 2* CD - the version on here is taken from a TV performance, while the *Missing Links vol 2* version is a full studio recording, properly EQd with reverb added. That version also features Chip Douglas, rather than Jones, taking the fourth harmony part. Both versions are absolutely lovely, though.

The Birds, the Bees and the Monkees

For this album, unlike any of the others under discussion, I'm afraid I have to discuss a lot of music which can not, at present, be legally acquired.

By late 1967, the Monkees were working to all intents and purposes as four solo artists, with only minimal involvement with each other's work. And by the time *The Birds, the Bees and the Monkees* came to be released, each man had recorded almost a full album's worth of material, which was cut down into one fairly strong single album, though some of the best tracks were left off.

Some of the tracks made their way onto future albums or onto compilations, but in 2010 Rhino Handmade released a comprehensive, exhaustive three-CD box set which showed the sheer depth of talent that went into making this album. And they made it a limited edition. So much of this music became unavailable within a month of two of release. Apparently Rhino Handmade don't like money.

But if you can manage to obtain the music (I would of course never countenance the illegal downloading of music, and would suggest instead you purchase one of the vastly overpriced second-hand copies which occasionally come up for sale at a hundred pounds or more, and from which all of the money would go to a speculator and none to the artists or record label) you can see that *The Birds, the Bees and the Monkees* should have been the Monkees' *White Album*.

The album released at the time, though, wasn't as strong as its immediate predecessor. While Nesmith's tracks, in particular, are outstanding, the album suffers from having far too many Davy Jones 'Broadway rock' tracks, and from the near-complete absence of Peter Tork (whose only contribution to the album as released is a piano part on "Daydream Believer"). It's much as if the *White Album* had been cut down to a twelve-track album by someone with a vendetta against George Harrison, and with tracks selected by tossing coins.

While the album's production credit is to the Monkees (with the exception of the previously-released "Daydream Believer", credited to Chip Douglas), in reality a variety of producers worked on the album, though usually employed as 'arrangers' to keep up the pretence, including Boyce and Hart and Shorty Rogers, though band members did also produce their own tracks.

Dream World

Writers: David Jones and Steve Pitts

Lead vocalist: Davy Jones

Other Monkees present: None

The album opens with the best of Jones' Broadway-rock tracks, one of several songs written in collaboration with his friend

Steve Pitts, apparently for submission for the Monkees' forth-coming film.

The song seems to have been an attempt at writing in the pre-Beatles early-60s style of Jones' pre-Monkees ColPix solo album, and has a whiff of Adam Faith about it, though the lyric is at times quite biting ("Always pretending that everything's fine when it's not/Why must you lie when you know that you'll always get caught?"). However, Shorty Rogers' arrangement, with its harpsichord part and horn solo, brings it up to date.

Still among the weaker tracks on the album, this is a pleasant enough opener.

Auntie's Municipal Court

Writers: Michael Nesmith and Keith Allison

Lead vocalist: Micky Dolenz

Other Monkees present: Michael Nesmith (guitar and backing vocals)

Nesmith's first composition on the album, a jangly guitar-led country-psych song, is one of only two songs on the album that could legitimately be called a track by the Monkees, plural, rather than a Monkee singular, having as it does two band members on it - along with several of the band's regular recent collaborators, like Harry Nilsson, Bill Chadwick and Eddie Hoh.

This is Nesmith at his most psychedelic, stringing together words almost without regard for meaning, in a vaguely skipping-rhyme rhythm ("fine man, crazy man, he can't see/Sound of the sunset, sound of the sea"), rather than the precise, affecting choices of his earlier and later work. However, the country guitar-picking clearly grounds this in Nesmith's comfort zone, at least until the psychedelic freak-out reverbed ending.

We Were Made for Each Other

Writers: Carole Bayer and George Fischoff

Lead vocalist: Davy Jones

Other Monkees present: None

This is actually the Monkees' third attempt at this track. The first version, recorded three months earlier, and available as a bonus track on the box set version of the album, is quite an interesting track, driven by fast picked banjo, though it's missing a lead vocal.

The finished version, on the other hand, is horrible. It sounds like Jones' voice has been sped up, making it sound ridiculously thin, and it's just a wash of bad strings and tinkling harpsichord, over which Jones sings Bayer's banal lyrics. The stereo version is moderately better than the mono version in this respect, with the rhythm section more to the fore, and the strings being used as colouring rather than the major feature of the track, but that just elevates it from terrible to bearable.

Tapioca Tundra

Writer: Michael Nesmith

Lead vocalist: Michael Nesmith

Other Monkees present: None

Another of Nesmith's forays into psychedelia, this is a surrealistic poem ("Silhouettes and figures stay/Close to what we had to say/And one more time a faded dream/Is saddened by the news") over a vaguely Latin-inflected backing track (almost all played by Nesmith, apart from the drums by Eddie Hoh), a wash of acoustic guitars and hand percussion.

The music seems to show the influence of both the pre-rock country music Nesmith had been listening to recently (especially in the fingerpicked-and-whistled intro, but it shows up more consistently in the acoustic demo of this track, which could almost be Jimmie Rodgers at times, and doesn't have the psychedelic effects on the intro) and of the newer hard rock music that was becoming popular.

In particular, the between-verses riff, although similar to a lot of the playing with suspended chords that the Byrds and the Searchers did in their early folk-rock songs (and the feel of this track is such that the first comparison that would spring to mind is the Byrds' "Feel a Whole Lot Better"), is identical to that used by LA bands Love and the Leaves in their proto-punk versions of "Hey Joe" from 1966.

It also actually shows Nesmith self-plagiarising slightly, as the melody for the middle eight of this ("Sunshine, ragtime, blowing in the breeze...") is near-identical to the middle eight of "The Girl I Knew Somewhere" ("Someway, somehow, the same thing was done...").

There's a very strange alternate mix of this with a double-tracked vocal, with one of the vocals emoting very differently to the performance used in the finished version, and with reverb drenched all over everything, but the finished version, with a filter on Nesmith's single-tracked vocal, is one of the most interesting records the band ever made. Certainly, I can think of very few other surrealist garage-punk Latin country-psych tracks to have made the top forty.

Davy Jones would often claim in interviews that Nesmith got his songs regularly on the B-sides of the band's singles, and that this made Nesmith far more money than the rest of the band, but in fact this was only the second of his songs to be released as a B-side (as the B-side of "Valleri") and the first lead vocal he'd ever taken on either side of a single. "Valleri" was so popular that this reached number 34 in the US charts on the back of that success.

Daydream Believer

Writer: John Stewart

Lead vocalist: Davy Jones

Other Monkees present: Micky Dolenz (backing vocals), Michael Nesmith (guitar), Peter Tork (piano)

In many ways, this is the last Monkees record. It's certainly the last studio recording of an actual song to feature all four band members until 1996's *Justus* reunion album. It's also the last track produced by Chip Douglas to be released during the band's career, though several of the bonus tracks on the CD versions of this album feature Douglas' bass playing.

Written by John Stewart of the Kingston Trio, this became the band's fifth consecutive gold single, and remains probably their most-loved track. Everything about the track is precisely right, from the *audio verite* at the beginning ("7a" "What number is this, Chip?", "7A", "OK, no need to get excited man, it's 'cause I'm short, I know"), to Tork's simple arrangement, to the oblique lyric.

The piano part and arrangement for this track turned out to be the only contribution Tork made to the finished album (several of his songs were considered for it, including the two that eventually made the *Head* soundtrack), but given that this record is such an absolute pop classic, one has to wonder what would have happened had the four members continued to work together, rather than drifting apart.

Incidentally, there was one lyrical change that was made by the band from Stewart's demo - where he sang "now you know how funky I can be", the word 'funky' was changed to 'happy', presumably because the idea of Davy Jones ever being funky was such an absurd one. In later recordings, Stewart himself changed the lyric of the last chorus, singing "and an old closet queen".

This track was reissued in the 1980s, in a remixed version with a new drum part (full of gated reverb and 'sonic power') and handclaps. That version should be avoided at all costs.

Writing Wrongs

Writer: Michael Nesmith

Lead vocalist: Michael Nesmith

Other Monkees present: None

And here we get to possibly the most controversial record in the Monkees' 'canon'.

There are two schools of thought about this track. One of them (which seems to be the one to which almost every Monkees fan belongs) thinks this is dreadful. The other (to which I, and very few others, belong) considers this possibly the best single track the Monkees ever recorded.

An epic at 5:05 (for the mono mix) or 5:09 (for the stereo), this is very much the Monkees' equivalent of "A Day in the Life" or "Surf's Up". Nesmith here plays all the keyboard and guitar parts on what is easily his most ambitious Monkees track.

Starting with a two-chord tick-tock rhythm on piano, Nesmith comes in on vocals with his most impenetrable lyrics yet. Seemingly apocalyptic ("Did you know the water's turning yellow?/Had you heard the sky was falling down?") the lyrics seem to reference things that have some meaning at least to Nesmith ("Have you heard about Bill Chambers' mother?"), while the piano keeps tick-tocking and an organ drones underneath.

Suddenly the piano changes to straight fours - "You have a way of making everything you say seem unreal..." - as the organ rises in volume. This, what we must consider the chorus, lasts for two lines, then we get eleven beats in $\frac{3}{4}$ time, and a sudden stop.

We then enter the jazz freak-out section. Over Latin-flavoured drums and a single, briskly strummed, guitar chord, the piano starts playing around with a couple of three- and four-note scalar riffs, while the organ plays different variations of the same patterns.

The whole thing is almost wilfully difficult. There is a consistent pulse to the music, but each instrument is playing against that pulse, rather than with it, and against the other instruments. Were one to listen to this instrumental piece out of context, the first thought might be that it was by Sun Ra or someone rather than the Monkees.

After two minutes and ten seconds of this - the length of many normal Monkees songs - we return to a shortened version of the original musical material, with similarly oblique lyrics ("And I hope Bill Chambers' mother's better/Oh dear, the moon just disappeared"), and fades on a repeat of the instrumental section.

It's a draining, exhausting piece of music, quite unlike anything else the band recorded, but quite astonishingly good.

I'll Be Back Up On My Feet

Writers: Sandy Linzner and Denny Randell

Lead vocalist: Micky Dolenz

Other Monkees present: None

This is a remake of a track that had originally been recorded during the *More of the Monkees* sessions with Jeff Barry producing. This version is much better, being faster paced, and with a very interesting arrangement by Shorty Rogers, especially a bizarre sound in the bass register which comes from a percussion instrument called a quica which is unlike anything I've ever heard.

The song itself is not hugely impressive, though, being patterned after the kind of material with which Sandie Shaw was having some success at the time, a sort of cod-Bacharach without Bacharach's harmonic or rhythmic unpredictability.

What *is* impressive, though, is the stylistic range of this album, where something like this could follow something like "Writing Wrongs" and have neither track sound more out of place than the other.

This song has recently had something of a revival, being included in many of Dolenz and Tork's two-person "Monkees" shows of 2015 and 2016.

The Poster

Writers: David Jones and Steve Pitts

Lead vocalist: Davy Jones

Other Monkees present: None

Easily the worst song on the album by a long way, this is "Being for the Benefit of Mr Kite" as rewritten by a very literal-minded five-year-old with no sense of poetry or imagery, and sung slightly out of tune. Except not as interesting as that sounds.

Jones got the idea for this song (and the quote he used on the back cover of the album) from one Edith Sidebottom, a woman in her mid-eighties who had written a song that ended 'and the circus is coming to town'. She later threatened to sue him, but he settled out of court.

P.O. Box 9847

Writers: Tommy Boyce and Bobby Hart

Lead vocalist: Micky Dolenz

Other Monkees present: None

This is actually a cover of a track Boyce and Hart had previously released under their own names, as a B-side. Boyce and Hart's original is actually rather better than the Monkees' version.

This song came from an idea by Bob Rafelson, one of the producers of the Monkees' TV show, about someone writing a classified ad. It's actually one of Boyce and Hart's cleverer songs, with each verse being a classified ad leading up to the chorus, which is just the title repeated, leading back into the verse with a different line each time, but all along the lines of "I've described me very poorly, better try again".

Not only is it an extremely good song as a song, it also manages to work very cynically on the teenage girl listener. Each verse is slightly more grounded and realistic than the one previous, and it's easy to imagine poor Micky trying vainly to describe himself, while only you - yes *YOU* teenage American girl - can really understand him.

Listening to Boyce and Hart's original version, it's very obviously inspired by John Lennon and George Harrison's work on *Revolver*, but the two versions by the Monkees move further from that inspiration (though the piano part in the released version bears a family resemblance to the "Taxman" riff).

There are two very different versions of this song recorded by the Monkees. The more conventional of the two, driven by an eerie Bernard Herrmann-esque string part, is the one that made it on to the album, but the other version, based around a Moog rather than the strings, is slightly better in my view. Either way, though, this is, other than "Daydream Believer", the strongest non-Nesmith track on the album.

Magnolia Simms

Writers: Michael Nesmith

Lead vocalist: Michael Nesmith

Other Monkees present: None

The most straightforward of Nesmith's songs on the album, this is a note-perfect attempt at recapturing the feel of 1920s and 30s 'old-time' music, from a time when country music and jazz were much closer than people now think (see for example Jimmie Rodgers and Louis Armstrong recording together).

There was a brief fad for this kind of nostalgia at this time, more in Britain than in the US, with bands like the Bonzo Dog Doo-Dah Band recording 1920s novelty songs, and even the Beatles would follow a few months later with "Honey Pie", which, like this song, had added surface noise to replicate the sound of an old 78. Nesmith also has a filter on his vocal, to sound more like the 1920s singers who used a megaphone to be heard above their bands.

The stereo mix of this song, in fact, only plays in one channel, because the music it was emulating was in mono. However, the box set reissue of this album contains a true-stereo remix, without the noises.

This is Nesmith's slightest piece on the album, but accessible and catchy, and shows his mastery of this style, both as a songwriter and a vocalist.

Valleri

Writers: Tommy Boyce and Bobby Hart

Lead vocalist: Davy Jones

Other Monkees present: None

This is another remake of a song recorded earlier in the band's career. In this case, the song had featured on the TV show, and was being played by DJs, but had never been released commercially.

The original version, produced by Boyce and Hart, was deemed unusable as all tracks now had to have a 'produced by the Monkees' credit. So Boyce and Hart were called back in to re-record it, as close as possible to the original recording, but had to give the Monkees credit for production.

The song itself has been called by Nesmith "The worst song I've ever heard in my life," and there's some truth to that assertion. Its genesis began when Boyce and Hart were asked by Kirshner if they had a girl's-name song for the TV show, said 'of course', then wrote it in the car on the way to see him. As a result, the song just consists of four chords repeated over and over - a descending sequence by whole tones from I to V7 - with the most moronic possible lyrics (rhyming "good" with "could" and "door" with "before", with the chorus just being the word "Valleri").

However the production and arrangement are a truly impressive piece of turd-polishing, with a fuzz-guitar riff inspired by "Satisfaction" (though sounding more like "Hungry Freaks, Daddy" by the Mothers of Invention), a Stax-esque horn section and blisteringly fast acoustic guitar playing from Louie Shelton. While the song may be dreadful, the record is a great piece of pop music.

Most Monkees fans prefer the first recorded version of the song (available as a bonus track on *More of the Monkees*) but there's actually little difference between the two – the main difference being the addition of horns on the remake, and the song opening with Louie Shelton's fast guitar rather than the riff.

This was the Monkees' last top ten single in the US, peaking at number three and going gold. Perhaps not coincidentally, it was also the last single they released to feature in their TV show.

Zor and Zam

Writers: Bill and John Chadwick

Lead vocalist: Micky Dolenz

Other Monkees present: None

A rather intense nursery-rhyme like song telling the story of two kingdoms preparing for a war that never happens because nobody showed up, this song is possibly best known for popularising the anti-war slogan "what if they gave a war and nobody came?", a paraphrase by the Chadwicks of "Suppose they gave a war and no-one came?", the title of a magazine article, which was itself a misremembering of a line from a poem by Carl Sandburg.

The line as used by the Monkees became one of the most powerful slogans of the Vietnam era, though few remembered where it had come from.

Bonus Tracks

Alvin

Writer: Nicholas Thorkelson

Lead vocalist: Peter Tork

Other Monkees present: None

A charming 24-second *a capella* piece by Tork's brother, about missing a pet alligator who's been flushed down the toilet.

I'm Gonna Try

Writers: David Jones and Steve Pitts

Lead vocalist: Davy Jones

Other Monkees present: None

Described (accurately) by Jones as 'just a throwaway thing, really'[10], this harmlessly pleasant example of Jones' 'Broadway rock' style would nonetheless have made a much better track than "The Poster", which was recorded at the same time.

Lady's Baby

Writer: Peter Tork

Lead vocalist: Peter Tork

Other Monkees present: None

This simple ballad by Tork, which went unreleased until the 1990s, was his obsession at this period, taking twelve sessions

---

[10]quote taken from Sandoval, p. 172

to record, including musicians like Stephen Stills, Dewey Martin (the drummer from Buffalo Springfield) and Buddy Miles.

It's odd it took so long, and went through so many versions (of which several are included on the box set version, and one more on a bonus single that came with the initial copies of the box set), as the basics of this simple song were in place from the start, and any of the multiple takes and mixes that have seen the light could easily have been released.

A nice, gentle song about being at peace with his then-girlfriend and her son, this is much better than much of the material that made it to the finished album, and it's a shame Tork's perfectionism drove him past a point of diminishing returns.

D.W. Washburn

Writers: Jerry Leiber and Mike Stoller

Lead vocalist: Micky Dolenz

Other Monkees present: None

This was the first Monkees song to be a flop, 'only' reaching number 19 on the US singles charts, thanks to being the first single the band released not to be featured on the TV show, and to the Coasters releasing a version almost simultaneously.

It's a shame, because this is an enjoyable Dixieland pastiche in a style that was suiting the Monkees well at the time, being stylistically close to "Cuddly Toy" in its mixture of rather dark lyrics (from the point of view of a homeless alcoholic refusing the help of the Salvation Army) and upbeat music. And Leiber and Stoller were one of the most reliable songwriting teams of their age.

Nonetheless, while this was not a big hit (though still far more successful than any singles from the rest of their career), it's still a great track, with the clanking banjo and Dolenz's mannered vocal bringing the song to life beautifully.

In recent years, Dolenz has added this to his shows, following his "A Little Bit Broadway, A Little Bit Rock And Roll" show, which combined Monkees hits with Broadway songs – "D.W. Washburn" had been included in the hit Leiber/Stoller musical *Smokey Joe's Cafe* and so bridged the gap between the two sides of the show – and it was a highlight of the Tork/Dolenz Monkees shows of 2015 and 2016.

It's Nice to Be With You

Writer: Jerry Goldstein

Lead vocalist: Davy Jones

Other Monkees present: None

Written by the co-writer of "I Want Candy" and "My Boyfriend's Back", this sappy ballad unfortunately has little of those tracks' energy, being exactly what you imagine Davy Jones singing a song called "It's Nice to Be With You" would sound like, with a plinky, over-orchestrated background. As the B-side of "D.W. Washburn" this scraped to number 51 in the US charts, but did better internationally.

Carlisle Wheeling

Writer: Michael Nesmith

Lead vocalist: Michael Nesmith

Other Monkees present: Peter Tork (banjo)

Musically, this is almost a rewrite of "Nine Times Blue", although lyrically it is very different, looking back with age at a happy romance that has almost but not quite dulled into complacency.

Nesmith was never very happy with this song, but nonetheless he attempted recording it several times - this version, a similar version during the *Instant Replay* sessions, a version on his big band instrumental album *The Wichita Train Whistle Sings* and a solo version in the early 70s.

It's easy to see both why he was unhappy with it and why he tried to make it work. Melodically it's quite beautiful, but lyrically the metaphors at times grow very strained. But then there are also moments of lyrical brilliance - "So forgive me my dear if I seem preoccupied/And if the razor edge of youth filled love is gone" is as good a couplet as Nesmith has ever written.

The result is a song that is more than listenable, and which I wouldn't want to be without, but which doesn't quite do what its composer intends. It's vastly preferable to much of what made the finished album, but it being left off is more understandable than with some other tracks.

Rose Marie

Writer: Micky Dolenz

Lead vocalist: Micky Dolenz

Other Monkees present: Peter Tork (acoustic guitar)

This horn-driven riffy soul track is as close to being funky as the Monkees ever got, and wouldn't sound out of place on an early-70s blaxploitation film. There are three versions of this track, all with different lyrics. The version on the *The Birds...* box set is an early mix with no lyrics at all on the bridge, the version on the *Missing Links* CD has the most properly-thought-out lyrics, but the best version by far is the version released as a bonus track on *Instant Replay*.

That version has Dolenz singing gibberish lyrics and imitating various musical instruments vocally, and is just superb. But all the versions of this - all of which derive from the same basic track - are an intriguing look at a musical direction the Monkees never really took, but to which Dolenz in particular was well suited.

My Share of the Sidewalk

Writer: Michael Nesmith

Lead vocalist: Davy Jones/Michael Nesmith

Other Monkees present: None

Lyrically, this is about as simplistic as Nesmith gets, but musically it's more interesting. This is the most metrically irregular thing the Monkees ever released.

Starting with an intro of four bars of $\frac{5}{4}$, it then goes into a first verse which breaks down as two bars of $\frac{7}{4}$, two of $\frac{4}{4}$ and one more of $\frac{7}{4}$. The second verse, while sounding similar, is actually six bars of $\frac{4}{4}$ and one of $\frac{7}{4}$. There's then a vocal bridge of eight bars of $\frac{12}{8}$, an instrumental break of four bars of $\frac{12}{8}$, then the whole thing repeats from the start, then repeats again til end of verse two and fades on a repetition of the $\frac{5}{4}$ intro.

What's interesting about this as well is it shows what a difference each Monkee could make vocally. When Nesmith sings this, in a rough version without the full orchestration, it sounds like a cool jazz piece, like it could be sung by Mose Allison or someone. By contrast, when Jones sings it, it sounds like the kind of all-round family entertainment that could easily have been used on any variety show of the period.

And while I've sometimes been harsh on Jones' vocals in this book, this shows that when he put his mind to it he could do a remarkable job. He sings this in his 'Broadway rock' style, but manages to navigate these horrendous changes (and some bad syllabics - the stresses to this lyric don't fall at all well) without sounding like he's even trying, as well as managing the rangey melody far better than Nesmith (who croaks his way through the high notes in what is, admittedly, a demo).

Little Red Rider

Writer: Michael Nesmith

Lead vocalist: Michael Nesmith

Other Monkees present: None

There are two versions of this recorded as the Monkees. The version on the *The Birds...* box set is a simple acoustic demo, while the version on *Missing Links vol 3*, later included on the *The Monkees Present* deluxe box set, is a country-soul number that sounds a lot like the music Elvis Presley was making at the time, or the country-soul blend Dan Penn, Chips Moman and Spooner Oldham had come up with. An enjoyable track, it's possibly more of a stylistic experiment than a proper song (though again, like "Rose Marie", it's interesting to see the soulful direction various band members were taking). Nesmith later rerecorded this with the First National Band on his first solo album, *Magnetic South*.

Ceiling in My Room

Writers: Don DeMieri, Robert Dick and David Jones

Lead vocalist: Davy Jones

Other Monkees present: None

A dreadful, dreadful song, this is some kind of self-pitying cross between "My Way" (though of course this was before that horror was ever written) and "It's Nice to Be With You", with some inspiration from the Beach Boys' "In My Room", and with backing vocals that are more bellowed than sung. Abysmal.

Come On In

Writer: Jo Mapes

Lead vocalist: Peter Tork

Other Monkees present: None

This song, in a sunshine pop version, was a hit for the Association, a harmony-pop band featuring Jim Yester, brother of occasional Monkees collaborator Jerry. This, however, is a drastically different arrangement. In fact, this track sounds like "Lady's Baby" part two, having the same slow/fast tempo changes, and like that track features Stephen Stills and Lance Wakely on guitars, along with Dewey Martin.

A nice, gentle song performed by excellent musicians, with a heartfelt vocal, this is nothing mindblowingly special, but it's a nice track. This kind of music would become incredibly popular a couple of years later, performed by people like Crosby, Stills, Nash and Young, but by that point Tork had retired from music.

Tear the Top Right Off My Head

Writer: Peter Tork

Lead vocalist: Peter Tork, Micky Dolenz

Other Monkees present: Micky Dolenz (backing vocals)

On the other hand, this kind of thing never became hugely popular, being as it is a novelty banjo-and-harmonica driven love song which occasionally turns into a hippy comedy hard rock number for a few bars.

There are a few versions of this track on the box set - Tork's original vocal, a version with Dolenz singing which doesn't really work, and a version (with Tork's vocal) sped up to be about a tone faster, which comes together much better than the other versions, but this never *quite* works, though no matter how often I listen to it I can't put my finger on why.

Merry Go Round

Writers: Peter Tork and Diane Hildebrand

Lead vocalist: Peter Tork

Other Monkees present: None

Musically an interesting track, this mournful organ-and-piano driven waltz was recorded in a few different versions. Easily the best version is the solo acoustic version on this box set. The two fuller versions that have been released, here and on *Missing Links vol 3,* both have interesting production choices, but are taken at too slow a speed for Tork's comparatively weak voice, and then fatally damaged by Tork double-tracking himself sloppily. There's an interesting idea in here, but other than the acoustic demo it's not something you'd want to listen to regularly.

War Games

Writers: David Jones and Steve Pitts

Lead vocalist: Davy Jones

Other Monkees present: Michael Nesmith (acoustic guitar, version one only)

Attentive readers will have noticed that I'm not the hugest fan of the songwriting talents of Jones and Pitts, and the two of them trying to write an anti-war protest song is about as poor as you'd expect.

But in fact, one of the two versions of this, the first version, works quite well. With a backing band led by Nesmith, the two-chord verse is slashed through at quite a fast pace, and the arrangement is a straight rip-off of 1965 Dylan, all Hammond organ and acoustic rhythm guitar.

Version two, though, is taken at a much slower speed, and mixes tinkly harpsichord with a marching band feel, to horrible effect.

Don't Say Nothin' Bad (About My Baby)

Writers: Gerry Goffin and Carole King

Lead vocalist: Micky Dolenz

Other Monkees present: None

A generic twelve-bar rock-and-roll track, this sounds like the kind of thing that could have been a minor hit for Danny and the Juniors in 1958 or Shakin' Stevens in 1981. It has absolutely no distinguishing features.

Laurel and Hardy

Writers: Jan Berry and Roger Christian

Lead vocalist: Davy Jones

Other Monkees present: None

This isn't actually a Monkees track at all. It's a Jan and Dean one, though neither Jan nor Dean appear.

To explain - Jan and Dean were a successful pop duo in the early and mid sixties, consisting of Jan Berry, who was a driven, unpleasant, ambitious man who wrote their hits (usually in collaboration with Roger Christian, Don Altfeld and/or Brian

Wilson), produced them and sang on them, and Dean Torrence, a nice person everyone liked, who didn't.[11]

Jones was friendly with both of them, and when Berry was seriously brain-damaged in a car accident stepped in to help, spending a lot of time helping Berry re-learn basic life skills.

Both Jan and Dean, separately, decided to record new 'Jan and Dean' material to try to keep the brand alive, with Torrence's solo concept album *Save For a Rainy Day* being released as a Jan and Dean album while Berry was still in hospital.

Berry responded with *Carnival of Sound*, a psych-pop album that remained unreleased until 2010, and Jones assisted with some of the vocals, as Berry was at the time unable to sing.

This track, which is based on a sitar rendition of the Laurel and Hardy theme before going into more familiar Jan and Dean musical territory, was written by Berry with lyricist Roger Christian, who had co-written many of Berry's previous hits as well as Beach Boys songs like "Little Deuce Coupe" and "Don't Worry Baby".

The track is very much in the novelty vein of albums like *Jan and Dean Meet Batman*, although this version, with Jones singing lead, doesn't go so far in the novelty direction as the version, with a different lead vocalist, released on the *Carnival of Sound* CD, which has a verse about Laurel and Hardy on a roller-coaster with the Maharishi.

---

[11]This is probably an exaggeration. But the vocal parts Torrence took live were, often, performed in the studio by P.F. Sloan or, less frequently, Brian Wilson.

Shake 'Em Up and Let 'Em Roll

Writers: Jerry Leiber and Mike Stoller

Lead vocalist: Micky Dolenz

Other Monkees present: None

There are two different versions of this track, both identical but for the vocal take used. It's a pleasant R&B number with an incongruously amusing trad jazz clarinet part, and in fact was recorded in 1970 as a single by Kenny Ball and his Jazzmen.

Astonishingly, though, this is the second time, after "D.W. Washburn", that Dolenz would sing a Leiber/Stoller song very shortly after the Coasters recorded a version. In this case the Coasters' version was recorded less than a fortnight before the Monkees' version was recorded, and one has to wonder what they were thinking. Perhaps wisely, after the Coasters' release had helped sink "Washburn" on the charts, this remained un-released despite being a very pleasant, though outdated, song.

Changes

Writers: David Jones and Steve Pitts

Lead vocalist: Davy Jones

Other Monkees present: None

A Jones/Pitts collaboration intended as a title track for the Monkees' forthcoming film (later retitled *Head*), this is actually not half-bad. The arrangement is in the same sort of muscular soul-rock range as that of "Little Red Rider", and while the song itself isn't particularly good, this has a nice *Dusty in Memphis* feel to it.

The Party

Writers: David Jones and Steve Pitts

Lead vocalist: Davy Jones

Other Monkees present: None

A very pleasant track, and one of the better Jones/Pitts collaborations, this has something of the feel of "Changes" about it, but a less impressive (and more string-dominated) arrangement - in fact an almost identical arrangement to that of "I'm Gonna Try". A minor piece, but enjoyable on its own terms.

I'm a Man

Writers: Barry Mann and Cynthia Weil

Monkees present: None

An unused backing track, produced by Chip Douglas in clear, blatant imitation of Phil Spector's style, this is actually one of the better Spector imitations I've heard, though the instruments are much clearer and more separated than Spector's usual style.

Head

And so we come to the last album the four Monkees would all appear on until the mid-1990s[12].

Head is a wonderful trivia-quiz question supplier - "What album, compiled by Jack Nicholson, features Neil Young, Frank Zappa and Bela Lugosi?" as an example - and by far the strangest album the Monkees ever released.

In late 1968 the Monkees released their film *Head*. Written by Jack Nicholson and Bob Rafelson from ideas that the group had supplied, the film is a collage of loosely-interrelated sketches mixed with what would now be called music videos, a psychedelic montage which tries to link the Monkees' status as plastic pop idols with the Vietnam War, with both being regarded as traps of the mind, to be escaped from by attaining mental or spiritual freedom. It features, among many other scenes, Peter Tork punching a female impersonator, the Monkees as dandruff in Victor Mature's hair, and Davy Jones beating Sonny Liston in a boxing match.

---

[12] Tork may have contributed some guitar to one archival track used on *Instant Replay*, and the deluxe edition of that album features him on some bonus tracks, but he left before work had properly begun on it.

The film is bizarre, and utterly unlike anything you might imagine from the phrase 'a Monkees film', but is in its own way a masterpiece. Probably the closest comparisons are Frank Zappa's *200 Motels* and *Monty Python's The Meaning of Life*, both of which came out much later, and neither of which were aimed at an audience remotely comparable to the Monkees'.

On top of this, the film had an...interesting...advertising campaign, based around the ideas of Marshall McLuhan, which didn't bother with giving information like the fact that *Head* was a film, or that the Monkees were in it, choosing instead just to show the head of advertising executive John Brockman with the cryptic slogan "What is *Head*? Only John Brockman's shrink knows for sure."

The film was, understandably, a gigantic flop, and inspires mixed emotions in the band members these days. Nesmith regards the film as a masterpiece. Tork is proud of it as a technical achievement, but dislikes what he sees as its overly cynical attitude. Jones, on the other hand, loathed it, blaming the film for the destruction of the band's career.

That may or may not be the case, though judging from their singles sales the band were probably doomed as soon as the TV show went off-air. But what *Head* did do, very successfully, was show future generations of fans that there was more to the band than the TV show and hits, when shown on late-night TV. Tork, Jones and Dolenz acknowledged this in their 2011 reunion tour, by opening the second half of their show with all the songs from *Head*.

It's not the place of this book to go into the film in any more detail, but anyone with any interest in the band should read the exhaustive analysis of the film and its making by comedy site Some of the Corpses are Amusing[13].

The soundtrack album is, in its own way, as interesting as the film. Edited together by Nicholson, the album was inspired by the Mothers of Invention's *We're Only in it for the Money*, and mixes the seven songs from the film with collages of dialogue (both from the film and from bits of other films excerpted in the film) and orchestral soundtrack music. All of this was taken out of context, so for example the line "Boys, don't never, but never, make fun of no cripples" from one scene in the film is followed by "Somebody come up and giggle at ya, that's a violation of your civil rights" from a vox-pop section, while the question "Are you telling me you don't see the connection between government and laughing at people?" is followed by Tork's "Well, let me tell you one thing, son, nobody ever lends money to a man with a sense of humour."

The result preserves many of the best lines from the film while recontextualising them, and the repetition of different snippets of songs and dialogue gives the album a through-line that's missing from many of the Monkees' other records. While this is the Monkees' most 'experimental' album, it's also, without a doubt, the one that has the greatest feeling of unity to it, thanks largely to Nicholson's editing.

It's also, after the largely solo *The Birds, the Bees and the Monkees*, slightly more of a group effort. While only "Ditty Diego" (and the live version of "Circle Sky" used in the film but not the album) features all four Monkees, the majority of the tracks feature two of them. And after Tork's near-absence from the previous album, and Dolenz's general lower profile,

---

[13]http://sotcaa.org/head

the two dominate this album at the expense of Nesmith and Jones, who only get one song each. The level of group control over the creative process in this album can be seen by the fact that it's the only 60s Monkees album to feature no Boyce and Hart tracks.

After this, the Monkees only did one more project as a quartet, the deeply strange and uncommercial TV special *33 1/3 Revolutions Per Monkee*, before Tork left, frustrated that the four were no longer working together in the studio as a unit.

While the two albums that followed have their moments, this is really where the Monkees meet their end.

All the actual songs on the album are credited as produced by the Monkees, with the exception of "Porpoise Song" which is produced by Gerry Goffin.

While a 3-CD deluxe edition of this album does exist, it has relatively little in the way of new music, featuring mostly alternate mixes, some live tracks from the concert that was filmed for the "Circle Sky" scene, and lots of promotional material (radio adverts, interviews with Jones and so on) that doesn't really come under this book's remit.

Opening Ceremony

This track starts as a collage of lines from various parts of the film, over sections of music from "Porpoise Song", "As We Go Along", "Daddy's Song" and "Circle Sky", while two people say, as dialogue, "Head" ,"Soon", over and over.

It then cuts to a speech from the opening scene from the film (the dedication ceremony for a bridge), overlaid by additional sound effects.

Porpoise Song (Theme from Head)

Writers: Gerry Goffin and Carole King

Lead vocalist: Micky Dolenz and Davy Jones

Producer: Gerry Goffin

Other Monkees present: None

This is Goffin and King being all cod-psychedelic, but it works here. While the lyrics are gibberish (where they're not in-jokes like "riding the backs of giraffes for laughs", a reference to Dolenz's child stardom on *Circus Boy*), the music is perfectly put together.

The verses are, roughly, inspired by "A Day in the Life", in their stately rhythm, especially with the piano chords early on, while the bridge and chorus are both tips of the hat to "A Whiter Shade of Pale", being as they are progressions based on a single chord each but with a scalar descending bassline. This is most notable in the organ part, which sounds near-identical to the Procol Harum song.

Both Dolenz (on the verses and bridges) and Jones (on the choruses) turn in stellar performances, but what really makes this track is the extraordinary arrangement by Jack Nitzsche, one of the great unsung heroes of American music in the 60s. He manages to combine a string arrangement perfectly in the style of George Martin (using only double basses and cellos) with the Procol Harum organ, but then adds reverbed, clanking bells to remind the listener of the sea.

This is especially effective on the extended mix used for the single, which features an extended instrumental coda for strings, bells, organ and cymbals that is one of Nitzsche's most beautiful pieces of work.

The whole thing seems to be a response to the Beatles' psychedelic work, saying in effect "Okay, we can top that" - an effect
which is added to on the album by the police sirens at the beginning, giving a reminder of "I am the Walrus". Unfortunately,
the Monkees weren't able to take the teen audience with them
the way the Beatles had, and this single only reached number
62 in the US charts.

Ditty Diego-War Chant

Writers: Bob Rafelson and Jack Nicholson

Lead vocalist: All four Monkees

The last pre-reunion track to be released featuring all four Monkees, this is a parody by Nicholson and Rafelson of the Monkees theme, with verses alternating between skewering the band
themselves ("Hey hey we are the Monkees, you know we love to
please/A manufactured image, with no philosophies" "Hey hey
we are the Monkees, we've said it all before/The money's in,
we're made of tin, we're here to give you more") and describing the film's plot and structure ("We know it doesn't matter,
'cause what you came to see/Is what we'd love to give you,
and give it one, two, three/But it may come three, two, one,
two, or jump from nine to five/And when you see the end in
sight the beginning may arrive").

This chant, spoken at times by the full band and at times by individual members, is spoken over a barrelhouse piano part reminiscent of silent-film comedy accompaniments, and the whole
thing is then sped up and slowed down to sound like the tape is
stretched and distorted, before there's a sharp cut to the band

exhorting a concert audience to "Give me a W! Give me an A! Give me an R! What's that spell?!"

This track is so breathtakingly cynical about the Monkees themselves, it may be the bravest thing ever recorded by a major band. It's not, however, worth listening to the twenty-two minute session excerpt on the deluxe box set more than once.

One of the oddest moments in Tork, Dolenz and Jones' reunion tour of the late 80s was that they performed an abbreviated version of this in a hip-hop style.

Circle Sky

Writer: Michael Nesmith

Lead vocalist: Michael Nesmith

Other Monkees present: None (studio version)/Micky Dolenz (drums),Peter Tork (bass), Davy Jones (maracas and organ) (live version)

The closest thing to a hard rock track the band ever recorded, this is for the most part just hammering away at a single chord in a manner inspired by Bo Diddley (apart from the instrumental breaks, which are just descending bar chords from B to D, and the middle eight, which is the minor-chord equivalent of the breaks). Lyrically, it's a stream-of-consciousness description of Nesmith's impressions of a Monkees tour ("Colours, sounds/all around"), although the themes of circularity and repetition ("it looks like we've made it once again") work well with the themes of the rest of the album and of the film.

This song was very specifically written to work well for the band in a live setting, and the performance in the film is taken from a real live show - possibly the first time a rock band had used actual live footage rather than mimed performances in a film like this. However, strangely, the version on the album is a nearly-identical studio take, performed by Nesmith with studio musicians.

This upset the rest of the band, especially Tork, who blamed Nesmith, but Nesmith himself now says that he prefers the live version and had nothing to do with its replacement on the album. Either way, the live version is now included on all CD reissues along with the studio performance.

The band later rerecorded this for the *Justus* album, making it the only song to have been released by the band as part of two proper albums. That version will be dealt with in that chapter.

Supplicio

Some Moog wind effects, a snatch of orchestral music, a cymbal with backwards reverb, and a voice saying "Quiet, isn't it, George Michael Dolenz? I said..." (the latter taken from a scene in the film where Dolenz becomes delirious in a desert).

Can You Dig It?

Writer: Peter Tork

Lead vocalist: Micky Dolenz

Other Monkees present: Peter Tork (guitar and vocals)

This is possibly the most 1968 piece of music ever, with pseudo-Indian sitarish acoustic guitar, bongos, and a chorus that goes "Can you dig it?/Do you know?/Would you care to let it show?", as well as a long instrumental freak-out at the end.

However, it's also the Monkees track that changed most from its original conception. Before becoming the minor pop-psych masterpiece it started out as a ragtime-ish acoustic guitar piece that sounded equal parts Blind Blake and Bert Jansch (this version can be heard on the *Headquarters Sessions* box set), with a bridge that didn't make it to the final version.

To my ears, that version is even better than the finished record, but the track as heard on the album, with its lyrics about the Tao and 'exotic' textures, is still one of the best things Tork ever brought to the group.

The song was originally intended to have Tork singing lead, but Dolenz recorded a new (and extremely good) lead vocal at the request of Rafelson, without any objection from Tork. However, the version with Tork singing lead is available as a bonus track on all CD releases, and Tork now sings this song live.

Gravy

Side one finishes with Jones saying "And I'd like a glass of cold gravy with a hair in it please".

Superstitious

A snippet from the 1934 Boris Karloff and Bela Lugosi film *The Black Cat*, briefly seen on a TV in the film. This just consists of David Manners saying "Sounds like a lot of supernatural baloney to me", with Lugosi replying "Supernatural, perhaps. Baloney, perhaps not."

As We Go Along

Writers: Gerry Goffin and Carole King

Lead vocalist: Micky Dolenz

Other Monkees present: None

The first proper song on side two is, like the opening track on side one, a Goffin/King ballad sung by Dolenz.

This gorgeous little ballad is notable for having possibly the most unnecessarily-stellar group of session guitarists ever. The wall of acoustic guitars in Jack Nitzsche's arrangement, mostly just strumming chords, includes Neil Young, Danny Kortchmar, Ry Cooder and Carole King.

The only song in the film to feature only one Monkee, this is a delicate, yearning ballad, which Dolenz sings perfectly, despite its difficulty. The song is one of the most metrically difficult things the Monkees ever did - starting out with an extended intro in $\frac{5}{4}$, once Dolenz's vocal comes in we have a verse of three bars of $\frac{5}{4}$ (in one of which the bass accentuates the wrong beat, adding to the metrical confusion - the bass seems to be implying that these fifteen beats should be broken up six, four, five rather than the five, five, five everything else implies) one of $\frac{6}{4}$, three of $\frac{3}{4}$ and one of $\frac{6}{4}$. The chorus, though, is in pretty straight sixes.

This is the kind of song with which King would later have a huge amount of solo success, but as the B-side of "Porpoise Song" this failed even to make the top hundred in the US. A shame, as while the song is very different from the rest of the *Head* material, it's a beautiful, gentle track that deserves a wider audience.

Dandruff?

A quick reprise of Lugosi's line, before brief snippets of three sections of the film - a factory tour in which the band are told "the tragedy of your times, my friends, is that you may get exactly what you want", a policeman calling them weirdos, and the band being directed to act like dandruff in a commercial.

Daddy's Song

Writer: Harry Nilsson

Lead vocalist: Davy Jones

Other Monkees present: Michael Nesmith (guitar)

This Nilsson song was originally recorded during a Nesmith session, with Nesmith singing lead (this version is available as a bonus track on the CDs, and is much better than the released version, with Nesmith's heavily-processed vocals working wonderfully with the muted trumpet).

The song is one of Nilsson's more heartfelt, talking about his relationship with his father as a small child, and his sadness and confusion at his father abandoning his family when Nilsson was aged three. Unfortunately, Jones seems to have ignored the lyrical content and treated this as "Cuddly Toy" part two - understandably, since the songs share a bouncy tempo and 1920s musical style.

There is a longer version of the track, which features both some Nilssonesque additional scat vocals by Nesmith and a much slower rendition of the verse starting "the years have passed and so have I", where Jones does seem to sing that part sadly - but there, he's hamming it up to the point of schmaltz.

It's a great song, but only an adequate performance. If you want a good version of the song, either listen to Nesmith's subtler vocal or get hold of Nilsson's own version (on *Aerial Ballet*).

Poll

A collage of spoken snippets from the film, starting with Frank Zappa's response to Jones' performance - "That song was pretty white", and followed with Nesmith saying "And I'll tell you something else too, the same goes for Christmas", from a different section of the film, before various other lines of dialogue, sound effects, bits of the vox-pop sections and snippets of "Circle Sky".

Long Title: Do I Have to Do This All Over Again?

Writers: Peter Tork

Lead vocalist: Peter Tork

Other Monkees present: Davy Jones (backing vocals)

This song was actually intended to have an even longer title, as Tork introduced it in a rare solo gig in the 1970s as "Long Title, colon, Do I Have To Do This All Over Again, question mark, Or, comma, The Karma Blues"

An enjoyable rocker with some extraordinarily mobile bass playing by Tork, this song's lyrics ("Do I have to do this all over again?/Didn't I do it right the first time?") do seem to sum up some ideas about karma (as does the music's brief drop into waltz time, like a turning wheel always getting back to the same place) but were written about Tork's frustration with being in the Monkees.

Another hard-rock song in the same style as "Circle Sky", this is obviously from the heart, and Tork is almost screaming with frustration by the end. It also, though, makes a perfect end point for the film, which ends at the same point at which it starts.

Swami–Plus Strings, Etc.

Abraham Sofaer, the actor who played the head Genie in *I Dream of Jeannie* and the judge in *A Matter of Life and Death*, recites some warmed-over Timothy Leary (with a bit of Thomas Kuhn thrown in, and a touch of Buddhism) as a Maharishi-esque character, while various other bits of the film are heard under him, before we get a chunk of the "Porpoise Song" and a sprightly Mozart-esque string instrumental by Ken Thorne from the film soundtrack.

The key part of this - and one of the messages of the film - is "Where there is clarity, there is no choice, and where there is choice there is misery."

Bonus Tracks:

Happy Birthday

Writers: Mildred and Patty Hill

Lead vocalist: Micky Dolenz, Peter Tork and Davy Jones

Other Monkees present: None

Some sepulchral (and very effective) block harmonies over a spooky church organ lead into an off-key rendition of "Happy Birthday to You" sung to Nesmith in the film.

California, Here It Comes

Writers: Buddy DeSylva, Al Jolson and Joseph Meyer

Lead vocalist: Peter Tork

Other Monkees present: None

A snippet from the end of the *33 1/3 Revolutions Per Monkee* special, this track consists of a heartbeat, TV producer Jack Good repeating "the end", and a busked banjo-and-trombone run-through of the old musical number for a few seconds. The lyric change to 'it comes' from 'I come' was apparently meant to imply an earthquake that will supposedly destroy California.

This really was 'the end' of the Monkees, at least as a four-piece band.

Decline and Fall (1969 and 1970)

Instant Replay

And here's where I start being harsher about these albums. *Head* was the last truly great album the Monkees released during their original career, and after that album and film flopped so badly, the rest of the Monkees' career was a panic, with the record label alternating between desperate attempts to regain the band's commercial success and utter apathy about a 'past it' band. Meanwhile, the Monkees themselves were getting sick of being in the band, and looking to get out.

The first to leave had been Tork, who had left after the recording of the *33 1/3 Revolutions Per Monkee* TV special, and as a result plans for the band's next album to be a double, with one side for each band member, were discarded. Instead, this hodge-podge was released, a mixture of *More of the Monkees* era outtakes (and remakes of those), a couple of experiments by Dolenz and Jones, and two decent-but-not-great tracks by Nesmith, who was clearly saving his best work for the solo career that would start within a year. While Tork is not pictured on the album cover or credited, he actually appears on one song, Nesmith's "I Won't Be the Same Without Her", meaning that he is featured as much on this album as on *The Birds, the Bees and the Monkees.*

It's surprisingly listenable, but could have been reduced to an EP without anyone even noticing. It's a fundamentally lazy album, and it's clear that everyone here is doing this, not because they've 'got something to say', or even to entertain, but because they've got a contract that says they must release two albums of pop-music-like product a year. Yet almost despite the efforts of everyone involved, it's still an enjoyable listen.

The deluxe box set version of the album contains several of the *33 1/3 Revolutions Per Monkee* tracks (some only in instrumental mixes as the masters for the finished versions no longer exist), featuring Peter Tork's last sixties work with the band.

Through the Looking Glass

Writers: Tommy Boyce, Bobby Hart and Red Baldwin

Lead vocalist: Micky Dolenz

Other Monkees present: None

Producers: Tommy Boyce and Bobby Hart

This plinky, McCartneyesque song about a girl who remains emotionally distant was first recorded during the *More of the Monkees* sessions, but passed over (that version is on the *More of the Monkees* deluxe edition, and is driven by acoustic guitar rather than piano, and has less orchestration). It was then rerecorded for *The Birds, the Bees and the Monkees*, and left off that album, but that recording was chosen to open this one.

It's not a bad song, as such, just thoroughly nondescript. Boyce and Hart at their best were capable of producing garage-rock classics like "She" or "Stepping Stone", and were also capable of pop like "Last Train to Clarksville". Those songs pop and spark with life, but this just sits there and says "Are we done yet?".

Don't Listen to Linda

Writers: Tommy Boyce and Bobby Hart

Lead vocalist: Davy Jones

Other Monkees present: None

Producers: Tommy Boyce and Bobby Hart

Oh dear. Another song with the same history as above - recorded for *More of the Monkees*, left off, re-recorded for *The Birds, the Bees and the Monkees* and left off again - this actually feels like a conscious piece of sabotage.

The original recording (available as a bonus track on the *More of the Monkees* deluxe edition) is a pleasant piece of chirpy pop, pitched somewhere between the country-pop of the Beatles' *Help!* album and the music-hall revivalism of Herman's Hermits, though somewhat closer to the latter.

Here, though, it's slowed down and over-orchestrated, and Jones actually attempts to emote (always a mistake). Slowed down, and sung like they actually *mean* something, lines like "You'll end up contender for the loser of the year" just sound abysmal.

Part of the problem, of course, is that these tracks were not intended for an album in 1969 – they were originally recorded in 1966, and music had moved on considerably in the intervening time. More importantly, though, these were songs that had been repeatedly considered and rejected, suggesting that everyone knew they weren't up to standard.

From this point on, the album gets much stronger, but opening with its two weakest tracks probably did it no favours commercially.

I Won't Be the Same Without Her

Writers: Gerry Goffin and Carole King

Lead vocalist: Michael Nesmith

Other Monkees present: Peter Tork (guitar)

Producer: Michael Nesmith

A truly unusual song for the Monkees, this was actually a left-over from the sessions for *The Monkees* (and alternate mixes of the track are available on the deluxe versions of that album), recorded at the same session as "Sweet Young Thing". This song seems to have been modelled on (and possibly intended for) Phil Spector, specifically the Righteous Brothers (whose lead vocalist, Bill Medley, sounded a little like Nesmith), though the stomping chorus is more Ronettes.

Either way, though, this track is *very* Spectoresque, from its Wrecking Crew backing track (with the Dano bass here used not as Nesmith usually did, to double a bass part, but rather to double a guitar line in a very Brian Wilson touch) to the female backing vocals buried in the mix. (Not that it was all Spector's influence - the drum pattern here is one that recurred in "You Just May Be the One").

But then adding Nesmith's distinctive vocals on top turns this into a country-soul song of a type that would not become normal for several years. By the time it was released, this song didn't sound hugely out of the ordinary (though it was better than almost anything else on the album by a long way), but at the time it was recorded it would have been hugely *avant-garde*. Of all the leftover tracks on here, this is the only one that cried out for a release.

Just a Game

Writer: Micky Dolenz

Lead vocalist: Micky Dolenz

Other Monkees present: None

Producer: Micky Dolenz

And so, with the fourth song on the album we finally get to something that isn't a reject from a previous album. This song had been demoed instrumentally during the *Headquarters* sessions (and that demo was released on the *Headquarters Sessions* box set), but at that time Dolenz hadn't yet written the lyrics.

Only the second song Dolenz wrote for the band, this is stylistically different from anything else the band did, even Dolenz's other songs. It seems, in fact, to be styled after French *chanson*, with flurries of conversationally-sung words gesturing at a melody, rather than singing every note precisely on the beat, and with Dolenz's feather-light vocal belying the lyric, which is painfully paranoid and insecure. The arrangement's lovely, as well, being mostly harpsichord and a few strings, but with some jazz clarinet noodling on the instrumental fade.

It's not hard at all to imagine someone like Scott Walker performing this on one of his early albums, and while it's only one minute and forty-nine seconds long, it has more invention in it than half the rest of the album put together. Tork has often said that in his mind the great tragedy of the Monkees is that Dolenz never fulfilled his creative potential, and on the evidence of the handful of songs he submitted to the band, it's definitely true. A lovely little track.

Me Without You

Writers: Tommy Boyce and Bobby Hart

Lead vocalist: Davy Jones

Other Monkees present: None

Producers: Tommy Boyce and Bobby Hart

Oh look, this Boyce and Hart song was only rejected from *one* previous album (*The Birds, the Bees and the Monkees*, the box set version of which contains some very slightly different mixes of this). And it's not actually terrible, as such, it just sounds like the theme tune to a bad sitcom. There's also a mix, included as a bonus track, with some hideously inappropriate fuzz guitar and lazy 'bop shoo-wop' backing vocals.

Don't Wait for Me

Writer: Michael Nesmith

Lead vocalist: Michael Nesmith

Other Monkees present: None

Producer: Michael Nesmith

This is a generic Nesmith country song in the same way the previous track was a generic Boyce and Hart song for Jones.

Admittedly that makes it one of the better songs of the album so far, but still the ultimate feeling one gets from this track, as with much of the first half of the album, is a sense of "Will this do?"

It's pleasant enough - I'd go so far as to call it good, in fact - and a definite highlight of side one. But it's hard to imagine that this *mattered* to Nesmith, in a way even a potboiler like "You Told Me" feels like it matters.

You and I

Writers: David Jones and Bill Chadwick

Lead vocalist: Davy Jones

Other Monkees present: None

Producer: Davy Jones

Now *this* is more like it!

Not to be confused with the song of the same name on *Justus*, this is far and away the best Monkees track for which Jones ever took responsibility, and one of the highlights of the album.

This is utterly, absolutely unlike anything else Jones ever did. The structure of the song is actually closer to his 'Broadway rock' than it might appear, with its drops into waltz time to emphasise the end of verses, but it's utterly transformed in the production.

Neil Young takes lead guitar here, and the track actually sounds far more like Young's own work with Crazy Horse than anything else - but while Young's guitar style is, of course, one of the most distinctive in rock music, this is actually a much harder rock track than anything Young had attempted himself at this point. In fact, given that Young's *Everybody Knows This Is Nowhere* wouldn't start recording til six months after this track, and given the incredible similarity in sound, it's not unreasonable to say that this track is where the loud, grungy Neil Young style starts.

But what really makes this track is the lyric. Originally by Chadwick, but rewritten by Jones, it's an attempt to look back calmly and understandingly at the way the Monkees' career had rapidly gone downhill. It starts resignedly ("You and I have seen what time does, haven't we?", probably the best opening line of any of Jones' songs) but soon becomes very bitter ("In a year or maybe two, we'll be gone and someone new will take our place/There'll be another song, another voice, another pretty face...")

For once Jones is singing about something that matters to him, personally. He's clearly utterly furious about what he perceives as his mistreatment by the record label and TV producers, and the result is Davy Jones inventing grunge in mid 1968. Utterly astonishing.

While I Cry

Writer: Michael Nesmith

Lead vocalist: Michael Nesmith

Other Monkees present: None

Producer: Michael Nesmith

A leftover from *The Birds, the Bees and the Monkees*, this is one of Nesmith's better ballads from this period, and has some nice backing vocals from Nilsson.

The problem is that at this point Nesmith's dragged his own baseline up so high that a merely very good song like this leaves little to discuss. We expect miracles from him, so when all we get is a nice country song, there's a vague feeling of disappointment. It's still one of the best things on the album, but it's just average for Nesmith.

Tear Drop City

Writers: Tommy Boyce and Bobby Hart

Lead vocalist: Micky Dolenz

Other Monkees present: None

Producers: Tommy Boyce and Bobby Hart

Dug out of the vaults and sped up, this recording dated back to October 1966 (the recording can be heard at its original speed on the *More of the Monkees* deluxe edition, but was hugely improved by being sped up), and was essentially a reworking of "Last Train to Clarksville", being based like that track on a train rhythm and three seventh chords.

This would have been rather racy had it been released at the time, with its mild drug reference (a sound of inhalation right before the line "I was high on top but I didn't know it"), but while it's pleasant and catchy enough, it's a filler track that should have been used for a romp scene in the TV show. As it is, though, it was released as the album's single, and only reached number 56 in the US chart.

It probably didn't help the album's commercial potential that by this point, Boyce and Hart had already released their own version on their album *I Wonder What She's Doing Tonite* –

the duo had started having hit records under their own name, although never quite reaching the commercial heights they had with the Monkees.

The Girl I Left Behind Me

Writers: Carole Bayer and Neil Sedaka

Lead vocalist: Davy Jones

Other Monkees present: None

Producer: Neil Sedaka

This Sager/Sedaka schlock had been tried three times in total, first during the *More of the Monkees* sessions, then for *The Birds, the Bees and the Monkees* (that version can be heard on the deluxe version of *The Birds...* and on the *Music Box* box set) and finally in late 1967. This version, however, is the original recording.

Frankly it didn't deserve even one go. It's not that it's bad, as such, although it is. It's just that like much of the rest of this album, this song is just there.

A Man Without a Dream

Writers: Gerry Goffin and Carole King

Lead vocalist: Davy Jones

Other Monkees present: None

Producer: Bones Howe

This track was produced by the legendary Bones Howe, who amongst other accomplishments was just about to produce the music for Elvis' comeback special. As a result, it feels more alive than most of the album, and Howe's pop-soul arrangements suit Jones very well.

There are hints in various parts of this album and the outtakes around it that the Monkees were considering going in a direction similar to, say, *Dusty in Memphis*, with slick, horn-driven soul-lite arrangements of pop songs. If you put together this with, say, "Rose Marie", "I Won't Be the Same Without Her", "Changes", "Little Red Rider" and a couple of others you could have had a truly interesting album in that style. But as it is, *Instant Replay* seems the work of people who aren't sure what they want to be doing. This track, at least, is the work of people working towards a clear goal, and it shows.

Shorty Blackwell

Writer: Micky Dolenz

Lead vocalist: Micky Dolenz, Coco Dolenz

Other Monkees present: None

Producer: Micky Dolenz

But the album ends on Dolenz's masterpiece, an attempt to write something in the style of "A Day in the Life", about Dolenz's cat.

Well, ostensibly about his cat, anyway. How many cats are involved in the record-making process ("Everybody's talking faster, 'Hurry up, get me a master,'"), are unhappy, spend a lot of money on cars, "speak very crude", own a house on top of a hill, and could be said to have "finally gotten everything you wanted/and you're taunted by the power/that you really don't want anymore,"? It just might be possible that this is about someone else.

Whoever the mystery subject of the song might be, this is a psychedelic masterpiece. We start with a huge bombastic fanfare, before cutting to Dolenz singing, off tempo and *a capella* in a silly voice, before the first verse proper starts, with McCartney-esque tack piano and Coco Dolenz singing lead (the first time on a Monkees record that someone other than the four band members has sung a lead vocal).

We then get the addition of horns, bass and Micky Dolenz doubling his sister for a second verse. So far, this sounds like a typical sunshine pop record of the kind that the Association or the Cowsills might make.

But then we get two verses with doomy orchestration, all trombones and tympani, both ending with the line "he's going mad". The song has started to get very strange. And it continues to as we have a long section with the Dolenzes singing "he's going mad" over and over more frantically as a trumpet squeals the opening vocal phrases, slowly turning into a full horn section fanfare.

We have one more verse with the same musical material as before, before going into a completely different section ("Black and shiny...") based on a tick-tock musical phrase, which then goes into a performance of "Sobre las Olas", with the Dolenzes eventually joining in and singing in sarcastic, high-pitched voices. We then get another verse with an orchestra overwhelming everything else, before going into a jazz version of the "Sobre las Olas" musical material in $\frac{5}{4}$ time to fade.

It's quite, quite bizarre, one of the most ambitious pieces the Monkees ever did, and comparable with great pop-psych tracks like "My World Fell Down" or "Heroes and Villains". This just shows what this band *were* capable of when they bothered.

A demo of this can be heard on the deluxe version of *The Birds, the Bees and the Monkees*.

Oh, and on a totally different subject. . .

> "The house, originally owned by Doris Day, sat high on top of a hill in Beverly Hills and cost Michael $200,000. Then he proceeded to spend an additional $50,000 in remodelling the house that he named "Arnold"."
> **Total Control: The Monkees Michael Nesmith Story** By Randi L. Massingill

Bonus Tracks

Someday Man

Writers: Roger Nichols and Paul Williams

Lead vocalist: Davy Jones

Other Monkees present: None

Producer: Bones Howe

Another Bones Howe production, this song shows how desperate for a hit the record label were - or how little concern they had for the Monkees at this point - as it's the first time they were ever allowed to record and release a song from a publisher other than ColGems.

And it's an absolute masterpiece. Easily the best Monkees single to feature a Jones lead, this song should have been as big a hit as "Daydream Believer", which it resembles slightly in the chorus. It's a dizzying kaleidoscope of different musical styles, but Howe's arrangement (which writer Paul Williams duplicated almost exactly when he used this as the title track to his 1970 solo album) guides us through the shifts in tempo and style so smoothly they're almost unnoticeable. And Jones steps up to the challenge, delivering one of his best vocals.

In a just world, this should have rekindled the Monkees' career. Certainly it's the first thing since "Daydream Believer" to have felt like 'the next Monkees single' ("D.W. Washburn" and "Porpoise Song" are great but don't feel like singles, and "Tear Drop City" feels like 'the Monkees single from two years ago'). Unfortunately, this isn't a just world, and this track only hit number 81 in the US charts, as the B-side to "Listen to the Band".

Smile

Writer: David Jones

Lead vocalist: Davy Jones

Other Monkees present: None

Producer: Davy Jones

One of Jones' best ballads, this sounds like nothing so much as early McCartney, with its brief descending chromatic guitar passages and two-part harmonies. It could very easily have been an album track on *Beatles For Sale* or something McCartney gave to Peter and Gordon. It also ends rather cleverly, building to a big climax that never actually happens. The only problem is some very poor multi-tracking on Jones' lead vocal.

Recorded at the same session as "You and I", this also features Neil Young on guitar.

St. Matthew

Writer: Michael Nesmith

Lead vocalist: Michael Nesmith

Other Monkees present: None

Producer: Michael Nesmith

And finally, in an unreleased bonus track, we get Nesmith on top form. This great sludgy, violin-led production sounds very like his early "Sweet Young Thing". Nesmith's yearning melody (with his vocal put through a Leslie speaker in the mix heard here, though not in the early mix available on *Missing Links vol 2*) contrasts wonderfully with the driving rock riffs underneath. This track sounds like nothing more than a country Phil Spector, with no individual element audible on its own; there are guitars, organs, violins, drums, but they all just merge into one great noise.

As for the lyric, it's one of Nesmith's most inscrutable. Fortunately, he's tried to explain it (that explanation can be found in the Sandoval book and in the liner notes for *Music Box*). Unfortunately, that explanation seems to bear no resemblance to the lyric itself. Apparently, this song was intended as a commentary on what Nesmith saw as Dylan's subconscious incorporation of the Biblical figure of the Holy Ghost into his lyrics. The acoustic demo also has slightly different lyrics.

But it doesn't really matter what it's about, this is one of the great Monkees-era Nesmith tracks, and it's a real shame this got left on the shelf while merely decent tracks made the album.

Look Down

Writers: Carole King and Toni Stern

Lead vocalist: Davy Jones

Other Monkees present: None

Producer: Carole King

An enjoyable piece of horn-driven bubblegum soul, this seems modelled after the Four Tops' recent hits, especially "Standing in the Shadows of Love" and "Bernadette", but with a chorus that almost goes into Partridge Family territory.

Jones turns in a decent vocal, straining a bit and delivering a more impassioned performance than he normally would, although his shout of "Hold on, I'm comin'" does raise comparisons to Sam and Dave which Jones could not possibly benefit from.

If I Ever Get to Saginaw Again

Writers: Jack Keller and Bob Russell

Lead vocalist: Michael Nesmith

Other Monkees present: None

Producer: Michael Nesmith

This orchestrated country ballad in Jimmy Webb mode features one of Nesmith's best vocals, a yearning, keening vocal in his high tenor range, occasionally dropping into a breathy chest voice. There are some lovely touches in the arrangement, too - the cello countermelody and the almost steel-band vibraphone part are gorgeous, all the more so for their incongruity.

The only problem is the lyric, which is essentially someone looking back yearningly at having sex with a seventeen year old girl and then leaving her to bring up the resulting baby alone.

Some of Shelly's Blues

Writer: Michael Nesmith

Lead vocalist: Michael Nesmith

Other Monkees present: None

Producer: Michael Nesmith

A musically rather lovely little country song, led by some nice steel guitar and harmonica playing, this song was left unreleased, eventually surfacing in an inferior re-recorded version on Nesmith's sixth solo album *Pretty Much Your Standard Ranch Stash*.

It's a shame, because while the lyric is macho posturing (it's a rewrite of "That'll Be the Day" in all but name), the music is far superior to the two Nesmith compositions which ended up on the album.

Nesmith has in recent years (notably on his "Movies of the Mind" tours) tried to promote a strained interpretation of the lyrics to this one that make it less lyrically dodgy, but the fact remains that the song is lyrically at best braggadocio and at worst actively threatening towards its subject.

Hollywood

Writer: Michael Nesmith

Lead vocalist: Michael Nesmith

Other Monkees present: None

Producer: Michael Nesmith

This song was recorded at the same sessions as "Some of Shelly's Blues", a set of sessions in Nashville where Nesmith worked with Elvis Presley's music supervisor Felton Jarvis.

In this version, this song about the fickle nature of Hollywood showbiz seems to point toward the country rock of Gram Parsons and the Flying Burrito Brothers. However, this didn't see release until the 1990s, and Nesmith ended up recording a far more boogie-based version for his *Magnetic South* solo album. Oddly, given the nature of the lyrics, this song was written before Nesmith even joined the Monkees.

The Crippled Lion

Writer: Michael Nesmith

Lead vocalist: Michael Nesmith

Other Monkees present: None

Producer: Michael Nesmith

And another song from the Nashville sessions, another one that Nesmith remade for *Magnetic South*. Nesmith seems to have regarded the light country sound he got in these sessions as a creative dead end, reworking the songs substantially into heavier, more ponderous arrangements for his solo albums.

But in truth, these tracks sound far less dated than the solo versions did. The heavier country-rock, with emphasis on rock, he went for later may have been more contemporary, but this is timeless.

One particularly lovely lyrical touch - "And then suddenly I see the light of something called the moon". Nobody would ever speak like that, but it's almost the quintessential Nesmith line.

That's What It's Like Loving You (backing track)

Writers: David Jones and Steve Pitts

Lead vocalist: None

Monkees present: None

Producer: David Jones

Had I been asked to listen to this without any information, I would have guessed it as a Nesmith track, being as it is a riffy country-soul number. This is only a backing track, but it's Neil Young on lead guitar (the track sounds slightly like Young's Buffalo Springfield song "Burned" at points) and Larry Knechtel on Booker T style organ (at one point seeming to play a few bars of "I Can See Clearly Now", though this was before that song was ever written).

It's clearly not a completed track - it sounds to my ears a tiny bit out of tune, in fact - but there's potential here, and it's a shame the track was never finished.

How Insensitive

Writers: Antonio Jobim, Vinicus DeMoraes and Norman Gimbel

Lead vocalist: Michael Nesmith

Other Monkees present: None

Producer: Michael Nesmith

This is an interesting experiment, from the Nashville sessions - a song by the great bossa nova composer Jobim, rearranged for banjo, fiddle and steel guitar.

The result is curiously Mediterranean, the banjos sounding almost like bouzoukis, as the complex harmonies of the Jobim piece get reinterpreted in a style which usually thrives on harmonic simplicity. It works, but it's easy to see why this was the only one of those tracks which was never mixed for release in the 60s.

I Go Ape

Writers: Neil Sedaka and Howard Greenfield

Lead vocalist: Micky Dolenz

Other Monkees present: None

Producer: Bones Howe

The *33 1/3 Revolutions Per Monkee* TV special, the last thing the band did together as a four-piece until the mid 1990s, was a very, very strange piece of television. Opinions are divided on its quality, but one thing that can definitely be said about it is that it is unlike anything else that was on TV at the time. Essentially a more cynical rewrite of *Head*, were such a thing possible, this show manages to embed the attacks on the Monkees' manufactured status in a psychedelic story about creation myths, which seems to combine Darwin with Prometheus with Frankenstein with the snake in the Garden of Eden and have evolution be the knowledge gained by eating the apple[14].

Unfortunately, while the show has many ideas, it has little or no merit musically, and the rest of these bonus tracks go to prove that. First up we have Dolenz covering a 1959 hit by Neil Sedaka, to illustrate a scene where the Monkees dress up in monkey costumes. Unfortunately, nobody seems quite sure whether they're meant to be taking this nonsensical piece of rock and roll fluff seriously or not, and the result falls between two stools, neither competent enough to be good nor incompetent enough to be funny, it's just lazy.

Wind Up Man (backing track)

Writer: Bill Dorsey

Lead vocalist: All four Monkees (TV version only, not on backing track)

Producer: Bones Howe

A short, mechanical sounding song about how the Monkees were a manufactured group, this is a much less interesting take on the same idea as "Ditty Diego War Chant". The isolated backing track, without the nagging vocals, is rather more interesting in its use of percussion to suggest clockwork, but still nothing special.

---

[14]Those who have read my book *An Incomprehensible Condition: An Unauthorised Guide to Grant Morrison's Seven Soldiers* will see why I find this show fascinating.

String For My Kite (backing track)

Writer: Bill Dorsey

Lead vocalist: Davy Jones (TV version only, not on backing track)

Other Monkees present: None

Producer: Michael Nesmith

A short, rather twee, waltz-time ballad, given to Jones as a brief solo number before the big finale of *33 1/3 Revolutions Per Monkee*, this has no redeeming qualities, or even interesting ones.

Naked Persimmon

Writer: Michael Nesmith

Lead vocalist: Michael Nesmith

Other Monkees present: None

Producer: Bones Howe

Performed as Nesmith's solo number in *33 1/3*, this song is Nesmith's attempt at writing about the manipulation he felt the group had been subjected to. In the TV show, this is performed by Nesmith in a split-screen (in front of a poster saying "Wanted for fraud") and the song itself is split, between the rock-flavoured patter song verses of "Monkee Mike" and the country waltz choruses of the Nudie-suited cowboy Mike.

The verses bemoan the band's treatment ("Well the devil incarnate was running music supervision") while the choruses are more relaxed ("So for now I'll just play my guitar/and sing a couple of tunes") but this was clearly conceived far more as a spectacle than as a song.

Goldilocks Sometimes

Writer: Bill Dorsey

Lead vocalist: Davy Jones

Other Monkees present: None

Producer: Michael Nesmith

Jones' solo number for *33 1/3* was this rather charming piece of toytown pop, all celeste and tack piano. It's the kind of thing that Jones' stage persona was suited to, and is pleasant in a "Cups and Cakes" sort of way, but has little worth discussing.

Darwin

Writer: Bill Dorsey

Lead vocalist: All four Monkees

Producer: Michael Nesmith

A very, very brief snippet of a song, sounding oddly like the Bonzo Dog Band, which for some reason seems to argue that Darwin invented evolution, and thus came before fish.

All The Grey Haired Men (Mono Backing Track)

Writers: Jack Keller and Bob Russell

Producer: "The Monkees" (Shorty Rogers)

No Monkee presence

This song, co-written by Jack Keller, who had co-produced much of *The Monkees* and co-written "Hold On Girl" and "Your Auntie Grizelda" among others, was a not-quite-hit for the Lettermen, reaching #109 in the Billboard chart, around this time, and the Monkees' version, arranged by Shorty Rogers, followed their version closely.

The song is in $\frac{5}{4}$ time, and frankly doesn't work very well — where other pieces sometimes sound like they were written naturally in odd time signatures because that's how the song should go, this sounds like an exercise in trying to force something into $\frac{5}{4}$ whether it felt right or not, with the result that it just sounds like people are dropping beats left and right.

No vocal was recorded, but this is a mild mercy, as the lyric is another example of that tired 60s staple of mocking conformist old people for being conformist and old.

The Monkees Present

The last Monkees album to feature Nesmith until the 1990s, and to all intents and purposes the last Monkees album full stop, this is a much better effort than *Instant Replay*, as everyone seems to have realised this would be the band's last chance to make an album on their own terms. While still not rising to the heights of the great run of albums from *Headquarters* through *Head*, it's a respectable effort, and everyone involved at least sounds like they're trying, though by this point there's absolutely no pretence at this being a group effort - each member gets his solo tracks, and that's it.

Interestingly, there had apparently been plans before Tork left for the next album to be called *The Monkees Present* and for each band member to get a solo side of a double album. It's possible that that plan continued (with the fourth side of the album to be a group side?) until fairly late in the day, which would explain both the cover of this album (with head shots of the three remaining Monkees over their names) and the relative weakness of *Instant Replay*. It's possible, though this is only speculation, that *Instant Replay* was a quickie release while they were working on a planned 'real' album.

Still, there's an air of resignation here that there simply isn't on the albums while Tork was a member, and an utter lack of coherence. This isn't an album, it's a semi-random assortment of quite nice tracks, with little to distinguish them. It's a better way for the band to go out than *Instant Replay* was, but it's the work of three talented individuals who are tired of having anything to do with each other, working solo.

Little Girl

Writer: Micky Dolenz

Lead vocalist: Micky Dolenz

Other Monkees present: None

Producer: Micky Dolenz

The album opens with this rather charming Latin pop effort by Dolenz, with session guitarist Louie Shelton reprising his blisteringly fast guitar playing from "Valleri", and Coco Dolenz adding backing vocals. The lyrics are rather bitter, but Dolenz sings them so sweetly that the track comes out as a light bit of pop.

Dolenz has consistently produced good material on these last few Monkees albums, and it's a shame he really only started once the band were a commercial flop.

This should not be confused with Tork's song "Little Girl", which appears on *Good Times!*

Good Clean Fun

Writer: Michael Nesmith

Lead vocalist: Michael Nesmith

Other Monkees present: None

Producer: Michael Nesmith

What on earth... ? It's... it can't be... it *is*! A Nesmith track where he's trying, released on a Monkees album rather than saved for his solo albums!

Easily the most poppy and commercial of Nesmith's Nashville session tracks, this is a wonderful banjo- and fiddle-driven train song (it's about an aeroplane journey, but the structure is absolutely that of a train song, right down to the boom-chicka-boom rhythm) about returning to a lover the narrator hasn't seen for a year.

The title, incidentally, is a dig at someone working for Screen Gems, who had told Nesmith that if he wanted to write hits, he had to stop writing that weird stuff and write something that was good clean fun instead.

Released as a single after "Listen to the Band" became surprisingly popular, this was Nesmith's second A-side for the band, and it went only to number 82 in the US charts, not helped by the fact that the title isn't mentioned anywhere in the lyric.

Some have claimed (allegedly including Nesmith himself, in a fanzine interview I have been unable to track down a copy of) that the last line, "I told you I'd come back and here I am", is sung in a more menacing tone than the rest of the song, and that this in some way gives the song a twist ending. This seems strained at best – there's nothing in the recording to support this interpretation.

If I Knew

Writers: David Jones and Bill Chadwick

Lead vocalist: Davy Jones

Other Monkees present: None

Producer: Davy Jones

According to Chadwick[15], he wrote this song by himself, and gave Jones credit to get the song recorded. Whether this is the case or not, it certainly sounds tailor-made for Jones, its acoustic soft pop stylings sounding premonitory of the Carpenters.

Jones turns in one of his very best vocals here, especially when harmonising with himself on the middle eight.

Bye Bye Baby Bye Bye

Writers: Micky Dolenz and Ric Klein

Lead vocalist: Micky Dolenz

Other Monkees present: Davy Jones (backing vocals)

Producer: Micky Dolenz

Yes, it's an actual track by Monkees, plural, as Jones adds some backing vocals to this Dolenz track. This seems to be an early attempt at writing the 'Indian chant' section of "Mommy and

---

[15] In Sandoval, p. 244

Daddy", but is a great stand-alone track in itself. The driving riff could almost be an early Led Zeppelin one, especially the way it keeps to a $\frac{4}{4}$ beat but varies the stresses within the bars, and the use of a banjo doubling a harmonica to give a sitar feel is reminiscent of some of Donovan's music of the time.

Dolenz seems to have had a real knack for riffy tracks around this time (see, for example, "Rose Marie"), and it's a shame we never got a period where he had creative dominance over the band in the way that Nesmith had earlier.

This song was co-written by Ric Klein, who was Dolenz's stand-in on the TV show and had various, mostly non-speaking, roles in the series. Klein and Dolenz were close, and were best men at each other's weddings. It's not known what Klein contributed to the song.

Never Tell a Woman Yes

Writer: Michael Nesmith

Lead vocalist: Michael Nesmith

Other Monkees present: None

Producer: Michael Nesmith

This track, the last of Nesmith's experiments in 1920s pastiche, sounds almost like it could have come from the pen of his friend Harry Nilsson, especially in the sections where Nesmith scat sings in clear imitation of him. This is one of Nesmith's most musically enjoyable songs in this style, all clanking banjo and silent-movie barrelhouse piano, but the shaggy dog story of the lyrics makes the song somewhat overlong.

Looking for the Good Times

Writers: Tommy Boyce and Bobby Hart

Lead vocalist: Davy Jones

Other Monkees present: Micky Dolenz (backing vocals)

Producers: Tommy Boyce and Bobby Hart

This is another left-over from the *More of the Monkees* sessions in October 1966, recorded at the same sessions as "Tear Drop City", but is far better than the rejects dug up for *Instant Replay*. In fact, had it been released in 1966, it would easily have been a Mod dance-floor filler, with its garage-band-by-way-of-LA-sessioneers R&B slickness.

Jones turns in a surprisingly good vocal, on a type of track on which he's normally weedy and underpowered, and Dolenz does a very creditable backing vocal turn (making this one of the increasingly small number of 'Monkees' tracks to actually feature multiple Monkees).

However, between 1966 and 1969, popular music had been revolutionised at least twice, and this sounded in that context about as dated as a madrigal. A shame, because it still stands up today.

The title of this song is the first appearance of the phrase "good times" in a Monkees song – a phrase which also appeared in "Daydream Believer", but now has more resonance due to its use as the title of the band's final album in 2016, and in the titles of two songs on that album.

Ladies Aid Society

Writers: Tommy Boyce and Bobby Hart

Lead vocalist: Davy Jones

Other Monkees present: Micky Dolenz (backing vocals)

Producers: Tommy Boyce and Bobby Hart

Another track left over from *More of the Monkees* (and a longer mix of this is available as a bonus track on the deluxe edition of that album), this is an attempt by Boyce and Hart at a piece of satire in the style of the Kinks' music of that time. In truth, though, between the lyrics about old ladies wanting to 'clamp down on the youth' and the terrible falsetto vocals in the chorus, this is closer to some of Jan and Dean's music from the period.

As a novelty song, this isn't as bad as some of the material they'd done at that time, but why on earth anyone thought it would be a good idea to dig this drivel up more than two years after it had been successfully buried, I can't imagine.

Listen to the Band

Writer: Michael Nesmith

Lead vocalist: Michael Nesmith

Other Monkees present: None

Producer: Michael Nesmith

This song was originally performed on the *33 1/3 Revolutions Per Monkee* special, in a slow version driven by Tork's harpsichord, but here it's a horn-driven country-rocker. At this point, the three remaining Monkees were touring with a nine-piece band (Sam and the Goodtimers) including a horn section, and many of their songs in this period seem to be geared to that kind of arrangement.

As a result, we have what is a more or less straightforward country arrangement, all twangy steel guitars and harmonica, but with a big band horn section overlaid. And just to make the genre-bending complete, there's a false fade, and we come back into the song with some psychedelic organ music.

This was released as a single - the first Monkees single to have Nesmith on the A-side - and only reached number 63 in the US charts (though it made the top 20 in Australia). Nonetheless, it has since become one of the band's most popular songs, and a highlight of live performances on the various reunion tours.

Rather oddly, Nesmith re-recorded this on his second solo album, *Loose Salute*, in 1970, the only time he ever put a re-recording of a previously-released Monkees track on one of his solo albums.

I was told by a friend (but unfortunately don't have a source) that Nesmith has said that this song was based around the chords for "Nine Times Blue" played backwards. There's certainly a resemblance there, but it doesn't seem to be a backwards one, and both songs are harmonically fairly simplistic anyway. But the movement I-V-vi on the lines "Hey, hey mercy woman/plays a song and no-one listens" and "Like a fool I tested you" has a similar melodic shape, and both songs move to III7 for emphasis ("Weren't they good, they made me happy" and "But you did it with such love").

So it's entirely possible that at the very least Nesmith was thinking of this as a reworking of the earlier song.

French Song

Writer: Bill Chadwick

Lead vocalist: Davy Jones

Other Monkees present: None

Producers: Davy Jones and Bill Chadwick

A rather nice lounge-jazz song, this track really is the epitome of lift music, between its cheesy organ and flute and the vibraphone solo. From the description of the session in Sandoval, it seems the musicians involved were rather unimpressed, but this is still an interesting track, if only because it shows Jones and Chadwick moving in a completely different direction to the rest of the band.

I find it hard to defend this song on any rational basis, but I have an instinctive love of anything with acoustic guitar, organ and vibraphone; thanks to the Beach Boys and Tim Buckley that combination of instruments can be relied upon to enthrall me. But on an objective level, this is one of the weaker tracks on the album.

Mommy and Daddy

Writer: Micky Dolenz

Lead vocalist: Micky Dolenz

Other Monkees present: None

Producer: Micky Dolenz

Easily Dolenz's greatest production (other than maybe "Shorty Blackwell"), the version of this on the released album is hamstrung by the insistence of Lester Sill, the music supervisor from the record label, that Dolenz bowdlerise his original lyrics ("tell your mommy and daddy they're living a lie" became "tell your mommy and daddy that you love them anyway"). Thankfully, the CD reissue contains both versions, although Dolenz's rewritten lyrics manage to still be almost as effective.

To be truthful, the lyrics here are frankly adolescent, shouting at the hypocrisy of adult society. Apparently parents hide the truth about sex and prescription drug use from their children, the genocide of the Native Americans was bad, war is wrong, and J.F.K. might not have been killed by a lone assassin.

Were Dolenz to have written about any one of those topics, he could have possibly come up with something powerful, but as it is this is just one of the many, many songs written in the 60s which seek to lay all the problems in the whole history of the world on well-meaning middle-class suburbanites.

However, Dolenz clearly means these lyrics, and so he turns in an impassioned vocal performance. He may even be playing the drums on this, for the only time in the sixties since "Cuddly Toy", and the song clearly meant a lot to him.

Musically, the way the song builds up, with the pseudo-Native American chanting chorus and unusual rhythm, to a huge brass band climax playing cheerfully away while Dolenz sings "living a lie, lie, lie" over and over is a masterstroke. For all its sixth-form lyrics, this is a highlight of the album, and there's an immense power to the music here. Dolenz seems at this point to have been growing immensely as an artist, and it's a real shame he more or less gave up writing after this album.

Oklahoma Backroom Dancer

Writer: Michael Martin Murphey

Lead vocalist: Michael Nesmith

Other Monkees present: None

Producer: Michael Nesmith

This is Nesmith's weakest track on the album, but is still pleasant enough. Written by Nesmith's former bandmate Michael Murphey, who also wrote "What am I Doing Hangin' 'Round?" and "(I Prithee) Do Not Ask For Love", this is a slice of Southern rock about watching a bar-room dancer that wouldn't have been out of place on a Creedence Clearwater Revival album, and far more straightforward than most of Nesmith's material from this time. One suspects it was included on the album more as a favour to Murphey than because of its own qualities, though it's still very listenable.

Pillow Time

Writers: Janelle Scott and Matt Willis

Lead vocalist: Micky Dolenz

Other Monkees present: None

Producer: Micky Dolenz

And we close with another Dolenz track, this time a lullaby originally demoed during the *Headquarters* sessions (and audible on the *Headquarters Sessions* box set).

This is another song that seems to owe a lot to Nilsson, more in the arrangement than anything else, but at times it sounds like a very close relation of Nilsson's own lullaby "Little Cowboy". It's perhaps a little twee lyrically, but a nice performance of a nice melody.

Bonus Tracks

Calico Girlfriend Samba

Writer: Michael Nesmith

Lead vocalist: Michael Nesmith

Other Monkees present: None

Producer: Michael Nesmith

This cowbell-driven samba track is one of Nesmith's most up-beat, enjoyable tracks of the period, but was left unreleased at the time, and Nesmith re-recorded it (in a more straightforward arrangement) for his *Magnetic South* solo album the next year. Rather improbably, Sandoval [p. 237] states that notes on the tape box suggest that this track was intended for Jones to sing. This would have been interesting, but as it is, it's hard to think of a more quintessentially Nesmith track.

(Incidentally, Sandoval states that the track as recorded had additional percussion overdubs by unknown people, after the basic track was cut. This track (with Hal Blaine on drums) was recorded at the first of two Nesmith sessions on this date, and on the second session Earl Palmer was the drummer. I'd be prepared to bet a reasonable sum of money that Palmer was the percussionist who did the overdubs, as it sounds very much like his playing.)

Time and Time Again

Writers: David Jones and Bill Chadwick

Lead vocalist: Davy Jones

Other Monkees present: None

Producers: David Jones and Bill Chadwick

This is one of the best things Jones was involved with as song-writer/producer. The lyrics are pap, but musically this is just lovely. It sounds, in fact, very like the Turtles, with its layered backing vocals by Jones and Chadwick inviting the listener to just sink in. And the calliope and Moog parts complement each other beautifully. This was apparently considered for *Changes* before being passed over for "I Never Thought It Peculiar", in one of the most baffling decisions in a career that was full of them.

Down the Highway (Michigan Blackhawk)

Writers: Carole King and Toni Stern

Lead vocalist: Michael Nesmith

Producer: Michael Nesmith

Other Monkees present: None

This song's release has caused no end of confusion for Monkees fans. A mix-up meant this King/Stern number, "Down the Highway", was released on *Missing Links vol 2* under the name of a track Nesmith recorded later in the same week, "Michigan Blackhawk".

A pleasant country-rocker perfectly suited to Nesmith's voice, this track is interesting because it shows that the band's normal LA session people were capable of getting exactly the same sound that Nesmith had been getting in his Nashville sessions. Louie Shelton's guitar-picking here is extraordinary - Shelton really was the unsung hero of the Monkees' session players, and this was his last real chance to shine, with some wonderful double-time fingerpicked arpeggios (though Al Casey, the other guitarist, also does a sterling job).

Steam Engine

Writer: Chip Douglas

Lead vocalist: Micky Dolenz

Producer: Chip Douglas

Other Monkees present: None

Having been dropped as producer by his former bandmates the Turtles, Chip Douglas decided to see if he could return to working with the Monkees in 1969. To that end, he actually financed a session out of his own pocket, from which this was the only track to feature a Monkee vocal.

Intended to sound like Wilson Pickett, this song fits well with the other Monkees material of 1969, having as it does a driving, R&B horn section, but with country guitar from Clarence White of the Byrds and steel playing from Red Rhodes (a favourite player of Nesmith's, who used him on almost all of his material from this point until Rhodes' death in the 1990s).

While this song was never released, it was used in repeats of the Monkees' TV show, where it was overdubbed over older footage in an attempt to make the show seem more up-to-date.

You're So Good

Writer: Robert Stone

Lead vocalist: Micky Dolenz

Producer: Michael Nesmith

Other Monkees present: None

Not to be confused with "You're So Good To Me", this is an R&B track recorded during the same sessions as "Oklahoma Backroom Dancer" and sharing much of that track's feel. There's nothing much to the song, but it has a catchy riff and Dolenz turns in a quite extraordinary soulful vocal. The band were clearly going in a somewhat unified musical direction in early 1969, with funky horn sections turning up all over the place, but somehow none of the actual releases of the time show this. It's a shame, because while this is no Otis Redding, it's a thoroughly enjoyable soul track.

We'll Be Back In A Minute

Writer: Micky Dolenz

Lead vocalist: Micky Dolenz

Producer: Micky Dolenz

Other Monkees present: None

This is a gorgeous little snippet of fun pop, recorded in 1969 for repeats of the TV show to use going into the commercial break. Two different versions of this Nilssonesque piece were released on *Missing Links vol 3*, one fast and one mid-tempo. Both featured Dolenz on guitar and vocals with Henry Diltz on banjo and Chip Douglas on bass.

In their 2011 reunion tour, Tork, Dolenz and Jones used this as the walk-off music before the interval.

Make Friends With Kool-Aid

Lead vocalist: Micky Dolenz

Other credits unknown

A jingle for Kool-Aid drinks, used in commercials featuring the band and Bugs Bunny.

Angel Band

Writers: trad. (William Bradbury and Rev. J. Hascall) arr. Nesmith

Lead vocalist: Michael Nesmith

Producer: Michael Nesmith

Other Monkees present: None

A beautiful rendition of the traditional country gospel waltz, a song now probably best known for its use in the film *O Brother, Where Art Thou?*

This is recorded as if to sound like a church performance, with acoustic instruments and harmonium (a pump organ used in many small churches), and a massed backing chorus. Nesmith's vocals are suitably yearning, and the whole track is just beautiful.

Good Afternoon

Writer: Unknown (Michael Nesmith)?

Lead vocalist: Instrumental

Producer: Michael Nesmith

Monkees present: none

At the start, this Nesmith backing track sounds like it might be trying to be "Ticket to Ride", before it goes into a very different direction, going for a soft Latin feel not unlike that of "Acapulco Sun" from the next album. It's a surprisingly full and imaginative sounding arrangement given the relatively small number of musicians on the track, just five Wrecking Crew members, but it's hard to judge what it would have been like with vocals.

Opening Night

Writer: Charlie Smalls

Lead vocalist: Davy Jones

Producer: Davy Jones

Other Monkees present: none

When the Monkees chose some of their favourite musicians to appear in guest spots on their show for the final four episodes, Tork chose Pete Seeger, who was unavailable, Dolenz chose Tim Buckley, who gave a stunning solo performance of "Song to the Siren", and Nesmith chose Frank Zappa. Part of Nesmith and Zappa's dialogue was a mockery of Jones' dialogue with his choice, the then-obscure composer Charlie Smalls.

Smalls would later go on to write the music for *The Wiz*, but at the time he was just at the beginning of his career, and this song is one of the earliest things he ever wrote. It's a song from the point of view of a performer with opening night nerves (though it could also easily be interpreted as being about nerves before trying other things), and is a curious hybrid of the Broadway rock style Jones liked and the sort of jazz-funk that would within a few years become a staple of cop shows and blaxploitation film soundtracks. It's more "interesting" than good, per se, but it's better than much of the stuff that Jones was working on that did see release around this time.

London Bridge

Writer: David Gates

Lead vocalist: Instrumental

Producer: Michael Nesmith

Monkees present: none

In this case, we can at least know what the song was that Nesmith was producing – "London Bridge" is a song by David Gates, who had written "Saturday's Child" on The Monkees, and who had now formed his own band, Bread. The song, which appeared on Bread's eponymous first album in 1969, was typical of that band, a soft-pop confection with a Moog hook that was perfectly suited for 70s AM radio.

This Nesmith-produced Wrecking Crew backing track, though, is just weird. It starts off with ninety seconds of atonal percussion experiment that frankly sounds like Edgard Varése or someone, before slowly coalescing into something that is recognisably Gates' song, but taken at a funereal pace, and driven by distorted guitar, tuned percussion, and what sounds like a distorted monophonic synthesiser, although there are various electronic effects on the percussion, especially, that make it difficult to tell what instrument is what.

It's absolutely nothing like the Bread version, and it's hard to imagine this one with vocals at all, but it's easily the most fascinating of these Nesmith experiments, and the one that is most worth listening to.

The Good Earth

Writers: unknown

Lead vocalist: Davy Jones

Other Monkees present: None

Producer: Davy Jones

A horrible piece of Hallmark-card doggerel, a spoken-word piece of 'poetry' about the environment, recited earnestly by Jones. Drivel.

Lynn Harper

Writer: Michael Nesmith

Lead vocalist: Instrumental

Producer: Michael Nesmith

Monkees present: none

Another of the large number of Nesmith backing tracks on the deluxe edition of *Present*, this is a slick, horn-driven R&B

riffer that wouldn't have been out of place coming from Muscle Shoals. It's frustrating how many of these tracks there are, as they all show a reasonable amount of potential, but Nesmith never took any of them further.

A Bus That Never Comes

Writers: Bob Russell and Jack Keller

Lead vocalist: Instrumental

Producer: Michael Nesmith

Monkees present: none

Another Nesmith backing track for a song by someone else, by the same writing team that wrote "All the Grey-Haired Men", this was most famously, if the word applies here, a B-side for an unsuccessful single by Shirley Bassey. Nesmith's arrangement of it takes the tempo up a bit compared to Bassey's version, and this soft-pop version shows the influence of Jimmy Webb – this could be right out of Webb's productions for the 5th Dimension, and the tuned percussion driving the track is a nice touch.

While obviously there are no vocals on the track, this sounds like it might have been an attempt by Nesmith to produce something for Jones to sing, as he had done with "My Share of the Sidewalk" and "Daddy's Song" – this is very much in Jones' stylistic range, and it's something one could easily imagine as a follow-up to "Someday Man". It's rather a shame that Jones wasn't given a chance to sing this one, as I expect he would have done so very well.

Storybook of You

Writers: Tommy Boyce and Bobby Hart

Lead vocalist: Davy Jones

Producers: Tommy Boyce and Bobby Hart

Other Monkees present: None

One of the few Boyce and Hart songs recorded by the band after 1966, this is from a session in 1969. A plodding, dirge-like ballad in $\frac{6}{8}$, it's easy to see why this went unissued, as even had the song been any good, its long sustained held notes do no favours to Jones' voice.

Thirteen is Not Our Lucky Number

Writers: Michael Cohen and Michael Nesmith

Lead vocalist: Instrumental

Producer: Michael Nesmith

Monkees present: Michael Nesmith (acoustic guitar)

An odd one this, another Nesmith backing track never taken any further, it alternates between two clearly distinct sections (possibly one written by Nesmith and one by Cohen). The first section is a mid-tempo garage rocker with stabbing guitar beats in the "She's About a Mover" style that Nesmith had favoured in his 1967 songwriting, albeit a little slower in tempo, and with long pauses which would presumably have been solo vocal parts.

After this section repeats, we go into the second section, which has a more straightforward rhythm (with a cowbell on every beat) and multiple guitars playing psychedelic freak-out music, before sharply transitioning back into the verse material. We then get another freak-out, another verse, and a sudden dead stop.

If You Have the Time

Writers: Bill Chadwick and David Jones

Lead vocalist: Davy Jones

Producers: Davy Jones and Bill Chadwick

Other Monkees present: None

An upbeat, catchy music-hall sunshine pop track, this would actually have made a good single. It feels like many of the Cowsills' songs of the period, but has the unusual touch of a Moog doubling the string part (and playing a solo). While it's not Jones' best work, it's odd that this was left off *The Monkees Present*.

Little Tommy Blues

Writer: Tommy Griffin

Lead vocalist: Instrumental

Producer: Michael Nesmith

Monkees present: none

The original of this was an obscure country-blues song recorded in 1936 by the almost-unknown Tommy Griffin. Griffin is so unknown that in most books on the blues he is only mentioned because at one session he was recorded accompanied by Ernest

"44" Johnson, a pianist who was well regarded by other pianists but who otherwise never recorded.

However, while this song is credited as being that song, I suspect this is a misattribution. Quite simply, while both songs are twelve bar blues, so it's theoretically possible that Nesmith could have sung Griffin's melody and lyric over this backing track, the track doesn't really fit Griffin's melody at all. Griffin's song is a country-blues song in the style of Charley Patton or Robert Johnson, while this is a honky-tonk blues jam which, honestly, doesn't sound like the musicians were trying for a specific song at all, as much as just playing some twelve-bar blues – it doesn't even sound like there's a head arrangement, as much as just a jam (albeit one by top-notch session musicians, so with a musicality that's lacking from many similar jams).

Penny Music

Writers: Michael Leonard and Bobby Weinstein

Lead vocalist: Davy Jones

Producer: David Jones

Other Monkees present: None

This Broadway-pop track, possibly featuring members of the Monkees' touring band Sam and the Goodtimers, is an unmemorable, bland song about a busking violinist. Jones does his usual cheery chappie routine, but the song has very little reason to exist.

Thank You My Friend

Writer: Michael Nesmith

Producer: Michael Nesmith

Monkees present: none

A rather listenable waltz-time soulful blues track, this has something of the feel of "Love Letters" or "Go Now" about it, and certainly sounds like it had the potential to be a good track, although it's clearly a backing track waiting for a vocal that was never recorded.

Till Then

Writers: Eddie Seiler, Guy Wood, and Sol Marcus

Lead vocalist: Michael Nesmith (laughter, no formal lead vocal)

Producer: Michael Nesmith

Other Monkees present: none

This is a song originally recorded by the Mills Brothers, a hugely popular vocal group from the 1930s and 40s who were a massive influence on the Ink Spots and, through them, on doo-wop and R&B music. A hit for them in 1944, this was one of many songs from the 40s sung from the perspective of a soldier telling his far-away girlfriend to wait until his return. The verse melody follows the standard I-vi-ii-V7 doo-wop changes for its first two lines, with a far more harmonically sophisticated third line in the style of the slicker big band music of the time, making it an interesting bridge between the style that was popular at the time of the song's release and the styles that would come into fashion a decade or so later.

Nesmith's arrangement of the song starts out with the same guitar intro that the Mills Brothers used, and is a fairly straight lounge-jazz rendition of the song, although featuring rather forced-sounding overdubbed laughter, possibly inspired by "America Drinks and Goes Home" by Nesmith's friend Frank Zappa, which did the same sort of thing on a similar-sounding lounge arrangement.

It's a real shame that Nesmith never recorded a vocal for this one, as the song would suit his voice perfectly. Interestingly, Peter Tork independently covered this song at many solo acoustic shows in 2010 and 2011, some of which can be found on YouTube. Tork's version is very pretty, too, and worth checking out.

How Can I Tell You

Writers:David Jones and Bill Chadwick

Lead vocalist: David Jones

Producer: Bill Chadwick

Other Monkees present: none

In part, this is a remake of "Smile" with different lyrics, but where "Smile" is a tight, coherent, song, this is musically sloppy – Jones and Chadwick seem to have reused the verse melody and hook of "Smile", and then added a lot of meandering lounge-singer melodic noodling that doesn't really go anywhere.

Omega

Writer: Michael Nesmith

Lead vocalist: Instrumental

Producer: Michael Nesmith

Monkees present: Michael Nesmith (acoustic guitar)

A Nesmith composition, this one is almost in the old Boyce and Hart style – a simple twist dance number, as the phrase would have been in the early sixties, although the piano is a little stylistically incongruous for this type of music and would possibly be more appropriate on Nesmith's more country efforts.

Michigan Blackhawk

Writer: Michael Nesmith

Lead vocalist: Instrumental

Producer: Michael Nesmith

Monkees present: none (other than Nesmith as producer)

Not to be confused with "Down the Highway", the Carole King song misleadingly released under this title, this is a Nesmith song based around standard blues changes and old Chuck Berry guitar licks.

Changes

As of 1970, Michael Nesmith was no longer a Monkee, having bought out the remainder of his contract as Tork had before him, and the band were reduced to a duo (and Jones was widely reported to be just waiting out his contract). The final humiliation came when Jeff Barry, who had produced the band during the *More of the Monkees* sessions, was brought back in to record this last album with Dolenz and Jones.

Other than Dolenz's song "Midnight Train", the band members had no creative input. In fact, Jones later insisted [Sandoval, p. 262] that the album was originally recorded as an Andy Kim record, and Kim's vocals wiped and replaced with Dolenz and Jones' when no record company would take it.

Certainly the mix suggests that something odd was going on. The entire album (apart from mono track "99 Pounds") is mixed in stereo - but it's a mix consisting of a mono mix of the full track dumped dead centre in the stereo mix, with a single extra overdub then added in each channel (usually a light percussion overdub) to make it nominally stereo.

The album, in fact, isn't at all bad - its low reputation is mostly down to those who've never bothered to listen to it - and is certainly more cohesive than the previous few efforts. But it's not really a group album - Jones only appears on five of the album's twelve tracks, and one of those is a backing vocal and two others are leftovers from earlier albums. The Monkees were definitely over, even if the corpse was still twitching.

There would be a brief reunion of Dolenz and Jones in the mid-70s (dealt with in the next section of this book), and Jones and Tork would perform together briefly as a duo in the 80s, but this would be the last time the Monkees would perform under that name until 1986.

All tracks produced by Jeff Barry except where noted.

Oh My My

Writers: Jeff Barry and Andy Kim

Lead vocalist: Micky Dolenz

Other Monkees present: None

Actually not a bad opener at all, this is a catchy bit of psych-soul, sounding mildly influenced by Norman Whitfield's productions for the Temptations, but also not far off the style that Dolenz had been heading in himself with songs like "Rose Marie". It's notable that Dolenz thinks far less harshly of this album than Jones did, and certainly he's better served by the material, having always had a streak of soul/R&B influence.

Released as a single, this was the Monkees' lowest-charting A-side to date, peaking at number 98 in the US. However, it's notable for having a promo video directed by Dolenz (who had also written and directed the last episode of the band's TV show). As Dolenz's musical career started to fail, he later moved into TV production and direction.

Ticket on a Ferry Ride

Writers: Jeff Barry and Bobby Bloom

Lead vocalist: Micky Dolenz

Other Monkees present: None

This acoustic track, in a style that wouldn't seem out of place on a Crosby, Stills, Nash and Young album, is pleasant enough, if overlong, but barely even features Dolenz, consisting mostly of stacked backing vocals in the CSNY style, with just the occasional solo line for Dolenz. This would have been a nice track at two minutes long, but there are simply not enough ideas in the song for its 3:29 running time.

You're So Good to Me

Writers: Jeff Barry and Bobby Bloom

Lead vocalist: Davy Jones

Other Monkees present: None

This isn't the Beach Boys song of the same name, but can only be described as bubblegum soul. This track shows Barry's way with a hook — much like "Sugar Sugar", this song doesn't go more than about two bars without another catchy phrase or riff, but whereas that song had been bright and cheerful, this struts and swaggers, and Jones, allowed to sing in his natural baritone range, doesn't do a half-bad job with the material.

The main problem with this track is its lyrical inanity, but other than that there's little so far on the album to suggest the travesty it's reputed to be.

It's Got to Be Love

Writer: Neil Goldberg

Lead vocalist: Micky Dolenz

Other Monkees present: None

A bright, cheery pop song so bland it actually gets forgotten before it's finished, this is notable only for how well Dolenz does with material with which he has absolutely no emotional investment. When you consider that Dolenz and Jones were essentially presented with this album as a *fait accompli*, the way Dolenz manages to sell the songs is nothing short of miraculous.

But as we get into this album, it becomes very apparent that while it's in no way a bad album, nor is it in any way an interesting one. While an album like *Instant Replay*, a much less listenable album, had tracks like "I Won't Be the Same Without Her" and "Shorty Blackwell" that repay relistening, this is all on the surface.

Acapulco Sun

Writers: Ned Albright and Steven Soles

Lead vocalist: Micky Dolenz

Other Monkees present: None

This Latin-flavoured track with a slight resemblance to the Beatles' "Here Comes the Sun" could, in the right hands, have been pretty decent (I can actually hear it in Nesmith's style). Unfortunately, nobody involved seems to have any idea whether they're meant to be taking it seriously or not, and the overly-silly backing vocals push it into the territory of bad parody, rather than entertaining pastiche.

There's also a horrific noise from 2:17 through 2:24, which sounds like the tape rubbing against the heads (possibly tape squeal caused by reusing an old, damaged tape) rendering the track almost unlistenable around that point.

99 Pounds

Writer: Jeff Barry

Lead vocalist: Davy Jones

Other Monkees present: None

Now, this is more like it! A stomping bit of fuzz-guitar freak-beat, this isn't too far from something like the Nazz's "Open My Eyes", and has a ferocious garage-rock organ solo. This track is actually a left-over from Jones' pre-*Headquarters* sessions with Barry (the sessions that had produced "A Little Bit Me, a Little Bit You"), and still has the enthusiasm of early 1967 about it.

Lyrically, the song is drivel, but Jones delivers one of his most impassioned vocals here, though it's buried in a strange mix. The mix, the only one on the album in mono, was created when this track was slated as the B-side to "A Little Bit Me" back in 1967, and doesn't seem to have had as much attention paid it as perhaps it should. Luckily, this is the kind of track where a sloppy mix doesn't matter too much, as it's all about the energy in the track.

Dolenz has sometimes claimed that he was made lead singer of the band because he was the only one who would let loose with full-throated screams for the rockers. This song belies that, with some of Jones' "Wow"'s sounding frankly Lennonesque.

Tell Me Love

Writer: Jeff Barry

Lead vocalist: Micky Dolenz

Other Monkees present: None

This attempt at a slow-burn R&B ballad sounds like nothing so much as the schlock that Elvis Presley spent his last few years performing. But Micky Dolenz, for all his undoubted talent, is no Elvis, and Barry's session backing vocalists are definitely no Sweet Inspirations, so a chorus that should be an impassioned howl, a roar of desperation, a yearning for reassurance, becomes instead just Dolenz singing slightly louder. This is the kind of song which needs absolute conviction in the performance in order to raise it to the heights of mediocrity, and while Dolenz does his best, it's simply not quite enough.

Do You Feel It Too?

Writers: Jeff Barry and Andy Kim

Lead vocalist: Davy Jones

Other Monkees present: None

Apparently "Life is like a cartoon movie, being with you makes it groovy". After a surprisingly-listenable side one, this and the previous track show a precipitous drop in quality on side two. For some reason this is generally considered one of the better tracks on the album, but I can find few, if any, redeeming features about it. Particularly bad is Jones' lead vocal, one of only two new lead vocals he cut for the album.

I've been harsh on Jones at times in these reviews, but one thing that could normally be said of him is that he was the consummate professional. No matter how bad the material, or how ill-suited to his style, he would always do the very best he could. Sometimes that best wasn't good enough, but that was never because of any laziness on Jones' part.

Here, though, his contempt for the material shines through. His double-tracking is sloppy as hell, making some of the lyrics almost incomprehensible, and he's exaggerating his Mancunian flat vowels, presumably as a joke in order to stave off boredom. Poor stuff.

I Love You Better

Writers: Jeff Barry and Andy Kim

Lead vocalist: Micky Dolenz

Other Monkees present: Davy Jones (backing vocal)

This is the only track on the album to feature two Monkees, but Jones might as well not have bothered as he's just barely audible in the usual Barry-backing-vocalist stack. This is quite enjoyable, in its call-and-response way, but the verses seem to be going for a set-up line/punchline joke structure, but then don't actually deliver a funny punchline.

This is just there, but after the last two tracks 'just there' is something of an improvement. This was released as the B-side of "Oh My My", but did not chart.

All Alone in the Dark

Writers: Ned Albright and Steven Soles

Lead vocalist: Micky Dolenz

Other Monkees present: None

This pleasant jazzy track is in fact just a demo by Albright and Stoles. Barry apparently liked the demo so much (or couldn't be bothered re-recording it) that he just got Dolenz to add a vocal to the demo, without even removing the original lead vocals.

It's a sloppy, demo-quality recording, but it has more spirit than most of the rest of the album, with its silly kazoo solo and falsetto vocals. It's just got absolutely nothing to do with the Monkees.

Midnight Train

Writer: Micky Dolenz

Lead vocalist: Micky Dolenz

Other Monkees present: None

Producer: Micky Dolenz

This song had a long gestation, starting out as a Kingston Trio-style folk track that Dolenz and his sister Coco used to perform as a duo pre-Monkees. The Dolenzes then cut a demo version of the song in 1967 (available on the *Headquarters Sessions* box set) in a strange hybrid of clean-cut *Hootenanny* folk on the choruses (anyone who has seen *A Mighty Wind* will be unable to hear the section where they drop down into half-speed without imagining the New Main Street Singers singing it) and Dylanesque talking blues on the verses.

This version, however, has slightly different verse lyrics, and is patterned equally on Dylan (especially listen to Dolenz's phrasing on "look who's crying, guess you lose") and Johnny Cash (the bass melody is nearly identical to that of "I Walk the Line"). Other than "99 Pounds", it's definitely the highlight of the album.

I Never Thought it Peculiar

Writers: Tommy Boyce and Bobby Hart

Lead vocalist: Davy Jones

Other Monkees present: None

Producers: Tommy Boyce and Bobby Hart

There seems to have been a sort of cargo-cult belief held by someone in the Monkees' organisation that because Boyce and Hart had written two hit singles (and two charting B-sides) early in the band's career, the secret to success was to dig up some piece of rubbish they'd done with the band in 1966 and stick it on the album, no matter how bad or dated.

This plinky piece of nonsense seems to have been patterned after some of Herman's Hermits' music-hall style hits of the mid-60s, and would have sounded dated in October 1966, when it was originally recorded. A mish-mash of oompah music-hall verses, a waltz-time middle eight and a pseudo-Hendrix solo (presumably overdubbed in 1969, when some additional work was done on the track), this is just a horrible mess, and has nothing to do with anything on the rest of the album.

An ignominious end to the last album the Monkees would release in their original time together.

Bonus Tracks

Do it in The Name of Love

Writers: Bobby Bloom and Neil Goldberg

Lead vocalist: Micky Dolenz

Other Monkees present: Davy Jones (backing vocals)

This pop-soul piece of fluff with rather sleazy lyrics from the point of view of a man begging his girlfriend for sex is the kind of thing Rod Stewart would soon build a career on, but for the last thing recorded by the Monkees, it's an embarrassment.

Or rather, not by the Monkees. While this was recorded as the last thing under Dolenz and Jones' Monkees contract, it was released as by "Mickey *[sic]* Dolenz and Davy Jones". Unsurprisingly, it failed to chart at all.

Lady Jane

Writers: Bobby Bloom and Neil Goldberg

Lead Vocalists: Davy Jones and Micky Dolenz

The B-side to "Do it in the Name of Love" is marginally better (in fact, musically, it sounds very much like the Wings song "Medicine Jar" from several years later). This isn't the Rolling

Stones song of the same name, but more of the pop-soul that Barry had been producing for the Monkees. Rather incredibly, this track was the first ever true duet between the Monkees' two main lead vocalists, with both splitting the lead vocal equally. But it's a sad end for a once-great band. They would be back though. . .

Dolenz and Jones (and sometimes Boyce and Hart)

Dolenz, Jones, Boyce and Hart

In 1975, the first attempt to reunite the Monkees happened. Bobby Hart had been put in touch, by a friend of his, with a promoter in Asia who wanted to book the Monkees for a tour. Hart got in touch with Micky Dolenz, who informed him that there was no way that Nesmith would do it, and that no-one knew where Tork could be found, but that he and Jones might be interested. To fill out the lineup, Boyce and Hart themselves agreed to perform with Dolenz and Jones, and they put together a new band, which also featured guitarist Keith Allison (a former member of Paul Revere and the Raiders who had also been a session player on several Monkees songs, and who had had a short-lived career as a wannabe teen idol in the sixties).

Throughout late 1975 and 1976 this band toured amusement parks throughout the US with some success, toured East Asia, and had a TV special broadcast in the US. As the band were not legally allowed to use the name "the Monkees", they performed as Dolenz, Jones, Boyce and Hart, but with the promotional tag "the great golden hits of the Monkees show: the guys who

215

wrote 'em and the guys who sang 'em". Their shows consisted of a run through of the Monkees' biggest hits, along with a few other songs Boyce and Hart had written for other artists, but they also recorded an album of new material, the closest thing to a new "Monkees" album since *Changes*. As well as Dolenz, Jones, Boyce, Hart, and Allison, a large number of other Monkee associates made a return here – Louie Shelton adds guitar, and all four of the Modern Folk Quartet feature instrumentally[16].

It's a surprisingly solid album. It's not, perhaps, up to the standard of most of the actual Monkees albums, but it's a very successful update of the formula from the first couple of albums, combined with a variety of styles that were popular in the mid-seventies – a little Elton John here, a little E.L.O. there, a touch of the Hudson Brothers. The result is, basically, what one would expect a Monkees album produced by Boyce and Hart to sound like in 1976.

Unfortunately, the album and its associated singles had little commercial success, and D,J,B, and H went their separate ways, although Dolenz and Jones would continue touring together for a while longer.

All tracks produced by Tommy Boyce and Bobby Hart. All tracks feature both Micky Dolenz and Davy Jones on either lead or backing vocals, so the "other Monkees present" category won't be used below.

---

[16]the MFQ had been Chip Douglas' old band, and as well as Douglas had featured sometime Monkees session bassist Jerry Yester, and Henry Diltz who had taken many photos of the band over the years and had added banjo to some tracks.

Right Now

Writers: Tommy Boyce and Bobby Hart

Lead vocalist: Davy Jones

The opening track on the album seems to be an attempt at pastiching the solo Beatles – the stately, plodding, piano chords, vocal melody (especially the melisma on the word "I"), and general reverby production sound are all very like Lennon's more cocaine-fuelled mid-70s work; the slide guitar part is a passable imitation of George Harrison; and the Moog at the start, and some of the chord changes, could be straight off a Wings album. This combination, along with the layers of acoustic guitars, makes this sound somewhat prescient of "Free as a Bird".

Oddly, though, the inspiration for the song seems to have come from a song that was a hit for a different Liverpudlian quartet – the opening line "And so it begins/needles and pins" is both lyrically and melodically taken from "Needles and Pins", a song that Jack Nitzsche and Sonny Bono had written for Jackie DeShannon, and which had been a hit in 1963 for Merseybeat group the Searchers.

It's a very different style from anything Boyce and Hart had written previously for Dolenz or Jones, and they do a decent job of this kind of more harmonically sophisticated song, although the lyrics are all on the "We've waited so long/And the feeling's so strong" level.

Jones does a creditable job on the lead vocal, but Dolenz manages to steal the show with some gospel wailing on the fade.

I Love You (And I'm Glad That I Said It)

Writers: Tommy Boyce and Bobby Hart

Lead vocalist: Bobby Hart

This is quite a pleasant ballad let down a little by the sequencing of the album – it's much the same kind of feeling and tempo as "Right Now", and has a similar arrangement – but it's a better song than that one, with the unusual-for-the-70s choice of opening with a sung intro that's made up of different musical material than the rest of the song, as used to be common in the 1930s and 40s.

Hart takes the lead on this ballad of unrequited love, full of lines like "If they ever give awards for the loneliest story/I'll be there when they give them out, and I'll win without a doubt", and he does a very creditable job. If Jones or Dolenz had sung this, it would have been too adolescent, but Hart's weathered baritone, with something of the feel of Bill Medley, brings the song into more adult territory.

That said, it's hard to understand the choice to release this as a single from the album – when the selling point of the Monkees semi-reunion was "the guys who wrote 'em and the guys who sang 'em", having one of the guys who wrote 'em, rather than the guys who sang 'em, as lead vocalist, seems a counterproductive idea.

The single was unsuccessful, but this is one of the better-loved songs from this album. Hart was a distinctive vocalist, and deserved to have more success as a singer, but his vocal style wasn't particularly suited to the pop sensibility he had as a songwriter,

You and I

Writers: Micky Dolenz and Davy Jones

Lead vocalist: Micky Dolenz

This isn't the same song as the one on *Instant Replay*, but is instead the *second* Davy Jones song called "You and I" to be better than one would expect.

The song itself isn't all that great, but it's catchy, and the subject (still being together after a long time and getting through adversity) is perfect for a reunion record – "it was you and I and promises not broken/you and I and magic memories". Indeed, twenty years later the Monkees would revisit the song for another reunion album, this time with Jones taking lead.

In the first edition of this book, I said that version, from 1996's *Justus*, was "infinitely superior" to this one. Seven years' hindsight make me revise that opinion somewhat – while I still think the 1996 version is superior, this has much to offer. Dolenz does a lovely, gentle, vocal right at the top of his range, and the arrangement suits this gentler take on the song, with its multiple layers of picked acoustic guitar, weeping steel guitar, and almost total lack of drums (for most of the song the only percussion is some maracas in the left channel).

Dolenz's vocal is extraordinary, especially at the end when he tails off into falsetto wailing in much the same manner as his friend Harry Nilsson often would. This was released as the B-side of the "I Remember the Feeling" single.

After Jones' death, Dolenz and Tork performed this song live once, as a tribute to him.

Teenager in Love

Writers: Doc Pomus and Mort Shuman

Lead vocalist: Micky Dolenz

And again we have the problem of this album's sequencing letting it down. We started with two ponderous piano ballads at a similar tempo, and now we've got a second mid-tempo acoustic-guitar-driven song with a Dolenz lead vocal. It's a shame, because this is really quite extraordinarily good, and easily the highlight of the album.

The mid-70s were a peak time for nostalgia for the late fifties and early sixties, with *American Graffiti*, *Happy Days*, and the phenomenal success of the Beach Boys' *Endless Summer* causing a revival of the popular music of fifteen years or so earlier, and so it made sense to cover an oldie from a few years before the Monkees' career.

"Teenager in Love" was written by the songwriting team of Pomus and Shuman – a great songwriting team who were, oddly, among the very few great Brill Building songwriters who never contributed a song to the Monkees, but who wrote many hits for the Drifters, Elvis Presley, and others.

This song was originally performed by Dion and the Belmonts, but was so popular when it came out that in May 1959 no fewer than three different versions were on the charts in the UK, with the Belmonts' version being joined by Marty Wilde and Craig Douglas.

Dolenz, Jones, Boyce, and Hart do something quite special with it though. It starts off sounding like a straightforward arrangement of the song, with acoustic guitar, piano, and drums – but then when Dolenz's vocal comes in, so do a banjo and a set of Caribbean-style steel drums. By the time of the instrumental break, there are strings, Jones singing strange "ha ha ha" backing vocals, what sound like angry crowd noises just out of earshot, a thumping drum, and Dolenz again singing in what sounds like an imitation of Harry Nilsson.

And then, we get a strange *a capella* break which layers distorted voices over each other (Jones in particular sounds sped up), before bringing all the other instruments in under the distorted vocals for the fade.

This might well be the most sonically inventive thing on any Monkees or Monkees-related record, and certainly it's the instrumental arrangement of theirs that pulls in from the most different areas of music. It's quite, quite extraordinary.

Sail on Sailor

Writer: Doug Trevor

Lead vocalists: Davy Jones, Tommy Boyce, and Bobby Hart

Not the Beach Boys song of the same name, this was written by Doug Trevor, a former member of the Cherokees, who had opened for the Monkees on an Australian tour in 1968. He'd stayed in touch with Jones, and had written a song for Jones' 1971 solo album, and he would continue to work with the Monkees on occasion in future, writing a track for Jones in 1981 and being a prominent part of the Monkees' late-80s touring band.

This is easily the least interesting song on the album – which is not quite the same as saying it's the worst. It's a country-rock ballad of a type that was popular at the time, and one can easily imagine this becoming an Elvis album track – the arrangement has a lot of the feel of the TCB Band (the band who backed Elvis Presley in the 70s, and who also worked with Gram Parsons and Emmylou Harris) about it. But as soon as the song is over, it's almost impossible to remember any details of it – it just slips out of the mind.

Each of Jones, Boyce, and Hart takes lead for a verse, and all four of the band sing the choruses – and fans of Davy Jones will be pleased to hear another lead from him after three songs in a row with him relegated to backing vocal parts – but somehow Dolenz still manages to steal the show, with his "sail on sail on" vocals on the tag.

As an example of proto-yacht rock this is fine, and there's some nice banjo picking buried in the mix, but this is forgettable.

It Always Hurts The Most In The Morning

Writers: Tommy Boyce and Micky Dolenz

Lead vocalist: Micky Dolenz (and Tommy Boyce?)

The only Boyce/Dolenz song ever to be released, on the evidence of this song they should probably have collaborated more – it's really a rather good track, and probably the best song, as a song, of the new material on the album.

Unfortunately, this is also a song where the poor mastering quality of the currently-available versions of the album is something of a let-down. The only CD release of the album (which is also the version available on Spotify and other streaming services) is a needledrop from a vinyl copy, and more than most tracks on the album this has audio artefacts and a muddy sound.

Put simply, Dolenz is multitracking his lead vocal here, but I sometimes think I hear someone else (presumably Boyce, who could sound very like Dolenz) also doubling him. But with the poor sound quality of the available version, I am not capable of telling for certain either way whether that's just an artefact of the multiple Mickys, or whether Boyce (or someone else) is being drowned out by Micky's stronger vocal.

Either way, what we have here is a quite gorgeous bit of breakup pop – a song that sounds like a classic Bee Gees chorus coupled to a Paul McCartney verse, with driving tack piano giving way later in the song to some glorious arpeggios running counter to strings, some Beach Boys vocals and fuzz guitar. A really lovely little bit of orchestral pop music to close side one.

Moonfire

Writer: William Martin

Lead vocalist: Micky Dolenz

And side two opens with the closest this band could ever come to hard rock. This song by Bill Martin, who had previously written "All of Your Toys" and "The Door Into Summer", and had since written several songs for and with Harry Nilsson (one of which, "Rainmaker", had also been recorded by Nesmith on *Nevada Fighter*).

Starting out with a vaguely gospel-inflected piano-and-organ verse with Moog bleepings, this goes into a surprisingly heavy chorus, and an instrumental break which sounds like it was inspired by Led Zeppelin. The whole thing feels very like early-70s bands like Argent – there's more than a little of the feel of "Hold Your Head Up" to this.

It's not a style of music I find particularly appealing, but Dolenz does a surprisingly reasonable job on the vocals – not that he's not usually excellent, but this is completely out of his normal stylistic range.

You Didn't Feel That Way Last Night (Don't You Remember)

Writers: Tommy Boyce and Bobby Hart

Lead vocalist: Micky Dolenz

Any Boyce and Hart fans who'd bought this album for the songwriters, assuming there were any, must have been feeling slightly disappointed listening to the album thus far – of the seven songs before this, only two and a half had been by Boyce and/or Hart, so by this point our hypothetical Boyce and Hart fan would be excited to hear a new song by them.

Sadly for them, they don't get a new song. Instead, after a brief announcement by a robot voice that sounds a little like a speak-and-spell, saying "this is radio DJBH", they get "Steppin' Stone" with different lyrics. And those different lyrics include a line about a "magic carpet ride" which in turn just points out how much "Steppin' Stone" itself owed to "Kicks" by Paul Revere and the Raiders (who recorded "Steppin' Stone" before the Monkees, but after "Kicks").

This is not a wholly bad thing – after all, "Steppin' Stone" was a great record, and hearing Micky Dolenz sing a near-identical song but with added Moogs and space blooping sound effects is perfectly fine – but it's not exactly a new song, and it just leaves the listener with the desire to hear "Steppin' Stone" instead of this.

Along Came Jones

Writers: Jerry Leiber and Mike Stoller

Lead vocalists: Group

A cover version of the Coasters' hit, this is usually picked out by people reviewing the album as a low point, but personally I find it quite endearing.

The Coasters' original is a comedy song in their usual style, with a group vocal describing watching an exciting Western on TV, in which a bandit called Salty Sam repeatedly tries to murder Sweet Sue, but "long lean lanky Jones" comes along and saves her. Each verse has a solo line for the bass vocalist Bobby Nunn, as Salty Sam threatening Sue, and a breakdown in which the group ask "and then?" and a single spoken voice repeatedly describes the exciting events before "along came Jones", the first line of the chorus.

The narrator eventually gets so excited/bored (it's not entirely clear which) that he gets up and turns the channel over, only to find the same thing playing out, in a fairly funny mockery of the omnipresence of formulaic Westerns on US TV in the late 50s.

Dolenz, Jones, Boyce, and Hart replicate the Coasters' version almost exactly, down to a King Curtis soundalike on the saxophone with one notable change – after Hart as Salty Sam has threatened Sue, and Dolenz as the spoken narrator has detailed her peril, we get a spoken line from Davy Jones as the eponymous Jones, interjecting in an exaggerated upper-class British accent "what seems to be going on here?" or "that's not cricket old chap!"

Now, there is an issue with this track that I'm not going to try to judge, because it's an area where my lack of sensitivity to cultural and racial nuance comes into play. But... it's a truism among critics that some of the power of the Coasters' original version of this came from the fact that it was black men mocking the extremely white genre of the Western. That's not the case with Dolenz, Jones, Boyce, and Hart – and indeed there's a case that could be argued that this is a rather racially insensitive recording.

The "Salty Sam" vocal on this track is a fairly good imitation of Nunn's comedy bass vocal, but that comedy vocal is sung in an exaggerated accent that is very definitely that of a black man. I can't convince myself that the same voice coming from a white singer is not problematic – but nor can I be sure that it is.

As a white British man, I am simply not in any position to make a sensible judgement. I'll have to leave the morality of the imitation aside, for those with a better understanding of the issue to judge, but I thought it should at least be mentioned.

Having said that, assuming that my qualms about it are wrong, aesthetically the track works, for me at least. The original was a great track, and while this version is such a close imitation that it loses points for that, it does have the added comedy value of Jones' interjections – and also of the resultant idea that the famously-tiny Jones could be described as "long, lean, lanky Jones" by anyone.

At the end, there's a little spoken-word joke, just a few seconds long, "nursery rhyme time with Davy Jones" (introduced by Dolenz's young daughter Ami), with Jones reading what starts as a nursery-rhyme but ends quickly as a dystopian science fiction story

Savin' My Love For You

Writers: Micky Dolenz and David Jones

Lead vocalist: Micky Dolenz

A glam-flavoured disco stomper which has more of Dolenz's fingerprints than Jones', the basic song here could easily have been one of Dolenz's R&B experiments from the late 60s, but the arrangement is absolutely mid-70s, with its skittering hi-hat and wah-wah guitar. It's a much better attempt at going disco than many of the band's contemporaries managed, and many people point to this as a highlight of the album.

For me, it's merely a decent attempt at the genre, though I love Dolenz's delivery of the line "Don't need the FBI, 'cause I'm a super spy". It's typical of this album, really – there are no special highs or lows here. Most of the album is very pleasant, but it only rarely reaches greatness.

The track ends with another interstitial – "And now, as a public service, Radio DJBH, in cooperation with United Galaxies, presents your Dolphin Joke of the Day", followed by some dolphin clicks and squeaks.

I Remember the Feeling

Writers: Tommy Boyce and Bobby Hart

Lead vocalists: Davy Jones and Micky Dolenz

This was the first single from the album, and makes a reasonable choice given the nostalgic theme of the lyrics, but it's not a particularly impressive piece of songwriting from Boyce and Hart. The verse, sung by Jones is a low-key, acoustic, one which sounds like a Bay City Rollers or Osmonds track. The verse has handclaps on it, which is often a sign that someone has tried to give a bit of extra excitement to a track that's sagging a bit, and the lyrics are doggerel.

The chorus, on the other hand, has Dolenz bursting out in his loudest voice, and actually does give the track an immense kick.

Musically, it's fairly simple, with the main point of interest being that Jones' vocal in the verse comes in five-and-a-bit beats later than one would expect, giving the song an odd structure and temporarily throwing the listener off. But really, this track stands or falls entirely on the power of Dolenz's vocal on the chorus, and luckily he delivers.

Sweet Heart Attack

Writers: Tommy Boyce and Bobby Hart

Lead vocalist: Micky Dolenz

And the album ends with a track combining elements of funk and heavy rock – the verse is all disco hi-hat, pulsing bass and electric piano, though in a darker mode than "Savin' My Love For You", with almost a blaxploitation soundtrack feel to it, while the chorus is dominated by loud fuzz guitar.

Underneath the arrangement, though, this is structured very similarly to many of Boyce and Hart's songs from the 60s, and it's easy to imagine it being recorded in the same style as, say, "Apples, Peaches, Bananas and Pears". Lyrically, again, it's nonsense – Boyce and Hart's lyrics on this album are in general nowhere near up to the standard of their better sixties work – but with some neat syllabics and internal rhymes that show a little more evidence of being crafted than some of the album's other tracks.

Dolenz does his usual exemplary job on the song, but it's a relatively weak track to end an album that's hard to sum up, one that – like Dolenz, Jones, Boyce, and Hart as a group – manages to be somehow both more than and less than the sum of its parts. It's an album with occasional moments of greatness, and which is never less than competent, but which somehow manages to leave one simultaneously feeling like the album is blander than it actually is and feeling like this is an unfair judgement.

It's an album that is more obviously of its time than the Monkees' sixties work was, and a lot of the styles it dabbles in are currently deeply unfashionable, yet it still feels like it could have had more success, both commercial and critical, than it did.

Concert in Japan

A live recording from 1976, this was originally intended to be released as a follow-up to the *Dolenz, Jones, Boyce and Hart* album, but sadly the commercial failure of that album meant this wasn't released until 1981, when a new burst of Monkee-mania in Japan meant that there was suddenly a hunger for any and all Monkee-related product.

Concert in Japan is marred by poor recording quality, and by the frankly insane decision to make so many of the songs into medleys. This is particularly harmful in the case of the hits that Jones sang – "Valleri", "Daydream Believer", and "A Little Bit Me, A Little Bit You" are all smushed together into a single medley, cut down to just a single verse and chorus each, and placed second in the show after "Clarksville". Anyone who came to the show to hear Davy Jones sing any of his Monkees hit singles could have left the show six or seven minutes in and not missed anything.

This is, fundamentally, a record of a band who seem unsure what they're trying to be. Are they a new band trying to do new material, or are they a nostalgia band? And if the latter, are they catering for nostalgia for the Monkees or for Boyce and Hart's writing for other acts? Any one of these could

231

make sense, and the combination could have made sense if it had been done with more thought, but as it is they seemed to be falling between multiple stools.

But all that said, Dolenz and Jones sound good, Boyce and Hart are better singers than you would expect given their back-room status, and the band are OK. It's a confused album, for completists only, but not as bad as its reputation suggests.

Line-up:

- Micky Dolenz – vocals, guitar

- Davy Jones – vocals

- Tommy Boyce – vocals, guitar

- Bobby Hart – vocals, keyboard

- Keith Allison – guitar, vocals

- Steve Johnson – keyboards

- Rick Tierny – bass

- Jerry Summers – drums

As Dolenz and Jones are both on every track as either lead or backing vocalists, the "other Monkees present" credit is dropped here.

I Wonder What She's Doing Tonight

Writers: Tommy Boyce and Bobby Hart

Lead vocalist: Tommy Boyce

This was a top ten hit in 1968 for Boyce and Hart as a duo, and was done in a very similar style to the Monkees records – indeed, Boyce was doing a very close imitation of Dolenz's vocal style on the record, so much so that it's honestly hard to tell if it's Boyce doing a particularly good imitation of Dolenz here or if it's Dolenz himself (helped by the fact that much of the time the vocals are doubled, and quite possibly both men are singing) – my best guess is that it's Boyce, but Boyce could sound spookily like Dolenz at times (and sadly, the credits for the album are not detailed enough for any judgement other than my own ears). Either way, it was a marvellous piece of pop music when Boyce and Hart had a hit single with it, and it's equally good here.

Medley: Come A Little Bit Closer/Pretty Little Angel Eyes/Hurt So Bad/Peaches 'n' Cream/Something's Wrong With Me/Keep on Singing

Writers: Tommy Boyce, Bobby Hart, and Wes Farrell/Curtis Lee and Tommy Boyce/Teddy Randazzo, Bobby Weinstein, and Bobby Hart/Tommy Boyce and Steve Venet/Danny Jansen and Bobby Hart/Danny Jansen and Bobby Hart

Lead vocalists: Tommy Boyce/Davy Jones with Bobby Hart/Bobby Hart and Davy Jones/Micky Dolenz/Bobby Hart/Micky Dolenz

A medley of songs which Boyce and/or Hart had written for artists other than themselves or the Monkees.

"Come a Little Bit Closer" was a hit in 1963 for Jay and the Americans, and was Boyce and Hart's first hit together as a duo – it's a Spanish-inflected rocker based very loosely on "La Bamba".

"Pretty Little Angel Eyes" was a hit in 1961 for Curtis Lee, produced by Phil Spector, and is a doo-wop pop song.

"Hurt So Bad" was originally a hit in 1965 for Little Anthony & the Imperials – as a soundalike for their earlier hit "Goin' Out of my Head" – and was later a hit for the Kingsmen and Linda Ronstadt. Dolenz, Jones, Boyce, and Hart's version seems modelled on the Righteous Brothers.

"Peaches 'n' Cream" was a 1965 single for the Ikettes, modelled on "Bread and Butter" by the Newbeats.

"Something's Wrong With Me" was a hit in 1972 for Austin Roberts, most famous for the "Scooby-Doo, Where Are You?" theme. "Keep on Singing" was also originally recorded by Roberts, but is best known for Helen Reddy's 1974 cover version, which was a minor hit.

These songs run to about forty seconds each, generally just one chorus of each song with very little coherence to the medley, which jumps around wildly from girl-group soul to country, from ballads to uptempo novelty doo-wop, without regard to musical coherence. A shame as several of these songs are, in their full versions, very strong.

Action (aka Where the Action Is)

Writers: Tommy Boyce and Steve Venet

Lead vocalist: Keith Allison

The theme song to the 1967 TV series "Where the Action Is", which Allison co-hosted, this was a 1965 hit for Freddy "Boom

Boom" Cannon, and was also performed by Paul Revere and the Raiders (who Allison joined after their recording of it) and shouldn't be confused with Allison's own song "Action, Action, Action", which appeared on Allison's "Where the Action is" tie-in album "In Action", and which was written by Boyce and Hart.

Allison sings lead on this version, and announces it as being written by Boyce and Hart, but it was actually written by Boyce and Steve Venet.

Got that?

The song itself is very much modelled on the songs that Brian Wilson was writing in 1964 and 65 – his Beach Boys music, obviously (particularly the repeated phrase "dance dance dance", which was the title of a Beach Boys hit in 1965), but even more blatantly his material for Jan and Dean. This is more obvious on Paul Revere and the Raiders' version, with its soaring falsetto, than this more garage-rock rendition, but the resemblance is still definitely there. There's also a more-than-slight resemblance to Cannon's earlier hits, especially "Palisades Park".

It's a fun enough track, but an odd way to end a Dolenz, Jones, Boyce, and Hart show and album, since it's sung by none of the principals and is also one of the sloppier performances.

Full tracklist (all songs sung by their original vocalists except as noted)

- **Last Train to Clarksville**

- **Medley: Valleri/Daydream Believer/A Little Bit Me, a Little Bit You**

- **I Wonder What She's Doing Tonight**

- (I'm Not Your) Steppin' Stone

- I Wanna Be Free

- Savin' My Love for You

- Pleasant Valley Sunday

- I Remember the Feeling

- A Teenager in Love

- Cuddly Toy

- Medley: Come a Little Bit Closer/Pretty Little Angel Eyes/Hurt So Bad/Peaches 'n' Cream/Something's Wrong With Me/Keep on Singing

- I Love You (And I'm Glad That I Said It)

- Action

The Point!

After the collapse of the Dolenz, Jones, Boyce, and Hart tour, Micky Dolenz and Davy Jones continued touring together for much of 1977, performing an odd show that was a mixture of comedy sketches, Monkees hits, and covers of songs like "Martha My Dear" and "Bye Bye Blackbird", mostly in small venues. Then, in late 1977, they were offered the opportunity to appear in a West End musical.

The Point! had originally been a concept album and cartoon by Harry Nilsson, a longstanding friend of the Monkees. In 1971, he had released the album, and with it an animated special from Murukami-Wolf, detailing the adventures of Oblio, a child who is born the only round-headed person in the Pointed Village, a village where everyone has a pointed head.

The story itself, written by Nilsson, Norm Lenzer, and Carole Beers from Nilsson's original idea, was acid-inspired whimsy, mostly endless punning on different meanings of the word "point", but both concept album and cartoon had been moderately successful, as they came out at the height of Nilsson's songwriting ability and, in the case of the cartoon, it didn't hurt that in its original version it was narrated by Dustin Hoffman, though more recent home video versions have Ringo Starr as the narrator instead. Incidentally, another longtime Monkee friend and collaborator, Bill Martin, also had a minor voice role in the cartoon.

Nilsson had actually written the original album during a period where he was spending much of his time at Dolenz's house – after the Monkees' breakup, Nilsson and Dolenz used to spend days together taking drugs and making music in Dolenz's home studio – but at the time he had sung all the parts on the record himself, in his then-beautiful voice. Six years later, Nilsson's recording career was deteriorating, after damage to his vocal cords meant he lost much of his singing ability, and he was looking to start writing musicals and films instead. As part of this sideways career move, he helped put together a stage version of *The Point!*

Originally, this ran at the Mermaid Theatre, London, over Christmas 1976, starring Wayne Sleep as Oblio. It was only moderately successful, but it was popular enough that it was brought back for Christmas 1977, for an eleven-week run, and as Sleep was no longer available, the role of Oblio went to Davy Jones.

This version was greatly expanded from the original version of the story, and indeed from the 1976 version, and incorporated several songs which had not been on the original album, but which had featured on other Nilsson records. It also included a new character, the Son of the Count, who was included for Dolenz to play after not having featured in the 1976 version of the show.

Dolenz's involvement was actually down to Jones, who had been on a trip to Japan with Nilsson and Ringo Starr to record a jingle for a suit commercial. While over there, Jones had suggested to Nilsson that a part be created for Dolenz, and Nilsson (who was friendlier with Dolenz than with Jones anyway) had happily obliged.

The show was not a massive success, and the run was not extended, but it was popular enough that a cast recording was produced, featuring all the songs from the show, and with both Jones and Dolenz involved – indeed, Jones takes the vast majority of the lead vocals.

Part of the reason for the lack of success, though, was that Jones and Dolenz did not get along during the run of the show. While they had been working together happily enough for a couple of years, cracks were showing in their relationship, not helped by Dolenz at the time suffering through the breakup of his first marriage and a period of depression. Their relationship got worse and worse during the show's run, and for much of the three months the show was on they weren't speaking at all offstage – at one point there was a fistfight between the two backstage at the theatre.

At the end of the show's run, Dolenz decided to stay behind in London, where he became a moderately successful television director, working on children's series such as *Metal Mickey*, *Murphy's Mob*, and the Bill Oddie vehicle *From the Top*. He and Jones would not speak to each other again for nine years, only getting back on civil terms after the Monkees' twentieth anniversary spurred the first of several reunions for the band in 1986.

The soundtrack album, which was reissued on CD in 2016, is a cast album, and many of the songs are credited to the full cast as performers, but Jones takes the lead on the bulk of the songs. All songs were written by Harry Nilsson, except for "Thursday (Here's Why I Did Not Go To Work Today", which was written by Nilsson and Danny Kortchmar. The arrangements were by the show's musical director Mike McNaught, adapted from George Tipton's arrangements for the original album.

Dolenz later criticised the show as a musical, primarily because the songs themselves didn't drive the story but acted as breaks in the narrative, but viewed purely as an album *The Point!* is one of the better products of the post-60s Monkees. Put simply, any album that largely consists of Dolenz and Jones singing songs Nilsson wrote during his creative peak is going to be worth listening to.

Overture: Everything's Got 'Em

Lead vocalists: Cast

The opening track to the album, this was also the opening track to Nilsson's original album. Where Nilsson's version was, typically of him at that time, largely backed by piano, this is a fuller arrangement, with a flute-led band playing to a semi-disco rhythm, and incorporating elements of melodies from other songs in the show (most notably a quote from "Lifeline") before the cast, in unison, sing the introductory lyrics – "this is the town and we are the people/This is the town where the people all stay... that's the way we wanted it, that's the way it's going to stay".

The "everyone's got one...wouldn't be without one" lyrics are one of several points in the show where there's a mild double entendre. Nilsson was fascinated with sexual and scatological humour, and while that's dialled back a little in what is ostensibly a show for children, it's still there if you look for it.

Me and My Arrow

Lead vocal: Davy Jones

Here's another example of that. "Arrow", in the context of the show, is Oblio's dog (portrayed on stage by a puppet), and that's how the song reads to me – yet several fans have hypothesised, with some justification, that this song about someone going everywhere with an "arrow" that's "straighter than narrow" and with him all the time, even when he wakes up, might be referring to the singer's penis rather than to the dog about whom the song is ostensibly about.

I prefer, however, to assume that in this case, even if Nilsson intended the double entendre, he also intended the song to be read on the literal level – and certainly Bill Martin always said that Oblio's relationship with Arrow was based on Nilsson's own relationship with his dog, Molly.

Nilsson's original version of this track reached number thirty-four in the US charts. Davy Jones' version of it is taken slightly faster, but otherwise follows the original fairly closely, although Nilsson's version has a multi-tracked vocal and various bits of instrumental layering which would not be possible to perform live, and so are missing here. This also has an extended instrumental break, in which Jones talks to Arrow ("here boy!" and so forth), presumably corresponding to bits of stage business which one can't fully appreciate from an audio recording.

The song itself is a fun, light, song with one of Nilsson's catchier melodies, especially in the middle eight, and Jones performs it well, in the lower voice he would increasingly use over the next few decades.

Poli High

Lead vocal: Cast

This is a song which Nilsson used to explain songwriting and song structure in one of his rare live appearances, on *The Smothers Brothers' Summer Show* in 1970. This is odd, as the song itself is one of Nilsson's less impressive works – the lyric mostly consists of the words "poli high, polytechnical high"[17] and "valley low".

It has a pleasant melody, but shorn of visual context the song doesn't provide much in the way of narrative, and the rather over-formal voices of the British musical theatre singers performing this don't have the charm of Nilsson's lead vocals on the original. In general this recording tends to steamroller the melody a bit, and to lose the quirkiness that made Nilsson's version so charming.

Remember

lead vocal: Veronica Clifford

Originally titled "Remember (Christmas)" this was one of the songs added to the show, having first appeared on Nilsson's *Son of Schmilsson* album from 1972. Here it's given to Veronica Clifford, who played Oblio's mother in the show, as a solo spot.

---

[17] A "polytechnic" was a type of further education college in the United Kingdom from the 1960s through the 1990s, which awarded degrees but taught technical, practical subjects rather than academic ones. Nilsson was spending a lot of time in the UK in the late 60s and early 70s, and the term would have been in the news there quite a lot as the polytechnics were just starting up.

Dolenz has always admired this song, and he's actually recorded two solo versions of it – on his 1991 album of classic rock songs sung as lullabies, *Micky Dolenz Puts You to Sleep*, and as the title track of his 2012 album of his favourite 60s and 70s songs, *Remember*.

Dolenz's solo versions, and Nilsson's original, are all superior to this – not because of Clifford's performance, which is fine (she's not as good as Nilsson, but she manages to perform this extraordinarily rangey song perfectly well) but because of a tedious instrumental section here which adds nothing musically (and which again was probably used for some stage business we can't see).

However, every version of this song is worth listening to – it's one of Nilsson's most beautiful ballads, and while Nilsson's original version was unsuccessful as a single, it's later gained the recognition it deserved thanks to its use in *You've Got Mail*.

To Be a King

Lead vocal: Noel Howlett

This is the only truly unsuccessful song on the album, and is so untypical of Nilsson that one could easily believe it wasn't his work at all – it's a typical example of musical-theatre writing, something that doesn't work at all as a song, and is just there as an exposition dump. Nilsson would later manage to do this kind of thing much better on the *Popeye* soundtrack, but here it's redundant and pointless.

This wasn't part of the original Nilsson album, and is one of a very few Nilsson songs not to exist in a version recorded by its composer. It's also, I believe, never been recorded by anyone other than Howlett.

He's Leaving Here This Morning (Bath)

Lead vocalist: Micky Dolenz

Originally from Nilsson's album *Aerial Ballet*, this was not part of the original version of *The Point!*, and was added to give Dolenz a solo spot, with parts of the first-person lyric changed to a third-person one, so Dolenz is singing "he's leaving here" about Oblio, rather than "I'm leaving here", though other parts are left in first person.

There are two other lyrical changes. One is minor – "hope for the human race" becomes "hope for the coming race" – but the other change gives the whole song a different meaning. The line "I'm awfully glad he's going to take a ride" makes the song about Oblio (Jones' character) being forced out of the Pointed Village by Dolenz's malicious character, and Dolenz's character's gleeful reaction.

However, in the original – in which the character going home to take a bath is the same person as the one whose eyes are heavy and knees are weak, rather than them being two people – that line is "I'm awfully glad you let me come inside", which gives the whole song a very different meaning. In the original, this song is about the immediate aftermath of losing one's virginity at a brothel. Everything Nilsson did contained at least one dirty joke song, though – remember that this is a man who once based a song for the Ronettes on a famous bit of toilet graffiti – and the song's utter sense of joy is contagious.

But here, those tiny lyrical changes make the song far more suitable for a family show, and Dolenz sings it with a wonderful sense of malicious glee, the leaps into falsetto that the song calls for being interpreted here as exuberance at the defeat of an enemy. Whereas Nilsson's original version had been fairly restrained, this one has Dixieland horns and Dolenz emoting all over it, and the result is one of the highlights of the album.

Think About Your Troubles

Lead vocalist: Davy Jones

The best actual song from the original version of *The Point!*, this is also the song from that album that is least connected to the general plot of Oblio, Arrow, and the Pointed Village. A simple "circle of life" type song, it tracks the course of a teardrop as it falls into a river, gets swept up into the ocean, gets swallowed by fish which in turn are eaten by bigger fish which are eaten (in defiance of biological plausibility) by a whale, who dies and decomposes in the ocean. The ocean water containing the teardrop is filtered and goes into the water supply, where it becomes part of a cup of tea drunk by the person who cried at the beginning.

It's a gentle, beautiful, song, typical of Nilsson's unique viewpoint on life, and simultaneously evokes both deep depression and a moving sense of hope. Jones does a very good job with the vocal, although as with other songs on the album it doesn't quite measure up to Nilsson's original.

Blanket for a Sail

Lead vocalist: Davy Jones

This was a new song for the musical, but it was also included on *Knnillssonn*, which came out in 1977 between the first and second run of the musical, and which was Nilsson's last album on RCA, the label on which he spent almost all of his career – he would only record one more album after that one. *Knnillssonn* is regarded as Nilsson's late-period return to form after a few less-than-stellar outings, and while this isn't the best song from the album, it's still good enough to fit in with the other songs here.

And musically, it's absolutely suited to Jones' vocals – it has much of the same bounce to it as "Cuddly Toy" or "Daddy's Song", but doesn't have the emotional complexity of either of those songs. Rather, it's a fun piece of kidpop – a song loosely based on "row row row your boat", talking about sailing through your dreams with a blanket for a sail. Indeed, this is possibly the only track here to be definitively better than Nilsson's own versions of the song (he recorded it twice), as it's more suited for Jones' innocent vocals than for the hoarse, weathered voice Nilsson had developed by 1977.

Life Line

Lead vocalist: Davy Jones

We return again to the songs from the original version of *The Point!*, and this time to the most depressive song on that album, and indeed one of the lowest, most depressive songs Nilsson ever wrote.

"Hello, won't you throw me down a lifeline/I'm so afraid of darkness and down here it's just like nighttime" is a typical line from the lyric, and the music matches it – it evokes the feeling of being trapped in a deep hole, simultaneously echoing and distant, but also claustrophobic and enclosed, with the music not moving much and giving the impression of being unable to move.

Jones does an excellent job here, on a song that's very much out of his usual style. One normally expects a Jones lead to be relatively fast moving – even on the ballads, there tend to be quite a lot of notes and syllables – but here he has to sing single-syllable words that last a bar or more at a time. He pulls it off well, for something that's so different from his usual work.

Thursday (Here's Why I Did Not Go To Work Today)

Lead vocalist: Felix Rice

This song was apparently written in something of a drunken haze by Nilsson and Danny Kortchmar, a well-regarded session guitarist. Van Dyke Parks was also present while they were writing the song, and may have contributed a couple of lines uncredited.

The song is a jazzy blues ballad, which originally appeared on Nilsson's *Sandman*, one of his lesser albums, and it seems to have elements both of the old standards which Nilsson had recorded for his *A Little Touch of Schmilsson in the Night* and of 50s R&B ballads – it may be that the song was somewhat inspired by Fats Domino's "Blue Monday", although it's a much more crafted song than that one.

Rice does a fine job of the performance, and this is a nice listen.

It's a Jungle Out There

Lead vocalist: Micky Dolenz

Another song that wasn't on the original *The Point!*, this one is from Nilsson's *Duit on Mon Dei*, where in its original arrangement it was based around steel drums rather than the more traditional rock arrangement used here.

In both versions, though, the song is very clearly modelled on the work of Nilsson's friend Randy Newman. The song is a reported conversation between Tarzan and Jane, in which Tarzan complains about aspects of domesticity that are hard when you're in the jungle (having to kill lions for Jane's dresses or kill crocodiles to make shoes), and it's a lot of fun, although it's cut down to about half its original length here (presumably in consideration of the family audience – it's another song where Nilsson included rather crude jokes, in this case about Tarzan's son accidentally trying to swing from Tarzan's penis instead of a vine).

Dolenz has a lot of fun yelping his way through this one, and it's a joy to listen to.

P.O.V Waltz

Lead vocalist: Davy Jones and Cast

And going back into the songs from the original album, we get a song that more than most of these sounds like it was written for an actual musical – a waltz (as the title would suggest), with a fairground carousel feel to it. It starts out with a Jones solo vocal, but he's soon joined by the whole cast, and by the end is completely buried by the chorus singing. This is one of those tracks that was definitely better in Nilsson's quirky original than in the rather overblown, bombastic, version here, but in either version it's pleasant but minor.

Are You Sleeping?

Lead vocalist: Davy Jones and Cast

The last song from the original *The Point!* to feature on the album, this is, like "P.O.V. Waltz", marred by being turned into a singalong for the whole cast for much of it. Jones' first verse works very well (although his pronunciation of "by your side" is... idiosyncratic) but then the whole cast come in and sing the rest of the song in unison, and the song is just not suited to that – it's a gorgeous melody, but a casual one, meant to be scatted and played with, and the casual nature is completely lost when half a dozen or so people are singing the "woah woah woah"'s simultaneously.

Gotta Get Up

Lead vocalists: Davy Jones and Micky Dolenz

And here's the last song proper on the album, this time taken from *Nilsson Schmilsson*, with Davy and Micky singing together almost throughout – like the last two songs it starts as a Jones solo vocal, but this time quickly becomes a duet with the two of them singing together, with Dolenz sometimes doubling Jones and at other times harmonising with him at the octave, in a manner similar to the way the two of them sang "Cuddly Toy".

It's surprisingly rare to hear only Dolenz and Jones' voices on a track together, given that they were the principal vocalists for the Monkees, but those few times where it happened always worked well.

This is another one that's been censored slightly – in this version, a sailor with a girl in town comes to "see her" for a couple of days, rather than "pound her", sadly but understandably losing a good laugh line that's also a nice internal rhyme – this is, as so often with these tracks, overblown and over-orchestrated compared to Nilsson's original studio version, but Jones and Dolenz both do an excellent job on the vocals

Overture (Reprise)

And the album ends with another, shorter, run-through of the instrumental portion of the overture. This is absolutely pointless, except to provide a sense of closure to the album (most of Nilsson's own albums were bookended in similar ways, but usually by more interesting material).

Overall, *The Point!* is an interesting attempt, which doesn't quite work as a coherent album but may well have worked extremely well in a live setting. To an extent it falls between the two stools of being a "Micky and Davy of the Monkees sing Nilsson's Greatest Hits" album and being a normal live musical cast album, and to my ears the former would have been far better than the latter – but then, I am a massive fan and admirer of both the Monkees and Nilsson, while I am not a particular fan of stage musicals.

How much this appeals to an individual listener will probably depend on their views on those three factors – I could imagine someone who was a fan of the Monkees, Nilsson, and of stage musicals getting more out of this – but I think most listeners would agree that this is, despite its flaws, probably the best Monkees-related album between *The Monkees Present* and *Good Times!*

That Was Then, This Is Now - reunion recordings, 1986 - 2016

Then and Now... the Best of the Monkees

And so we jump forward to 1986. Michael Nesmith has spent the intervening time pursuing a successful (critically if not commercially) solo career and has had a lot of financial success with his home video company. Jones and Dolenz have not worked together in nearly a decade.

Tork, meanwhile, had mostly been working as a teacher, with occasional abortive attempts to start a new music career (most notably with his band the New Monks, who released one very strange single coupling a New Wave interpretation of "Stepping Stone" and a banjo-driven arrangement of "(Your Love Keeps Lifting Me) Higher and Higher)".

Then, for the twentieth anniversary of the band's formation, a number of factors converged to make the Monkees one of the most popular bands in the world again. Most importantly, MTV started playing old episodes of the TV show, as did Nickelodeon, and a reissue campaign started up.

Dolenz, Tork and Jones took advantage of this, reuniting and licensing the Monkees' name for a series of tours which would last the next four years (Nesmith joined them occasionally for guest spots on Californian shows, but had no interest in reuniting on a permanent basis). They were also asked to contribute three new songs to the latest hits compilation. Jones refused to be involved (reports variously say that he had no interest in just adding vocals to pre-recorded tracks, and that he had business problems with Arista records), but Dolenz and Tork did. The resulting tracks were released as by 'Micky Dolenz and Peter Tork', but have been included on Monkees compilations.

That Was Then, This Is Now

Writer: Vance Brescia

Lead vocalist: Micky Dolenz

Other Monkees present: Peter Tork (backing vocals)

Producer: Michael Lloyd

The first of the reunion tracks was this, a cover of a Ramones-esque powerpop single by the Mosquitos from the previous year. And it's not half bad. The track sticks closely to the original's template, except for the unfortunate replacement of the rhythm guitar with a synthesiser playing the same notes.

It sounds dated now (and far more dated than the lower-budget original), but allowing for the dodgy 80s production techniques this is still catchy and enjoyable enough, and it's certainly no worse than anything the band's contemporaries were doing at the time; the Beach Boys, the Kinks, Paul McCartney... all had become seduced by the lure of synthesisers, squealing guitars, and gated snares.

But at the time, this is exactly what a Monkees comeback single should have been - a catchy pop song, nothing too clever, with a good vocal from Dolenz (Tork is essentially inaudible here) and a lyric that hints at nostalgia without going too far and making the band sound like they're irrelevant. Surprisingly, given it wasn't released as by the Monkees, it reached the top 20 in the US, and deservedly so. I do have to wonder if anyone ever thought Micky Dolenz was "tough and kinda wild" though.

Anytime, Anyplace, Anywhere

Writers: Bobby Hart and Dick Eastman

Lead vocalist: Micky Dolenz

Other Monkees present: Peter Tork (backing vocals)

Producer: Michael Lloyd

This, on the other hand, is exactly what one might have feared a Monkees reunion track would sound like. Plodding and unoriginal (the title of this song was also used by everything from a Martini ad to an album by the Rossington Collins Band to a track by Nena around this time), this song sounds like it was designed to be heard playing in the background in a John Hughes film set in a high school.

Boyce and Hart were, at this point, no longer working together, and Hart was writing hits for acts like New Edition and LaToya Jackson with his new writing partner Dick Eastman, so it's understandable that Eastman and Hart would have been chosen to supply a new song, but this is not Hart's best work by a long way.

Kicks

Writers: Barry Mann and Cynthia Weil

Lead vocalist: Micky Dolenz

Other Monkees present: Peter Tork (backing vocals)

Producer: Michael Lloyd

And this is better, but anyone who's heard the Paul Revere and the Raiders original will know how good this *could* have been, had it not been recorded in the 80s with its 'sonic power' and synth obsession. Put Dolenz's vocal here over a track in the style of the Raiders' original, with its jangly guitar and throbbing bass, and this could have been a garage rock classic on a par with "Stepping Stone", rather than this rather unimpressive nothingness.

20th Anniversary Tour

For the band's twentieth anniversary, for the first time in seventeen years the Monkees toured again – without Nesmith, but with Davy Jones, Micky Dolenz, and Peter Tork.

Indeed, this live album, originally released as a double vinyl record for sale on tour, but later issued as a fan club CD, is credited to "Micky Dolenz, Davy Jones, Peter Tork" rather than to the Monkees – while it was recorded at and sold at Monkees concerts, it wasn't released by the company which owned the rights to the Monkees' name at the time, and Dolenz, Jones, and Tork had licensed the name for the tour but not for the record.

But however it is credited, this is a Monkees live album, from a brief time period in which the band were once again almost as successful as they had been in their 60s heyday. Even given the possibility that it's been doctored (and the audience noise does sound extremely suspicious at times) it's clear that this was a band that was once again playing to ecstatic audiences.

Setlist-wise, this was one of the least interesting tours the reunited band ever did. While every configuration of the band since the eighties has performed all the hits and the expected songs – this is, after all, a band who pride themselves on being entertainers as much as artists – they have also usually included a fair amount of unusual or obscure songs, whether that be things like the 1989 tour's short acoustic section and hip-hop reworking of "Ditty Diego: War Chant" or the decision in 2011 to perform the whole of the *Head* album live.

For 1986, though, the band were performing together for the first time in nearly twenty years, and so it was enough to perform a setlist that essentially consisted of everything one would find on a "Best of" collection for the band, along with two new songs ("MGB-GT", discussed below, and "I'll Love You Forever" which would be included on the *Pool It!* album).

For the most part the arrangements stick closely to the versions of the songs that the audience would be familiar with from the records, with very little in the way of variation – this is, of course, what the audience wants to hear, but it also means that the album is less than essential – there are no radical reinventions here, nothing that will make you listen to these songs in a new light, and nothing that is going to surprise the listener. The main difference is that the arrangements usually incorporate horns (mixed very low in the mix) and synth pads, and generally thicken the sound in the way most bands would when performing live, especially at that time. It sounds exactly what you'd expect a Monkees reunion tour from 1986 to sound like, in other words.

It's pleasant, but there's nothing on here that anyone but the most obsessive of fans will need – although unlike the live albums we've covered previously, it at does the virtues of sounding professionally recorded and competently performed throughout.

MGBGT

Writer: Peter Tork

Lead vocalist: Peter Tork

Other Monkees present: Micky Dolenz and Davy Jones (backing vocals)

Producers: Micky Dolenz, Davy Jones and Peter Tork

This track by Tork was one of two new originals included on the album (the other being Jones' "I'll Love You Forever", which was later included on *Pool It!*). A rather odd track, this seems to be an attempt to meld Beach Boys style car songs with banjo-driven bluegrass.

This is an enjoyable bit of fluff (with Jones and Dolenz making racing car noises in the background) and apart from an ill-advised lounge sax solo has little of the production horrors that accompany the studio reunion tracks. The audience obviously love it, and nobody's taking it too seriously. This later became the B-side to "Heart and Soul", and Tork also rerecorded it for his 1994 solo album *Stranger Things Have Happened*.

Full tracklisting:

- **Last Train to Clarksville**

- **A Little Bit Me, A Little Bit You**

- **(I'm Not Your) Steppin' Stone**

- **Cuddly Toy**

- **Goin' Down**

- **Pleasant Valley Sunday**

- I Wanna Be Free

- Your Auntie Grizelda

- She

- For Pete's Sake

- That Was Then, This Is Now

- Shades of Gray

- Look Out (Here Comes Tomorrow)

- No Time

- Daydream Believer

- Listen to the Band

- Zilch/Randy Scouse Git

- I'll Love You Forever

- MGB-GT

- Valleri

- I'm a Believer

- (Theme From) The Monkees

Pool It!

And so, after the success of the reunion single and tour, it was decided that Dolenz, Tork and Jones should record a reunion Monkees album. Unfortunately, they were touring so intensively that they could not actually record as a band. Instead, they merely added vocals to pre-recorded tracks, with little creative input. None of the recordings featured more than one Monkee.

This *should* have still worked, as the producer chosen for the project was Roger Bechirian, who had engineered many of Elvis Costello's albums and (with Costello) co-produced Squeeze's *East Side Story*. He was known for getting a sound based on real instruments, recorded mostly live, which sounded close to classic 60s pop but was still acceptable for 80s radio, and for working with great songwriters. He should have been a perfect safe pair of hands for the Monkees.

But sadly (and here I depart from the text of the original edition of this book, in which I blamed Bechirian for the faults of this album – I've read interviews since which clarify what happened) there was disagreement between the Monkees as to what kind of album they wanted to make. Tork and Dolenz wanted an album that would have used Bechirian's talents and been something closer to the work he was doing. Jones, on the other hand, wanted something very different, and the result came out closer to Jones' vision. Sadly the result is a soulless, uninspiring, mess, and very easily the worst thing ever released under the Monkees' name.

Heart and Soul

Writers: Simon Byrne and Andrew Howell

Lead vocalist: Micky Dolenz

The opening track and lead-off single is one of the less objectionable tracks on the album. It's just a bland landfill-AOR track, all crunchy guitars and bad snare sounds, of the kind that was being produced by the metric tonne in the mid-80s.

At least, that's the case until the synth solo, when one of the most unforgivable bad production decisions I've ever heard happens, and a percussion part comes in in the right channel and remains for the rest of the song. This percussion part has a delayed reverb added, so it's a doubled beat (tish-tish) and the delayed reverb is very subtly out of time with the rest of the track, later sounding like the emphasis is on the second part (tish-*tish*), when everything else about the track is urging it to emphasise the original strike (*tish*-tish).

It may sound like a small thing, and it's buried in the mix, but it rubs against everything else in the track the wrong way. I guarantee you could give any decent drummer in the world a nervous tic by playing them this track from 2:28 onwards.

A slightly edited version of this track was released as a single. Unfortunately for the band, the Monkees' then-manager had double-booked them on the day of an MTV Christmas event they were meant to attend. They had to cancel the MTV appearance, and this was regarded as such a snub that all Monkees material was removed from rotation on the channel, and without their support this only just scraped to number 87 in the charts, and was the last Monkees track to even do that well.

(I'd Go The) Whole Wide World

Writer: Eric Goulden

Lead vocalist: Micky Dolenz

This is an improvement, but not much of one. Wreckless Eric was a labelmate of Squeeze, Elvis Costello and Nick Lowe, all of whom Bechirian had worked with, and this two-chord song had been the closest he'd ever come to a hit, so it's unsurprising that Bechirian saw some commercial potential in it and revived it for this album.

Unfortunately, the lack of subtlety of the production steamrollers the song flat, losing all its humour. When Eric sings "When I was a young boy, my mother said to me/There's only one girl in the world for you and she probably lives in Tahiti", you can believe that this slurring, ridiculous figure might actually have to travel the whole world to find a girlfriend. It's slightly less believable when sung by Micky Dolenz to a synthpop backing.

Still, this is a brave attempt, and the type of material that the band *should* have been doing for the whole album.

Long Way Home

Writers: Dick Eastman and Bobby Hart

Lead vocalist: Davy Jones

Jones does his best with the material here, giving one of his best performances, but between the mawkishness of this mid-tempo pop ballad, the cooing backing vocals, and the abysmal drum sound, his best efforts are in vain. Just horrible.

Secret Heart

Writers: Brian Fairweather and Martin Page

Lead vocalist: Micky Dolenz

I am very aware that this section of this book is repetitive, but there are only so many ways to say 'bland AOR shlock with a terrible drum sound, too many synthesisers and too much reverb'. Unfortunately, the band had no such compunction about repetitiveness, and so this is, once again, bland AOR schlock with a terrible drum sound, too many synthesisers and too much reverb. There is a very slight difference here, with the addition of a bad saxophone solo - one which sounds like it was played on a synth, rather than with a real instrument.

Martin Page, the composer of this song, went on to write "We Built This City" for Starship and "King of Wishful Thinking" for Go West, and this track bears a slight musical resemblance to both those songs. This is not a good thing.

Gettin' In

Writer: Peter Tork

Lead vocalist: Peter Tork

This is easily the highlight of the album, as well as being the only track to feature any instrumental contribution from one of the band (Tork added some guitar). While it's still slathered with synthesisers, they're being used in a more interesting way here. Tork has clearly been listening to David Bowie's early 80s work, and to Talking Heads, and the result is this moderately funky glam/New Romantic synthpop outing, with a very mannered vocal by Tork, occasionally leaping into a falsetto reminiscent of Sparks. This could easily have been a Talking Heads track, down to the slightly creepy, obsessive lyric.

(I'll) Love You Forever

Writer: David Jones

Lead vocalist: Davy Jones

The other song to have any Monkee creative contribution, this had been previously recorded by Jones for a self-released cassette, and had featured on the live album the band had recorded the year before. Unfortunately, it's awful, a slow, maudlin ballad in the vein of Barry Manilow, backed almost entirely by synth-celeste and synth-strings (plus an acoustic guitar solo, to show it's soulful). This track does, however, have the interesting production touch of the album - sampled, heavily-processed, backing vocals, sounding a little like those on "I'm Not in Love" by 10CC.

Every Step of the Way

Writers: Mark Clark and Ian Hunter

Lead vocalist: Davy Jones

This track at least has some energy to it, being pretty much a note-for-note cover of an album track by Ian Hunter, the former lead vocalist of Mott the Hoople. The result is a strange hybrid between New Wave pop (sounding at times a little like Bechirian's work with Lene Lovich) and Springsteen-esque muscle rock, with Jones trying his best to sound like he's heard of the existence of punk, while the guitarist still thinks he's playing "Heart and Soul".

It's by no means a good track, but it made sense that it was released as the album's second single. It didn't chart.

Don't Bring Me Down

Writers: Bill Teely and Glenn Wyka

Lead vocalist: Micky Dolenz

Neither the Pretty Things nor ELO songs of the same name (either of which would, actually, have been interesting choices for the Monkees to cover), this is another bit of nondescript 80s AOR.

Midnight

Writer: David[18]

Lead vocalist: Micky Dolenz

By this point, this album has become actively painful to listen to. The omnipresent digital sheen, the dead-sounding drums and the lack of air in the mixes combine so that after listening this far I've usually got a migraine. This track sounds like a B-side by Survivor or Toto. I actually can't imagine who could find listening to this in any way a pleasant experience.

She's Movin' in with Rico

Writer: Andrew Howell

Lead vocalist: Davy Jones

As this piece of bad faux-calypso nonsense, complete with synthesised steel drums, is written by one Andrew Howell (who also co-wrote "Heart and Soul"), I feel like I should apologise on behalf of the Andrew Hs of this world. We are all very, very sorry that one of our own could commit such an atrocity.

Since You Went Away

Writer: Michael Levine

Lead vocalist: Peter Tork

This is another highlight of the album, a lovely, jaunty, McCartneyesque uptempo pop song that Tork had previously demoed

---

[18]No first name is given for this writer, and many Monkees fans seem as unable as I to find out any more about the writer.

in 1980, a late-Beatles pastiche worthy of Neil Innes. There's still too much bad synthesiser on this, but this is really good. Had the rest of the album been up to the standard of the two Tork tracks, this would be regarded as one of the band's best albums, instead of their absolute worst.

Counting on You

Writer: Alan Green

Lead vocalist: Davy Jones

A variation on the lyrical conceit of "I Got a Gal in Kalamazoo", this songs lyrics are clearly intended to be clever, with lines like "five, four, three, two, one of these days..." and "one, two, three, four, five, six, seven, eight, nine, tentatively..."

Equally clearly, they're not clever, and nor is the pun on the two meanings of the word 'counting' that holds the song together. This is just appalling drivel. Unlistenable.

Justus

And so we come to 1996, and the only time all four Monkees ever reunited.

With the thirtieth anniversary of the TV show, all four band members reunited for a UK tour, a TV special, *Hey Hey It's The Monkees* (written and directed by Nesmith, and a wonderful recreation of the spirit of the original series), and this album.

The band clearly had something to prove, as this was the first and only Monkees album to be written, produced and recorded entirely by the band without any outside contributors. The result is rather odd - while still definitely better than *Pool It!*, this album suffers from a desire to be relevant, which makes it sound a bit too much like 90s college radio. It's not terrible, by any means - in fact it's fairly decent, for what it is - but it is the sound of four men in their fifties trying too hard to sound like men in their twenties.

Unfortunately, while Nesmith performed on the 1997 tour, he backed out of any future performances with the band, and the Monkees feature film he was apparently writing never got made. He wouldn't be involved with the Monkees again until 2012, after Jones' death.

For a long time, this album was the last ever Monkees album. Thankfully, that's no longer the case, and we can look at it as a little less of a lost opportunity – although the fact that this would be the last time Nesmith and Jones would ever work together hurts now we know that *that* opportunity can never arise again.

All Monkees perform on all songs - credits are:

Davy Jones - Vocals, Guitar, Percussion

Michael Nesmith - Guitars, Vocals

Peter Tork - Bass, Keyboards, Vocals

Micky Dolenz - Vocals, Drums

Circle Sky

Writer: Michael Nesmith

Lead vocalist: Michael Nesmith

The opening track is a remake of Nesmith's track from *Head*. It's curiously pointless, as there are lyrical changes - but neither set of lyrics are any more comprehensible or audible - and the track is very, very close to the original, but with more distorted guitar. Of course, being close to the original also means it's an excellent track, but it's an odd way to open an album.

Never Enough

Writer: Micky Dolenz

Lead vocalist: Micky Dolenz

A competent enough sludgy rocker built around a simple chordal riff (and with the ending from "With a Little Help

From My Friends" tacked on at the end) reminiscent of some of XTC's early work, this is far from Dolenz's best song, but it's still a pleasure to hear the Monkees actually functioning as a unit. Nesmith turns in a good, reverb-heavy guitar solo, and it's good to hear all the band's voices singing on the repeated chorus at the end.

Lyrically, the song is quite heartfelt, apparently about the breakup of Dolenz's second marriage, and the vocal matches that intensity, but possibly too much attention was paid to self-expression and not enough to the craft of songwriting.

Oh, What a Night

Writer: David Jones

Lead vocalist: Davy Jones

This is one of the better songs on the album, its vaguely Latin flavour bringing out the best in both Jones and Nesmith, who provides some gorgeously husky backing vocals. The only problem with it is that it's been sequenced following "Never Enough", which comes to the same kind of full close and ends with the same drumbeat-full-stop.

Clearly this similarity comes from a fundamentally good reason - these are songs and arrangements that have been worked out for live performance as a four-piece unit, and so they can't really fade, and they have to take into account Dolenz's limited drumming repertoire - but sequencing them back to back highlights these limits.

You and I

Writers: David Jones and Micky Dolenz

Lead vocalist: Davy Jones

A reworking of the track from *Dolenz, Jones, Boyce and Hart*, this is generally considered the better of the two versions, and I can't disagree. A pleasant singalong, with more than a little of the Beatles about it, this is unexceptionable, friendly, pop music that's hard to get worked up about, but equally hard not to like.

Unlucky Stars

Writer: Micky Dolenz

Lead vocalist: Micky Dolenz

This track is a straightforward 50s pastiche, with Dolenz's vocal slathered in slapback echo in the manner of Gene Vincent or early Elvis, and Tork's piano part being identical to Fats Domino's part on "Blueberry Hill". The only stylistic inconsistency is Nesmith's guitar, which while it has the proper amount of reverb is too busy and distorted for the time period.

How much one enjoys this will be entirely down to how enjoyable one finds this kind of pastiche - it's good of its kind, but it's clearly not trying to do anything new.

Admiral Mike

Writer: Michael Nesmith

Lead vocalist: Micky Dolenz

This is the closest the Monkees ever came to grunge, and is sung by Dolenz with a huge amount of fury. The song attacks journalists who tell lies in order to sell advertisements, and blames them for a suicide ("He killed himself/You killed him first/Because you're only 'only selling ads'").

The song appears to be about the death of Admiral Jeremy Michael Boorda, the Chief of Naval Operations, who shot himself in May 1996. Boorda had been depressed because of reports in *Newsweek* that he had been wearing, along with his medals, V-for-valour devices that he wasn't properly entitled to, and he had been worried that this would adversely affect the US Navy's reputation.

This was a *cause celebre* at the time, and while it was later shown that the *Newsweek* report had been largely correct, Nesmith clearly at the time believed it wasn't, and this song is full of righteous fury against journalists who would hound a man to death.

This is probably the Monkees song with fewest defenders (other than "She's Moving In With Rico") but I have a soft spot for it, not only because for a long time it seemed like it would be the last ever Nesmith song for the band, but also because there's a genuine passion to this that is missing from much of the rest of the album, although some of the lyrics seem curiously childish, calling the target of his anger "slimy toads" and "stupid twits".

Dyin' of a Broken Heart

Writer: Micky Dolenz

Lead vocalist: Micky Dolenz

One of the best tracks on the album, this seems to have been inspired by Harry Nilsson's "Coconut", a song with a similar rhythm, obsession with a single chord, and which also features a visit to a doctor. This, though, takes the idea in a more bluesy direction, with Nesmith's guitar quoting "Johnny B Goode" and Tork and Dolenz providing their tightest ever performance as a rhythm section.

Lyrically, this is another song that seems inspired by Dolenz's divorce, but he seems able to take a more humorous look at his own pain here.

Regional Girl

Writer: Micky Dolenz

Lead vocalist: Micky Dolenz

This, on the other hand, is just unpleasantly cynical, and rather nasty - a song about provincial people travelling to the big city to try to make it in entertainment, but with the narrator concluding "I think you're gonna end up making burgers for some bitch".

The mean-spirited lyrics combine with music that sounds like a fuzzed-up, angrier Dire Straits, to make easily the low point of the album.

Run Away from Life

Writer: Peter Tork

Lead vocalist: Davy Jones

A rather simple, wistful song about wanting to get away from it all, this is let down by a sledgehammer production until 1:37, when a wonderful multiply-overdubbed analogue synth solo comes in. Utterly unlike anything else the Monkees ever did, this sounds like nothing so much as some of Don Preston's *avant-garde* experimental jazz-prog instrumentals, and raises the whole track from 'failure' to 'interesting experiment'.

I Believe You

Writer: Peter Tork

Lead vocalist: Peter Tork

By far the best thing on this album, this is an obsessive, exhausted song based around a single cramped three-note phrase (tonic, flattened second, flattened third) played over and over again on a piano in straight waltz time, while over it the bass, drums and another piano play more exploratory, experimental material. Nesmith[19] has complained about critics calling this track 'jazzy', but Thelonius Monk is certainly one of the musicians to have influenced this, at the very least.

And lyrically, this is about obsession and desperation, too, about believing in a lover without any reason, without really any hope, just clinging on to that belief as its own reason and its own object in the face of the almost certain destruction of

---

[19]Posting to alt.music.monkees 15/10/96

the relationship. This is extraordinary, mature, intelligent writing, and while it's a lot less fun to listen to than many of the other tracks, as emotionally draining as it is it's possibly Tork's best work.

It's My Life

Writer: Micky Dolenz

Lead vocalist: Micky Dolenz

And this is what most people would have expected a Monkees reunion album to sound like - a mawkish inspirational piano-based ballad, vaguely like some of John Lennon's least interesting music. Another song about getting over divorce, this at least is about actually getting over the divorce, rather than wallowing in the misery of it, but I can't imagine who, other than the participants, would want to listen to this.

It's Not Too Late

Writer: Davy Jones

Lead vocalist: Davy Jones

And as we get to the end of the album, the main question one has to ask is who it is who keeps telling musicians in their fifties that we want to hear about their mid-life crises, and how can we stop them? Here Jones, whose own second marriage was breaking up, sings a big ballad about how "it's not too late to turn this ship around." I'm sure it was very meaningful for him on a personal level, and obviously it's awful when any longstanding relationship breaks up, but he didn't have to share the pain with the rest of us.

Overall, *Justus* is nowhere near as bad as its reputation suggests, with at least half the tracks being pretty good - a better standard than any of the other post-*Head* albums. But it's easy to see why it wasn't a success, having little of the pop wonder of the band's 60s music, and replacing it with 90s college rock cliches. This is an album that screams 'mid-life crisis' almost as much as the little ponytail the balding Micky Dolenz was wearing at the time. Sometimes it's best not to look back.

Live Summer Tour

Live Summer Tour is a DVD recorded in Anaheim, California on the final night of the Monkees' 2001 US tour – the last time Peter Tork would play with the band for a decade (Dolenz and Jones continued touring together as the Monkees for another year after that before the band split up for nine years). While Tork left the band rather acrimoniously this time round, whatever backstage problems the band were having don't show up at all onstage, where there is a clear rapport between the three of them, of the kind that could only come from thirty-five years of working together off and on.

This is, undoubtedly, the best document that exists of the Monkees as a live band. Two versions of the DVD were released – a longer, two-hour, one with almost the entire show on it, which was only given a limited release and is now almost impossible to get hold of (although illegal copies of it float around if you know where to look, and it can often be found on YouTube) and a shorter, fifty-nine-minute version which is still available. There have also been several CD releases, under various titles, containing excerpts of the music from this show, although no audio release has been made of the full show. This review is of the long DVD version, but comments here will apply to any of the other releases.

While Nesmith is sadly missed from this version of the lineup, what watching this performance clearly demonstrates is just how much all of the Monkees contributed to the band. This is something that may sometimes not have been clear enough in my discussions of the albums – Dolenz and Nesmith have far superior voices to the other two, Tork never sang much on record, and Nesmith was far and away the best songwriter of the bunch, so while I try to be fair to all of them and point out where they all shine and where they all fall down, the very fact that this book deals solely with the recordings, and not with the live performances, or the TV series and specials, or *Head*, means that I am ignoring a large part of what made the Monkees an important cultural phenomenon, and so I am inevitably going to be unfair to some of them.

But here, on this live DVD, you can see what each man brings to the band, and why they were all chosen. Dolenz, of course, is the voice – it's him who acts as the musical centre of the show, taking the lead on the vast majority of the hits, and doing so superbly. Anyone who's read this far will know exactly what he adds to any Monkees show.

But Tork is hugely important to the show. He takes more leads than on record (taking over from Dolenz on a couple of the songs he wrote himself), plays guitar, keyboards, and banjo – taking a lot of the most prominent instrumental lines – and most importantly adds a huge element of physicality to the performance. Tork has an almost Harpo Marx-esque onstage persona, and a gift for physical comedy and mime that works hugely to his advantage. He chooses to use a radio-mic headset rather than a handheld mic or using a mic stand, and so he's free to roam the stage while playing guitar and singing, and generally manages to be constantly watchable, even during songs for which he's not the musical centre of attention.

(This is an important note about the Monkees' stage show, at least while Jones was alive – they were not a "rock band", but were, rather, entertainers. There's a lot of comedy business in the act, mostly scripted, and usually of a rather corny vaudevillian nature, but this is an entirely positive, and endearing, part of the show.)

And he does get to show off his instrumental prowess, with a performance of Bach's "Two-Part Invention #8 in F". It's not quite as impressive a performance as in the 2011 reunion shows, where he would play French horn as well as banjo, keyboard, and guitar, but it's still enough to show him as a multi-instrumentalist with real chops.

And then there's Davy Jones. I've been rather harsh on his vocals in this book, but as this DVD reveals, the problems with his vocals were not of his making. Jones was a natural baritone, forced by the record company to sing in a tenor range to sound younger, and his vocals suffered because, for the most part, he was singing outside his natural range.

Here the keys on his songs are dropped a little, allowing him to sing in his more natural range, and he sounds *really bloody good*. The difference in his vocals between the live performances and the studio ones are substantial enough that I consider the live performances of many of these songs to be the definitive ones, not the weaker studio versions. He was done a real disservice by the decision to have his leads be out of his range, and every criticism I've made of his singing should be read with that taken into account. Here, and in many other performances in the last few decades of his life, he shows that he was better than the records showed.

And he was a truly great frontman. Here he acts as MC throughout, introducing almost every song, talking to the audience, and providing the feed lines for the others' jokes. He's constantly dancing, often playing maracas and tambourine, and on stage for almost the entire performance – the other Monkees each take one song as a solo spot to allow the others to take a break and get off stage, but Jones takes four – "I Wanna Be Free", "I'll Love You Forever", "Girl", and "It's Nice to Be With You" are all performed as solos without the other Monkees present. Jones is also constantly interacting with the audience, and if Dolenz is the musical centre of the show, Jones is the structural centre around which everyone else revolves on stage.

And since this is the place where I'm talking about this, I should say that that is also true for the TV series. It's very easy to underrate Jones' contributions to the show, as he was the straight man while the other three were comedians. Jones often compared the Monkees to the Marx Brothers, and in that comparison he would definitely be the Zeppo Marx of the group. And that sounds like a criticism of him – except that anyone who thinks that should try comparing *Duck Soup* to *Love Happy*. Zeppo was essential, and the fact that it looked like anyone could do what he was doing just shows how good he was at making difficult work look effortless. And the same goes for Davy Jones.

Instrumentally, the arrangements for the show tend to stick largely to those on the records, although often with the addition of a horn section. Dolenz and Jones often add additional acoustic rhythm guitar, especially on songs on which they're not singing lead (Dolenz only plays drums on two songs – "Mary Mary" and "Your Auntie Grizelda" – though he does an extremely creditable job on those). Sometimes, this can add a little too much slickness to the arrangements than the songs really call for. But for the most part, the arrangements and performances work extremely well, capturing the essence of the original recordings, while not having the instrumental sparseness that can sometimes seem like sloppiness when transferred to the live stage.

More notably, the vocal arrangements are often slightly rearranged to provide more of a group role. While each song is still performed by its original lead singer (with a couple of notable exceptions), often the other two Monkees will be double-tracking the lead live on parts where there's no backing vocal part – they're down in the mix, but still present. This serves two purposes – firstly, it thickens the vocals the way that the studio double-tracking did, but it also means that there's a more cohesive feel to the performances. Sometimes, the records can sound like a collection of disconnected solo performances that only belong on the same album because someone's chosen to apply the "Monkees" label to them all.

Here, everything sounds like the same band, and I think it's not a coincidence at all that the critical rehabilitation of the Monkees' music has largely tracked with their presence as a live band. After seeing them live, or even after seeing this DVD, it's much easier to say "yes, this music, varied and disparate as it is, does belong together. This is a band, not just a label that's been stuck on records made by other people

I'll only provide full reviews here of those songs which are not available on any other recordings, but it should be noted that these are among the weaker tracks — the live versions of several of the more well-known songs are well worth hearing.

Girl

Writers: Charles Fox and Norman Gimbel

Lead vocalist: Davy Jones

Other Monkees present: none

This song was originally an unsuccessful single for Jones, released in 1971 to tie in with an unpopular Neil Simon film for which it was the theme. While it didn't sell much at the time, it featured in an episode of the US TV series *The Brady Bunch* in which Jones had a cameo appearance and which was repeated so often that it became Jones' most-known solo song as well as the single most popular episode of the series — in the 90s, TV Guide magazine ranked the episode in which Jones appeared as number thirty-seven in its hundred greatest TV episodes of all time.

It was popular enough that in 1995 Jones reprised his performance with a grunge version of the song for *The Brady Bunch Movie* (Tork and Dolenz also have a brief cameo in the film, appearing with Jones as talent-show judges).

Thankfully, this isn't the grunge version, but sticks to the original arrangement. It's a harmless enough piece of middle-of-the-road pop, with a vague swing feel to it, that wouldn't have been out of place for any number of other 70s MOR acts but which has little to distinguish it other than the chance event of it having been used on an immensely popular episode of a popular TV series.

Higher and Higher

Writers: Gary Jackson and Carl Smith

Lead vocalist: Peter Tork

Other Monkees present: Davy Jones (guitar and vocals), Micky Dolenz (guitar and vocals)

One of the more bizarre inclusions in the show – though in a good way – is this cover version of Jackie Wilson's soul classic. Tork had recorded this in 1981 with his band the New Monks, as the B-side to a remake of "Steppin' Stone".

This live arrangement sticks closely to the New Monks' version, and it's very strange, but it works – it starts as, essentially, a bluegrass version of the song, with Tork performing solo, accompanying himself on the banjo (Tork's favourite instrument, and the one he's most impressive on). But then the other Monkees come in, singing the backing vocals – and the rest of the band comes in, playing a close approximation of the original Jackie Wilson arrangement, while Tork continues to sing and play more in the style of Pete Seeger than of Jackie Wilson.

The most notable difference in the instrumental arrangement, other than Tork's banjo, is the drumming, which has none of the funk or swing of Wilson's original but is instead a very regimented kick-snare-kick-snare, almost like playing a polka – this is necessary to fit with the pattern Tork's playing on the banjo.

So we have a bluegrass-polka-soul song, dominated by banjo and horn section, performed by the Monkees. That's not a combination you'd expect to make any sense, but oddly it works pretty well. And it's the kind of thing that shows how odd a band the Monkees were and are.

Since I Fell For You

Writer: Buddy Johnson

Lead vocalist: Micky Dolenz

Other Monkees present: None

Dolenz's solo spot is a version of a song that his mother used to sing around the house when he was a child. The song itself is a blues torch song, a standard that has been performed by singers as varied as Doris Day, Nina Simone, Tom Waits, Mel Tormé, BB King and Andy Williams.

Dolenz's version seems fairly closely modelled on Nina Simone's performance, though he showboats a little more on the song than she does, changing the dynamics around so it builds from a whisper to almost a bellow, while Simone stays on one level throughout. As a result, Dolenz's version lacks some subtlety compared to Simone's take on the song − but the fact that one can make the comparison at all, that the performance can be spoken of in the same breath as Simone's without it being utterly ridiculous, says a lot about how great a singer Dolenz actually is.

The one downside of this performance is the totally unnecessary lounge sax solo, which almost wrecks it before Dolenz's vocals come back in for the last verse.

Lucille

Writers: Albert Collins and Richard Penniman

Lead vocalist: Peter Tork

Other Monkees present: None

Tork's solo spot is, unfortunately, one of the weaker moments of the show. A cover version of Little Richard's classic R&B track, it's let down by an overly slick arrangement that manages simultaneously to be too busy and to just clomp along rather than have any kind of groove. And while I'm much fonder of Tork's vocals than many Monkees fans, he's no Little Richard.

He seems to be enjoying himself, though, and it's fun enough all things considered.

Tracklisting

The tracklisting below is for the longer version of the DVD. Songs marked with an asterisk aren't on the shorter version of the DVD. All songs are sung by their original lead vocalists, except where noted.

- Instrumental medley

- Last Train to Clarksville Look Out Here Comes Tomorrow For Pete's Sake (Peter Tork lead vocal)

- The Girl I Knew Somewhere

- Valleri

- Randy Scouse Git

- Mary Mary

- Your Auntie Grizelda*

- I Wanna Be Free (Davy solo)*

- I'll Love You Forever (Davy solo)*

- Goin' Down

- Can You Dig It? (Peter vocal)

- Girl (Davy solo)

- Higher and Higher (plus brief snatch of Cripple Creek on banjo)

- No Time (Micky sings lead on first verse, Peter second, Davy third)*

- Bach Two Part Invention #8 in F (Peter solo, with other Monkees still on stage) *

- A Little Bit Me, A Little Bit You

- Long Title: Do I Have To Do This All Over Again?*

- She Hangs Out (with instrumental snatches of "Day Tripper")

- Since I Fell For You* (Micky solo)

- Lucille (Peter solo)*

- It's Nice To Be With You (Davy solo)*

- That Was Then This Is Now

- Porpoise Song*

- Listen to the Band* (unison vocal by all three, Micky highest in mix)

- Daydream Believer

- I'm A Believer

- Steppin' Stone

- Pleasant Valley Sunday

- Monkees Theme (instrumental walk-off music)

Good Times!

For the Monkees' fiftieth anniversary, the band were in a strange position. After Davy Jones' death in 2012, just after the band's massively successful forty-fifth anniversary tour, it had seemed that the band would no longer continue – but then, suddenly, it was announced that Michael Nesmith, who had just per-formed a handful of solo shows for the first time in decades, would rejoin the band for a US tour celebrating the forty-fifth anniversary of the *Headquarters* album.

This new lineup of the Monkees – Dolenz, Tork, and Nesmith – spent much of 2012, 2013, and 2014 touring the US, and by all accounts put on a magnificent show. But then something – no-one is talking publicly about exactly what – happened to make Nesmith lose interest again. In 2015 another Monkees lineup – Dolenz and Tork, without Nesmith – performed a handful of shows. (I was lucky enough to see two of these, as unlike the Nesmith lineup they played two nights in the UK. Both shows were exceptional, and the end of their performance at the Moseley Folk Festival, when they invited the Polyphonic Spree on stage for a mass performance of "Porpoise Song", was one of the greatest musical events of my life. Nonetheless, Nesmith was missed).

So going into 2016 and the band's fiftieth anniversary, and the resulting celebrations, it wasn't even sure what, if anything, "the Monkees" referred to any more – and when the fiftieth anniversary tour was announced without Nesmith's participation, it seemed like "the Monkees" was just Dolenz and Tork. As it happens, Nesmith agreed to fill in for Tork on a handful of shows when Tork had to deal with a family illness, and all three Monkees played the final show of the US tour at the Pantages in LA, which Nesmith announced beforehand would be his last ever Monkees show[20].

So, when rumours started to leak out about a possible new album, at first it sounded like it might be a missed opportunity – while Andrew Sandoval and John Hughes at Rhino were good guiding hands for such a project, it seemed like this would only involve two of the Monkees. Assurances that Nesmith would be involved in some capacity were made – but from the early press material it looked like Nesmith's involvement would be limited to having played guitar on the backing track to "Good Times", a track which had been recorded in the sixties, and to contributing a song, "I Know What I Know", which he'd already released as a solo track through his own website, and which Dolenz was intended to sing.

However, after Sandoval and Hughes visited Nesmith at home and talked him through the project, he seemed to become much keener on it – suddenly, he was a full participant in the making of the album, both vocally and instrumentally, although he refused to record his portions of the tracks with Dolenz and Tork present. In the end, this is possibly the most Nesmith-flavoured

---

[20] And, just as this book is coming out, Nesmith has changed his mind again. Now in June 2018 Nesmith and Dolenz – but not Tork – are planning to tour as "The Monkees Present: The Mike and Micky Show".

Monkees album since *Pisces* – while he only contributes one song as a writer, he takes three lead or co-lead vocals, and is all over the backing vocals very prominently. While Nesmith had been the producer on *Justus*, and far more actively involved with the other band members, the final album didn't have very much of him audible. Here, by contrast, even though all his contributions were recorded in a couple of sessions away from the other band members, he sounds like a full participant, and many of the tracks have the Dolenz/Nesmith vocal blend that was such an important part of the band's greatest work. Nesmith, like Dolenz, still has almost as strong a voice today as he did in the sixties, and hearing the two of them together, as we do on seven of the album's thirteen tracks, is always an absolute joy.

The album, when it came out, was an absolute marvel. It was produced by Adam Schlesinger, of the band Fountains of Wayne (with bonus tracks produced by Sandoval), and went back to the technique that the band had used around the time of *Pisces, Aquarius, Capricorn, & Jones Ltd* – performances by a strong, consistent, band of studio musicians (consisting of three of the four members of Fountains of Wayne – Schlesinger, guitarist Jody Porter and drummer Brian Young, plus Schlesinger's frequent collaborator Mike Viola) but with Nesmith and Tork contributing instrumentally to almost every track, and all three living Monkees adding vocals. Davy Jones was represented by his 1969 vocal (on a 1967 backing track) on "Love to Love", a Neil Diamond track which had previously seen release on various compilations, and to which Tork and Dolenz added backing vocals for this release.

While Dolenz, Tork, and Nesmith all contributed one new song each, songs were also solicited from outside contributors – usually musicians of Schlesinger's own generation or the one preceding it. So Andy Partridge of XTC, Rivers Cuomo of Weezer, Noel Gallagher, Paul Weller, and Ben Gibbard of Death Cab for Cutie also contributed new songs.

To these tracks were added finished versions of a handful of songs for which instrumental tracks, but no vocals, had been recorded in the 1960s. This could, in many hands have led to an album that sounded like a patchwork – with tracks from 2016 jostled against others from 1967 or 68, there was the possibility of a serious stylistic mismatch. Luckily, Schlesinger is a master of stylistic mimicry, especially of 1960s records (he and Viola had recorded the soundtrack for *That Thing You Do!*, a Tom Hanks film which has some of the most fascinating examples of 1960s pastiche I've ever heard – and Viola had also worked on *Walk Hard, The Dewey Cox Story*, which likewise had to emulate a huge variety of recording styles).

Schlesinger managed to create a coherent whole from these recordings from different time periods, ending up with something that is sonically closer to 1990s powerpop than to either the Monkees' 60s recordings or contemporary 2016 material. The result – aided by Dolenz's miraculously-preserved voice – is curiously timeless, which is a huge relief after the band's 1980s and 90s attempts to sound "contemporary". It's also easily the best album they've released since at least *Instant Replay*, possibly *Pisces*.

The album had its detractors – among them Peter Tork , who at least in some interviews considered it less his album than an album put together by Rhino records (though Tork is a very inconsistent interviewee, and at other times has praised the record to the skies) – because of the comparatively light feel of a few of the tracks, but this is entirely in keeping with an album that manages to do what seems impossible, and celebrate every aspect of the Monkees' work while also being a viable, artistically valid, album.

And it really does manage to find a balance between these two seemingly-incompatible goals. All four Monkees get their solo spots, all of the living Monkees are all over the album – even though Nesmith and Dolenz never recorded together, their harmonies are intact and as joyful as ever – there are contributions from Boyce and Hart (and Bobby Hart adds keyboards to some of the 2016 tracks), Neil Diamond, Jeff Barry, and Goffin and King, as well as from the more recent songwriters, and even Nesmith's son Christian, Dolenz's sister Coco, and Tork's brother Nicholas contributed. So the celebration aspect is present – but this is also one of the band's most artistically robust albums, especially the run of songs that would make up most of side two on a vinyl album, where the band and their producers manage to bring in a maturity that's lacking from any of their earlier records without sacrificing the essential pop quality of the band's most famous work.

It's very much an album of two halves — much like the Beach Boys' mid-sixties albums, it has a first half made up mostly of light pop music, while side two is much heavier, darker, and meatier. This can make the album seem, perhaps, deceptively lightweight on first listen, as the fun stuff is the first impression, but it's an album that repays careful listening.

This is not a perfect album, but the Monkees never were a perfect band. It's certainly a fair criticism to say that this is an album that is very much targeted towards a particular segment of the band's fanbase – this is music that is likely to be most enjoyed by a particular type of white man in early middle age with an extensive record collection, a description which applies to many of the people involved in putting the record together, and the album got some criticism from other elements of the fanbase as a result.

Those criticisms should be taken into account, of course... but at the same time, *I* am a white man in early middle age with an extensive record collection, and while I can see that this is a record that is micro-targeted at me, specifically, it is so well targeted at me, and pushes so many of my buttons, I can't help but love it. It's not a record I can be objective about – this is an album that's been put together by people whose remit is basically "make an album that Andrew Hickey will love" (not literally me, but people who share my tastes). If this is the last Monkees album, as seems likely, I can't imagine a better way for them to go out.

All tracks produced by Adam Schlesinger, except for the bonus tracks "A Better World" and "Love's What I Want" produced by Andrew Sandoval. In some cases, a track is based on a 60s recording – for those, the "original producer" credit refers to the production on the 60s elements.

Good Times!

Writer: Harry Nilsson

Lead vocalists: Harry Nilsson and Micky Dolenz

Other Monkees present: Michael Nesmith (guitar)

Original producer: Michael Nesmith

The opening track is a Harry Nilsson song, originally released by Nilsson in 1966 as the B-side to an unsuccessful solo single, "The Path That Leads to Trouble". A basic backing track for the song was recorded in 1968 by Nilsson, Nesmith, bassist Rick Dey, and drummer "Fast" Eddie Hoh, along with a guide vocal by Nilsson. This 1968 track was used (with additional guitar by Schlesinger) as the basis for this finished track, with Dolenz performing a posthumous duet with Nilsson.

I usually have mixed feelings about such recordings, but given that Nilsson was one of Dolenz's closest friends, and that he wanted to pay tribute to his friend, and given the unusual nature of this album, I think it works. It's helped by the fact that Dolenz's voice is so miraculously preserved that this sounds like a 1968 duet – it's done so well that it's hard to believe that the interaction between the two of them is faked. It also makes Hoh, who played on many of the Monkees' best records but died in 2015, part of the album as well, and frankly any excuse to hear the voice of Harry Nilsson is fine by me.

The song itself is a simple one – a four-chord gospel-flavoured rocker, loosely inspired by "Dancing in the Street" – but it's a great, fun, opener, and immediately sets the tone for the album as a whole.

You Bring The Summer

Writer: Andy Partridge

Lead vocalist: Micky Dolenz

Other Monkees Present: Peter Tork (organ, vocals) and Michael Nesmith (guitar, vocals)

Andy Partridge was an obvious choice for someone to write for a new Monkees album. The principal singer/songwriter of the post-punk band XTC, he was a Monkees fan from his childhood, and indeed the Monkees were tied into the very start of his musical career – his earliest attempts at recording himself making music were done on a tape recorder bought with money he made from sending a caricature of Micky in to the letters page of a Monkees fan magazine as a child. Apparently when Andrew Sandoval asked Partridge if he wanted to be involved (over Twitter – the first public acknowledgement I saw that the project was happening), Partridge immediately went and recorded four songs the next day, he was so enthused by the idea.

"You Bring the Summer" sees Partridge returning to the musical ideas of his 1992 song "Dear Madam Barnum" (from XTC's ,*Nonsuch* album), but recasting what was originally a bitter, angry, breakup song into a joyous, upbeat, pop song, with hints not only of Monkees hits (especially the ones written by Neil Diamond[21], although the guitar motif is reminiscent of tracks like "Last Train to Clarksville" and "Pleasant Valley Sunday"), but of Partridge's own more pastoral work – while melodically this owes a lot to "Dear Madam Barnum", in tempo and feel it's closer to "Earn Enough For Us" from the *Skylarking* album – and to the Beatles and Beach Boys.

It's a gorgeous, lovely, track that sums up everything about the best summertime sixties pop – this would fit in perfectly in a playlist with "Daydream", "Good Day Sunshine", and other such tracks.

Lyrically, this does something Partridge does a lot, where the whole song features a single conceit – in this case, that it's winter, but when the subject of the song is present, it's suddenly summer. It's frothy fun, but it's perfectly crafted frothy fun.

---

[21]Partridge claimed of the song that he was conjuring up his inner Neil Diamond, because conjuring up his inner Goffin and King was too hard.

Nesmith adds some gloriously dumb "baby" backing vocals, and the song takes a nice sideways turn in the tag, where a new melodic line ("Summer baby, you bring the summer...") comes in, along with some *Revolver* style backwards guitar, and at the end some distorted laughter. *Revolver* is one of those touchstones we'll be returning to again and again – *Good Times!* is an album that's in constant dialogue with the past, and not only the Monkees' own past but the pasts of their contemporaries, most notably the Beatles, and this is the first sign of that.

"You Bring the Summer" was released as the second single from the album. It wasn't wonderfully received by the fanbase, largely because it's similar in feel to "She Makes Me Laugh", the first single, and people were understandably worried that the album would entirely be bubblegum-powerpop. As it turns out, the album has more depth to it than that, but personally I'd have been more than happy if the entire album had sounded like this. It's a wonderful song, and it became a regular part both of the Monkees' live setlists and of Micky Dolenz's solo show.

She Makes Me Laugh

Writer: Rivers Cuomo

Lead vocalist: Micky Dolenz

Other Monkees present: Peter Tork (banjo, vocals) and Michael Nesmith (guitar, vocals)

Another bubblegum-powerpop song, this time written by Rivers Cuomo of Weezer (who, as Peter Tork pointed out in many interviews promoting the album, went to the same high school

Tork(had attended, and was partially inspired to become a musician by the knowledge that a pop star had attended his school so it was possible).

This is possibly hurt by its placement on the album right after "You Bring the Summer". The two songs are similar instrumentally and in their general feel, and both feature solo Micky lead vocals, so this feels a little bit like an inferior sequel to the other song when heard in sequence. But that's rather unfair – while this is not as good as Partridge's song, on its own merits it's still an excellent track, and it makes for a great single.

The best aspect of the song actually seems to have come from Dolenz. Apparently he wasn't comfortable with some of Cuomo's original lyrics for this song, which he believed were inappropriate for a man in his seventies to be singing, and so he and Cuomo brainstormed some replacement lines for the sections describing the relationship between the singer and the subject of the song.

The relationship described, with the couple wearing pink party hats and playing Scrabble, is utterly delightful and very different from anything else I've heard described in this kind of pop song – in fact I've seen several people suggest that the relationship reads to them as a father/daughter one, rather than a romantic one. I don't believe that was the intention, but it says something about how rarely this kind of fun, affectionate, relationship appears in pop lyrics that that interpretation would be the natural reading for many people.

It's not a great classic, but it's still better than almost anything on any of the other reunion albums. A fun, catchy, little track that makes me smile. It's also fascinating to hear Dolenz's vocal choices here — he sings in a surprising number of voices, and it's a much more subtle performance than you might think at first. And as always, it's a pleasure to hear Nesmith harmonising with Dolenz.

Our Own World

Writer: Adam Schlesinger

Lead vocalist: Micky Dolenz

Other Monkees present: Peter Tork (keyboards, vocals) and Michael Nesmith (vocals)

Producer Adam Schlesinger's solo songwriting contribution to the album could almost be mistaken for a Paul Williams song. A simple two-chord verse with Dolenz backed by staccato harpsichord chords playing the I and IV leads into a lovely rising bridge/chorus. This could easily be a song written for a Muppets film – and that's meant entirely as a positive.

This is a song that's as light and frothy as the previous song, but while those earlier tracks were Beatlesque 60s pop as interpreted through the filter of post-punk powerpop songwriting – they don't sound like 60s songs, but rather sound like the kind of song that people say sounds like a 60s song (this is not a criticism, and could describe much of my favourite music) – this one is absolutely rooted in its idiom. And that idiom is songwriters like Williams or Bacharach, and sunshine pop performers like the Association or the Cowsills.

This is a close cousin to such almost-saccharine 60s pop tracks as "The Rain, the Park, and Other Things", and the only thing keeping it from sounding exactly like those records is the comparatively sparse instrumental backing – just keyboards, guitars, bass, and drums, where the records it's modelling would normally have a horn section or woodwinds as well – and the guitar solo, which is a little more distorted than that kind of record would generally have.

(Another referent that a friend pointed out is "Never Let Her Slip Away" by Andrew Gold, which does sound very similar to this).

This is completely uncool, utterly unconcerned with notions of what popular music in 2016 should sound like, or what critics will think – and it's utterly lovely, charming, and one of the less obvious, but no less pleasurable, minor treasures on the album.

Gotta Give It Time

Writers: Jeff Barry and Joey Levine

Lead vocalist: Micky Dolenz

Other Monkees present: Michael Nesmith (vocals)

Original producer: Jeff Barry

And here we go back in time to January 1967. One of the great things about this album is the way it manages to incorporate aspects from throughout the band's career, and in doing so include contributions from almost everyone who helped make the band great. Here we have a backing track recorded by Jeff Barry during the the final sessions under Kirshner's supervision; the sessions which produced "A Little Bit Me, A Little Bit You" and "Love to Love" among others.

No vocals were recorded for this track in the 60s, so Dolenz (sounding just like he did in 1967) added lead vocals, with backing vocals by Nesmith, to complete it. The result is a wonderful two-minute garage-punk stomper, full of adolescent sexual frustration that feels desperate to burst out. Given that all the songs from the 67 sessions had Jones on vocals, it's unlikely that this would have been given to Dolenz to sing back then if the band had continued working with Kirshner – but if it had, this would have been a classic for the band up there with "Steppin' Stone".

Everything on this track works toward the same end – the expression of teenage frustration – with the exception of Nesmith's backing vocals. Nesmith's voice has, like Dolenz's, remained remarkably preserved, but it's still noticeably aged, and his "give it time now baby" backing vocal chants are a little too laid-back to add to the tension. That said, there's a charm to them that means the incongruity works in the track's favour.

Five songs in, everything's been insubstantial, but great. You wouldn't want an entire album of this kind of thing without any variation, but this is quite superb.

Me and Magdalena

Writer: Ben Gibbard

Lead vocalists: Michael Nesmith and Micky Dolenz

Other Monkees present: none

Here I have to depart from the consensus wisdom among Monkees fans, and I hope that no-one takes offence at my disagreement with them over this track. I have many friends who love this song, and know many people who would say that this song by itself justifies the existence of the album. I'm afraid I simply can't agree.

To me, this is the one real clunker on the album. It sounds like utterly generic 90s American landfill college rock, of the kind that ten million bands all tried to make after the success of R.E.M's *Automatic for the People*, all "tasteful" acoustic guitars, simple, sparse, piano motifs, and pseudo-profound lyrics. It's written by Ben Gibbard of the band Death Cab for Cutie, and while I'm not massively familiar with his other work (he's the only one of the songwriters on here I can say that about), a cursory scan through the highlights of his back catalogue suggests it all sounds like this.

It's not unpleasant, but there's just nothing there to latch on to, to the point where I not only don't like the song myself, I can't even understand what it is that other people are liking about it (apart from the combination of Nesmith and Dolenz's voices, which is always wondrous – here Nesmith takes the lead line while Dolenz takes a high close harmony, in the manner of the Everly Brothers, and I could listen to the two of them sing like that all day, no matter what they were singing.

But the song itself, and the arrangement... there's just nothing there. Nothing at all.

But... I'm in the minority on that one. Everyone else absolutely loves it, and I'm prepared to accept that it's me, rather than the song that's at fault. You'll probably love this, and I'm happy that it gives many other people pleasure, even if I'll never see the appeal.

An alternative version of this, with a more jangly, uptempo, instrumental track (basically imagine the song influenced by *Green* or *Out of Time*-era R.E.M. rather than *Automatic for the People* era) was included as a bonus track in some versions of the album. It's no better.

Whatever's Right

Writers: Tommy Boyce and Bobby Hart

Lead vocalist: Micky Dolenz

Other Monkees present: Peter Tork (keyboards) and Michael Nesmith (vocals)

A Boyce and Hart song originally recorded during the *More of the Monkees* sessions, though a vocal was never recorded at the time, this version is almost unrecognisable from the 60s attempt (which can be heard on the *More of the Monkees* Super Deluxe box set). While that was an acoustic, mellow, track in the vein of the Lovin' Spoonful's "Daydream", this is a garage stomper in a style similar to Boyce and Hart's own single "I Wonder What She's Doing Tonight", but with a prominent organ part (played by Bobby Hart, working with the band again after an absence of decades) something like that on "I'm a Believer".

Musically, this is very similar to "Gotta Give it Time", but lyrically it's surprisingly sensitive for a Boyce/Hart song (which would more usually have a slightly aggressive, contemptuous, attitude towards love and relationships) – "whatever's right, don't let me change your mind/If I'm the one then you'll find out in time/You know I love you but I'll leave it up to you/And I know that you'll do whatever's right". A song about not putting pressure on a partner makes a nice contrast to the many, many, many songs of the same vintage that sound like this recording but mostly consist of the words "oh come on, *pleeeeeeease?*"

This works much better than the 60s recording would have had it been completed, and is a welcome if minor contribution to the album, and it's lovely to hear Hart working with the band again.

Along with Bobby Hart's appearance, this is also the first of several songs on the album to feature backing vocals from Coco Dolenz, Micky's sister, who since 2012 has sung with the Monkees' live band and who made several vocal contributions to her brother's late-sixties Monkees songs.

Love To Love

Writer: Neil Diamond

Lead vocalist: Davy Jones

Other Monkees present: Micky Dolenz and Peter Tork (vocals)

Original producer: Jeff Barry

Much of the publicity material around the album described this as "an unreleased track featuring Davy Jones". That's not really true – the track, which dates from the same sessions as "A Little Bit Me" (but for which Jones rerecorded his vocal in 1969), had been released many times since 1979, appearing on numerous compilations with either Jones' 1967 or 69 vocal takes. It wasn't released at the time, but almost every Monkees fan will have had a copy of the track.

When this was announced as featuring on the album, John Hughes said that the version on the album would be very different from the versions fans had heard, but in fact the only noticeable difference is the addition of backing vocals by Dolenz and Tork, which weren't on the original track. Otherwise, this is the same 1967 track and 1969 vocals that had been released numerous times previously.

It's a shame to have something that was already widely available appear on the album, though I can see the logic – they needed to have Davy represented in order to make this a celebration of the whole band, there were no actually-unreleased Davy Monkees vocals, this song had never been included on a non-compilation album, and by including this one they could also include Neil Diamond, whose contribution to the band also deserved celebration.

And as a track, it's still an excellent one. It's Diamond in a slower, more moody, mode, in the manner of "Girl, You'll Be A Woman Soon" or "Solitary Man", and the track is driven by a prominent bass and Hammond organ part. This would probably have been a single in 1967, had it not been for the decision shortly after recording to concentrate on recordings featuring the whole band. The chorus, in particular, which is based on the standard "Hang on Sloopy"/"Twist and Shout"/"Louie, Louie" changes, is very effective.

It's a fun track, but says little in itself about where the Monkees were artistically at this point. However, while my original reaction to the song's inclusion was mild disappointment, I've later come to appreciate its place on the album. This is a deeply, deeply, intertextual album, which gets most of its power from the way it references and responds to other works – not only the band's own back catalogue, but the music of their contemporaries and of the people they influenced. It's not so much an album as it is a statement – "this is who the Monkees were, this is what sixties pop music was". While it's definitely the work of a still-vital, creative, band, it works as a monument – almost a tombstone.

As the Monkees' generation of musicians have a relatively small, finite, working life ahead of them, this album seems almost to be an intentional summary of what that old generation had to say. In that context, including this song makes sense.

Little Girl

Writer: Peter Tork

Lead vocalist: Peter Tork

Other Monkees present: none

Going into the last part of the album, we hit a run of songs which are unlike anything most people would think of as Monkees songs, but which elevate the album to a whole new level.

First up, we have Tork's "Little Girl" (not to be confused with the Dolenz song of the same name from *The Monkees Present*), which he originally wrote in 1967 for Davy Jones to record as a follow-up to "I Wanna Be Free". They never recorded it, but Tork had occasionally performed it live under the title "Sunny Side Up".

Tork's songs had been highlights of the previous two reunion albums, where the rest of the band's contributions had been rather sub-par. Here, one could be forgiven for having lowered expectations of him, given the way the other band members and contributors have stepped up, but once again Tork's one songwriting contribution is one of the best things here. It's a metrically-irregular country-jazz-folk blend, mostly in waltz time but with odd beats dropped here and there. The overall impression is something like the gentle, genial, kindness of the Lovin' Spoonful's later records (especially *Hums of the Lovin' Spoonful*) and after the majority of the album has been either stomping garage-rock or frothy powerpop, having such a gentle, warm, song is a very welcome change of pace.

It's just absolutely lovely – though again I am departing from fan consensus, as everyone seems agreed that this is the weakest song on the album. And what's particularly impressive is

Tork's voice. Those who are only familiar with Tork's studio work, and hadn't heard him live since the early 2000s, would be forgiven for thinking it was a totally different person singing.

Tork, sadly, was diagnosed in 2009 with adenoid cystic carcinoma, a type of slow-growing cancer of the throat and, in Tork's case, tongue. He had a major operation, removing the tumour, which permanently altered his voice – he now sloshes his sibilants slightly, and has a gravelly rasp in his singing that wasn't there before.

But Tork had also taken several years of vocal lessons in the early 1990s, and had become a much better singer then than he ever was in the sixties, fixing the pitching problems that had plagued him.

The combination of Tork's improved skills (and he put in even more work on his voice as part of his recovery from the operation) and the change in his vocal timbre turned him from a mediocre vocalist into one who is in his own way the vocal equal of his bandmates – he sounds now like no-one so much as Willie Nelson.

So here we have a song written by 60s Peter Tork, but sung by 2016 Peter Tork, and the result is quite, quite, beautiful. The single best track Tork ever brought to the group.

Birth of an Accidental Hipster

Writers: Noel Gallagher and Paul Weller

Lead vocalists: Michael Nesmith and Micky Dolenz

Other Monkees present: None

This song was one that Gallagher (songwriter for the 1990s band Oasis) and Weller (whose long career included the Jam and the Style Council, as well as his own solo work) had started working on together and had thought sounded vaguely Monkees, but had put aside until they were asked if they would contribute to the album. Gallagher has said in interviews that they'd not finished the song when they were asked, and were quite surprised when their tentative agreement turned into a firm commitment in a press release, and had to finish the song in a hurry.

Nonetheless, this is quite probably the best thing Gallagher has ever done, and is in the upper echelon of Weller's work. It is, as one would expect from the writers, very derivative, but the chain of influences is so strange that it makes for a fascinating and wonderful record. This is a California pop band's interpretation of Madchester interpreting the phased psychedelia of the Creation. It keeps going from sounding like the Happy Mondays to sounding like *Revolver*, often in the middle of a phrase, and Nesmith's phased lead vocals are extraordinary. This is up there with "Shorty Blackwell" and "Writing Wrongs" — and I mean that in a good way.

The song has the most complex structure of any of the songs on the album. Starting with ringing guitars and a shoegazing beat that could come from any number of early-nineties records (for example "Vapour Trail" by Ride), Nesmith sings a verse whose melody is lifted from "I Can See Clearly Now" (this is lampshaded in the second verse, where a couple of lines of lyric are also taken from that song). Then the last part of Nesmith's verse vocal ("nobody else but my own sweet self") overlaps with a bridge sung by Dolenz ("do you know...") which is sonically similar but has a straight four on the floor beat.

After the bridge, we then go into a swing section ("high on a rooftop, singing a song/choirs of angels all sing along") sung by Dolenz, with Coco Dolenz on backing vocals, over a simple descending chord seq. This has more than a little musical similarity to "Cuddly Toy" or "Daddy's Song", and it's a shame no-one thought to have Tork add some banjo on this section, as it would have perfectly complemented the piano/bass/percussion backing. However, the musical referent here was probably "Feeling Lonely" by the Small Faces, to which it bears more than a little resemblance, though this section is in swing time rather than the waltz time of that song.

At the end of this swing section Dolenz sings "feeling low", and phasing is added to his voice, taking us into a guitar solo starting over an F# chord (a tone and a half below the chord at the start of the song) and rising until the start of a second verse, which is taken a full tone higher than the first verse. The verse/bridge continue as before, but at the higher key, until Dolenz's "do you know" section, which here continues for sixteen bars rather than the eight bars of its initial appearance. Over the second eight bars (which also have slightly different changes) Nesmith sings a countermelody ("Old friends say 'oh he's lost his way', but they can't see what I can see/I'm heading out in the sunshine baby").

We then go into another round of the swing section, which is identical to the first, except at the end of the "low" the piano and cymbals extend the last note for five and a half bars, before going back to the F# for an instrumental fade which sounds something like the Beatles' "Rain".

The whole thing is, frankly, a masterpiece, and even the lyrics (which fall into Gallagher's usual patterns of meaningless nonsense with lots of references to sunshine) manage to sound evocative rather than pedestrian. Nesmith sounds like some sort of Texan Old Testament patriarch, with his voice sounding aged but still as strong as ever, and some of the vocal choices he makes here (almost yodelling the psychedelic sections, while calmly singing the "old friends say" section) are absolutely perfect.

Wasn't Born to Follow

Writers: Gerry Goffin and Carole King

Lead vocalist: Peter Tork

Other Monkees present: none

Original producer: "The Monkees" (Shorty Rogers)

Goffin and King are another songwriting team who needed recognition if this was to celebrate every aspect of the Monkees' career, and "Wasn't Born to Follow" was a particularly appropriate song to choose – the original version of this, by the Byrds, from *The Notorious Byrd Brothers*, famously appeared in *Easy Rider* – the first film made by Bob Rafelson and Bert Schneider after they stopped working with the Monkees. Indeed, Peter Tork wrote a rejected theme song for that film (which he occasionally performs at solo concerts), and so having Tork sing a song from it now once again added many extra levels of resonance to the album.

Happily, there was also a vintage Monkees backing track for the song, recorded in 1968 (after the Byrds' version of the song was released, but before *Easy Rider*) during the sessions for *The Birds, the Bees and the Monkees*. This track also features the Wrecking Crew, allowing them, too, to appear on this album. (The track, without any vocals, appears on the deluxe version of *The Birds, the Bees and the Monkees*).

To that vintage track, Tork added a banjo part (which lifts the track to a whole new level – it pulls the whole backing track, which had otherwise been a little unimpressive, together) and his lead vocal. Tork, singing right at the top of his range, reverts to Carole King's original melody, rather than the less-impressive altered version that Roger McGuinn sang on the Byrds' version.

The combination of the original melody and Tork's weathered voice makes the similarities of this song to Leonard Cohen's "Suzanne", which came out shortly before Goffin and King wrote this song, very apparent – the two songs are so similar that it's hard to believe that Goffin and King weren't inspired by Cohen (when I first mentioned this on my blog, I believed Cohen's song was slightly later than Goffin and King's, but in fact it was the other way round).

There are several exceptional versions of this song available – Carole KIng's own versions (both solo and as lead singer of the City) and Dusty Springfield's version in particular are excellent – but I do think this may well be the definitive version of this song.

I Know What I Know

Writer: Michael Nesmith

Lead vocalist: Michael Nesmith

Other Monkees present: none

This is a song that Nesmith originally recorded in 2012 and released on his downloadable EP *Around the Sun*, on which it was a rather overblown mess of ambient synths that managed to hide a good song behind bad production. When it was announced that this would be Nesmith's only songwriting contribution to the album (and initially it was announced that Dolenz would be singing it, before the extent of Nesmith's participation became clear) I was rather disappointed, as I'd found that EP unimpressive.

However, this version is a revelation. Adam Schlesinger, who played every instrument on the track, has stripped the arrangement down to absolute basics – there's a piano playing just the chords on the beat, a bass, a strummed acoustic guitar and, for the solo solo, a string statement of the melody played on a Chamberlin, with a single cymbal splash at the end of the solo.

Stripped down like this, and with Nesmith's unprocessed, undoctored voice, the song reveals its simplistic beauty. The almost haiku-like simplicity of the lyrics ("I know what I know, and what I know is I know nothing without you") become direct expressions of emotional honesty, unlike most of Nesmith's earlier cleverness, when coupled with his fragile melody. The end result is spookily like many of John Lennon's 70s demos, with its rudimentary piano playing and single-take vocals, and like them it has a natural beauty that the more produced, slicker, version lacks.

This is a simply breathtaking conclusion to the run of more mature songs that has made up much of the second half of the album. Stunningly beautiful.

I Was There (And I'm Told I Had A Good Time)

Writers: Micky Dolenz and Adam Schlesinger

Lead vocalist: Micky Dolenz

Other Monkees present: none

And we finish on a joke, though a fairly layered one – one that is far more complex and referential than the simple song it's attached to would suggest.

The phrase "good times" of course echoes through the Monkees' career from "Daydream Believer" ("and our good times start and end..."), and as well as being the title of the album, it's also the title of the opening track, so it makes sense for the closing song to also refer to "good times".

And Micky Dolenz had a bit of patter that would suit such a song – he always introduces the song "Randy Scouse Git" on stage by talking about visiting the Beatles while they recorded *Sgt Pepper*, and how they threw him a party. "I'm told I had a great time".

And since Dolenz hadn't otherwise written a song for the album, or played drums on it, it made sense for Dolenz and Schlesinger to write a song based around that line, for Dolenz to sing and play drums on, so Dolenz would get his solo spotlight as Tork and Nesmith had.

And since Dolenz's anecdote was about the Beatles recording *Sgt Pepper*, it made sense for the song to be a soundalike for that album's title track, so what we have here is a fun song which gently mocks Dolenz's own tendency to repeat the same lines on stage, while also bookmarking the album and referencing both the Beatles and the Monkees' own career.

Except... I think there may be another reference there.

You see, the Monkees weren't the first band to be called "the prefab four" – the term has been applied to them a lot, but it was originally applied to the Rutles, a Beatles parody group featuring Eric Idle and Neil Innes. And oddly, Neil Innes had a fair bit of influence on some of the contributors here. Death Cab for Cutie, Ben Gibbard's band, took their name from a song Innes co-wrote, while Noel Gallagher was sued by Innes because Oasis hit "Whatever" stole the melody line from Innes' "How Sweet to be an Idiot".

And it turns out that Innes also did a "Sgt Pepper's Lonely Hearts Club Band" pastiche, for the Rutles' reunion album, *Archaeology*. And to my ears, at least, this song, with its references to "repeating all your good lines, 'cos the word is you heard them all from me", sounds more like a take-off of Innes' take-off than it sounds like the original song.

Which might be a coincidence, were it not for the name of Innes' song... "Major Happy's Up and Coming Once Upon a **Good Time** Band".

Of course, I may be reading more into this than was intended – the song itself is a frivolous bit of nonsense, just two minutes of silliness at the end of the album. The Rutles reference may not have been intended by either songwriter.

But at the same time, this is an album that tends to invite such readings. This is, fundamentally, a postmodern album. That may sound like a stretch, but I think that the album fits almost precisely Umberto Eco's description of the postmodern attitude (from *Reflections on The Name of the Rose*):

> The postmodern reply to the modern consists of recognizing that the past, since it cannot really be destroyed, because its destruction leads to silence, must be revisited: but with irony, not innocently. I think of the postmodern attitude as that of a man who loves a very cultivated woman and knows that he cannot say to her 'I love you madly', because he knows that she knows (and that she knows he knows) that these words have already been written by Barbara Cartland. Still, there is a solution. He can say 'As Barbara Cartland would put it, I love you madly'. At this point, having avoided false innocence, having said clearly that it is no longer possible to speak innocently, he will nevertheless have said what he wanted to say to the woman: that he loves her in an age of lost innocence. If the woman goes along with this, she will have received a declaration of love all the same. Neither of the two speakers will feel innocent, both will have accepted the challenge of the past, of the already said, which cannot be eliminated; both will consciously and with pleasure play the game of irony. . . But both will have succeeded, once again, in speaking of love.

I think that works very well to sum up a lot of what this album is doing, and given that it uses postmodernist techniques like pastiche, self-referentiality, collage, and intertextuality, I think it's safe to say that the death of the author applies here –

while I can construct a valid argument that the dense level of resonances in this song, and in the album as a whole, was put there deliberately, even if it wasn't it's still in the album that we have. This track closes the album, and quite probably closes the Monkees' career as recording artists. And despite being a silly little ditty, it manages to encapsulate everything about the Monkees in 2016.

We are here, and we're going to have a good time, like we did before, supposedly.

Bonus tracks:

As with all albums nowadays, various bonus tracks were included on copies of the album sent to different retailers, as exclusives. The three songs discussed below, and an alternate version of "Me and Magdalena" were used as bonuses on these versions, and were later collected on a Record Store Day EP. The chances are that your copy of *Good Times!* will have one or more of these tracks included, but not all of them.

Terrifying

Writer: Zach Rogue

Lead vocalist: Micky Dolenz

Other Monkees present: Michael Nesmith (guitar) and Peter Tork (keyboards)

An outtake from the album sessions, this song by Zach Rogue of the band Rogue Wave is a pleasant but unexceptional acoustic strumalong song. There's very little here to latch on to, positive or negative, and it's easy to see why it was dropped from the album, but it's also nicer to have it than not.

Love's What I Want

Writer: Andy Partridge

Lead vocalist: Micky Dolenz

Other Monkees present: none

This and the following track were produced by Andrew Sandoval, after the main album sessions had ended, and feature different musicians from the album proper – in this case the backing is provided by Sandoval on guitar, Bobby Hart on keyboards, Pete Thomas of the Attractions on drums, and Erik Paparozzi on guitar and bass, with Coco Dolenz adding extra backing vocals.

The song itself is a lesser effort than Partridge's "You Bring the Summer", but it's still enjoyable enough, having much the same feel to it as lighter Boyce and Hart tracks like "Apples, Peaches, Bananas and Pears", but with lyrics extolling the virtues of peace and love in much the same manner as "For Pete's Sake". It's light and frothy and Partridge not on his best form, but Partridge is almost incapable of writing a bad song, and so this is still extremely pleasant.

A Better World

Writer: Nicholas Thorkelson

Lead vocalist: Peter Tork

Other Monkees present: Micky Dolenz (vocals)

This song, by Tork's brother, was hyped in all the interviews Tork gave about the album as the kind of thing he would have done if he'd been given full control of the album. Sadly, it's not very good at all – it's a plodding, dull, finger-wagging song about how we all need to pull together to make a better world, without any specific details other than bland motivational speech stuff with much the same tone as a million similar songs from the eighties. Musically it sounds like dull eighties middle-of-the-road radio rock, and one can easily imagine this as having been an unsuccessful single for Eric Clapton or Peter Gabriel or someone of that "tasteful" ilk.

The only musically interesting element is Sandoval's string arrangement, which sounds like it deserves a much better song, but the rest of the backing track, played by members of Tork's blues band Shoe Suede Blues, is sadly pedestrian.

Appendices

The Pre-Monkees Recordings

Before they were signed up to be part of the Monkees, three of the four band members had recording careers in a minor way. Michael Nesmith recorded a solo single, "Wanderin'"/"Well Well", which had fewer than two hundred copies pressed total, before forming "Mike and John and Bill", a garage-pop band who recorded two singles. Nesmith then went on to record a handful of tracks under the name of Michael Blessing, before joining the Monkees.

Jones recorded an album and a non-album single before joining the band, after gaining a certain amount of fame as the Artful Dodger in the Broadway version of *Oliver!*, and Dolenz recorded two sides which remained unreleased until the Monkees' success, after which they were backed with two instrumentals with no Dolenz involvement and released as unsuccessful singles.

(Oddly, Peter Tork, who of all the band members was the best musician, was the only one not to have recorded anything at all before the band's success).

As both Jones and "Michael Blessing" were signed to ColPix, the same label that put out the Monkees' records, those tracks were made available on the bonus disc of the 2015 special edition of *The Monkees*, and so are part of the band's catalogue. For completeness' sake, I've decided to briefly cover the other singles by Nesmith and Dolenz here as well. I've also included a handful of tracks that are not part of the band's main discography.

David Jones

Davy Jones was, of all the Monkees, the one who was most well-known immediately prior to the Monkees TV show starting. While Micky Dolenz had been a child star, he had made few appearances on TV since *Circus Boy* had finished in the 1950s, and while he'd recorded a handful of tracks, none had seen release. Michael Nesmith had released a couple of singles to little success, and Peter Tork had been a jobbing folk singer.

Davy Jones, though, had appeared on the most successful episode of TV in US history. As a member of the Broadway cast of *Oliver!*. he had appeared on *The Ed Sullivan Show* on the day the Beatles first appeared, singing "I'd Do Anything" as a duet with his co-star Georgia Brown. After that appearance, he had been groomed for stardom, being signed by Ward Sylvester and appearing in episodes of several TV series.

He also recorded a truly odd debut solo album, *David Jones*, presumably produced in an attempt to emulate the success of Peter Noone of Herman's Hermits (who, like Davy Jones, was from Manchester but sang in a Mockney accent, and who had also appeared in *Coronation Street* before his pop career). This album consists mostly of old music-hall songs, much like those with which Noone was having some success in the US, and the plan seemed to be that it would sell entirely on the basis of Jones' face on the cover.

Certainly no-one can have thought much of the contents, which are fairly risible. The album barely made a ripple, and even after Jones' later stardom with the Monkees it sold hardly anything. It was out of print for most of the ensuing decades, until the Internet made it possible to re-release almost anything as a download, at which point several downloadable versions and CDs became available, all taken from needledrops of old vinyl copies rather than from the master tapes, which have long since been lost.

For the 2014 "Super Deluxe" edition of *The Monkees*, Andrew Sandoval and his team put together the best possible copy of the album from surviving vinyl copies, in both mono and stereo (except for the song "Dream Girl", which was never mixed in true stereo). The sound quality on that copy is almost indistinguishable from recordings taken from the master tapes, at least to my ears, and those are the versions I'll be using to talk about this album.

Various other CD releases are available, but this album is really for completists only. It was largely disowned by Jones himself, and it's very much a false start in his pop music career. Both with the Monkees, and in his later solo career, he would do some excellent work, but this shows few signs of his talents, and is best forgotten.

All lead vocals Davy Jones. Produced by Hank Levine.

What Are We Going to Do?

Writers: Hank Levine, Murray MacLeod, and Smokey Roberds

Very much in the style of the songs Jones had been performing in *Oliver!*, this is a bouncy singalong, written by the album's producer Hank Levine, with Jones backed by a guitar band plus a tinkly celeste. The most notable thing about this performance, perhaps, is the inconsistency of the accent in which Jones is singing – for the most part he's singing in the Mockney accent he would put on for most of his performances, but one can still hear the flat Manchester vowel in the word "love" at the end of each verse. That's more noticeable because Jones is singing that one word in a different range – it's the lowest note in the song, and while he sings the rest of the song in the rather nasal head voice he used when singing in his tenor range, he drops into his throat voice for that single note.

He also chooses to overenunciate his "t"s, presumably in an effort to accentuate his Englishness, rather than go for the softer mid-Atlantic "d" sound most singers would use when recording.

Arrangement-wise, this, like many of the other songs on the album, is modelled on Herman's Hermits' number one US hit "Mrs Brown You've Got a Lovely Daughter", which has the same tempo, same Manc-Mockney accent, and same muted guitar. Like much of the album, this is utterly unexceptional. Released as the first single from the album, it peaked at number 93 in the Hot 100 – the first chart entry for any of the Monkees.

Maybe It's Because I'm A Londoner

Writer: Hubert Gregg

A hit for Bud Flanagan (of Flanagan and Allen) in 1947, this
is one of the last of the music hall songs, having been written
in 1944 by Hubert Gregg. Gregg was a rather unusual figure,
who in his ninety-year life managed to be a film actor, radio
presenter, scriptwriter, and theatrical director.

Like the album's opening track, this is in the actual music hall
style (rather than what many pop music critics refer to as music hall, which has nothing to do with that style of music). But
while the song is still much loved in London, it's not a particularly good or even interesting one. Jones manages to keep
the Mockney accent up while singing, never letting his vowels
drift as he did in "What are we Going to Do?", although his
spoken interlude has a rather different accent, one presumably
designed to be comprehensible to US listeners.

Put Me Amongst The Girls

Writers: C.W. Murphy & Dan Lipton

This is a music-hall song originally published in 1907, and pop-
ularised by Billy Williams, one of the most prolific of Britain's
pre-World War I recording artists. It's a third song in a row
with the same plinkety-plink backing and Mockney vocals (the
muted guitar is back again), but at least there's a tiny bit of
charm in the song itself, which is a typical example of its type
– alternating sixteen-bar verses with different mildly comical
anecdotes, all of which lead up to the main character in the

verse requesting "put me amongst the girls", which is then expanded upon in a sixteen-bar chorus.

Jones changes the name of one of the characters in the song to that of his own father, Thomas Harry Jones, but otherwise there's nothing much to distinguish this.

Any Old Iron

Writers: Charles Collins, Fred E. Terry, and E.A. Sheppard

"Any Old Iron" is another old music-hall song (and one which some have claimed had hidden gay innuendo in it, although personally I think it's a bit of a stretch), and was first recorded in 1911, by Harry Champion. However, here the arrangement isn't the standard rinky-plink one copied from "Mrs Brown You've Got a Lovely Daughter" by Herman's Hermits. Instead, it's copied from Herman's Hermits' *other* 1965 US number one, their cover of the music hall song "I'm Henery the Eighth I Am".

Like "Any Old Iron", "Henery" was a signature song of Harry Champion, but Herman's Hermits reworked it into a beat group arrangement, with a rock guitar solo, and that arrangement is replicated near-perfectly here. A few songs in and it seems apparent that the people in charge at ColPix thought that Herman's Hermits were going to be a signal of the way the charts were going, and had decided to jump on that bandwagon. Sadly for all concerned, that bandwagon got no further.

Theme For A New Love

Writers: Hank Levine and Berdie Abrahams

A rather gloopy $\frac{12}{8}$ instrumental, somewhat in the style of the Beach Boys' "Summer Means New Love", with perhaps a little of "Lara's Theme" from *Dr Zhivago*. Over this, Davy talks about how you, yes you, teenage American girl, are the most lovely special person in the world, describing you in carefully generic terms that could apply to anyone.

It's the same kind of thing that Davy would later do so appallingly on "The Day We Fall In Love", and this is equally horrible.

It Ain't Me Babe

Writer: Bob Dylan

And in case they were wrong about Herman's Hermits being the wave of the future, here's a complete change in style, with a folk-rock version of the Dylan song. This version possibly owes something to the Turtles' hit single version, although it lacks that track's dynamics, but almost everyone was recording their own version of this song in 1965. Easily the best thing on the album, this is still not very good at all, though it does interestingly point the way forward to some of Boyce and Hart's more anti-romantic songs for the Monkees (most notably "I Wanna Be Free", which in its fast version shows the influence of Dylan very clearly).

Face up to It

Writers: Gerry Robinson and Roger Atkins

A rather unimpressive attempt at a stirring bolero[22] ballad, in the vein of Roy Orbison's "Running Scared" or Gerry and the Pacemakers' then-recent version of "Walk Hand in Hand", with a rather martial arrangement. Jones' voice is really unsuited to the material, which has a soaring melody line which requires more power on the higher notes – Jones gets weaker, rather than stronger, as he goes up in range, and gets completely overpowered by the strings and backing vocals.

Dream Girl

Writer: Van McCoy

The best of the original songs on the album, this song by Van McCoy, who later became famous with "The Hustle", was de-moed as a soul track in the style of singers like Arthur Alexander, but also has a smattering of Brill Building slickness to it – the verse melody could easily have been written by Neil Sedaka, while the middle eight with its harmonic twistiness sounds very like Carole King. Indeed, the song has some nice harmonic moments throughout – the use of a couple of out-of-key passing chords in the intro, and the change up to the VI on the line "tell me that you love me", are both nice little bits of craft that show a little more thought has gone into this than might at

---

[22]in the way in which that term is usually applied to popular music having some influence from Ravel's "Bolero", rather than in the meaning of an actual bolero rhythm

first be apparent – it's just slightly better crafted than it needs to be.

Jones' version ups the Brill Buildingness, and the result is something that sounds similar to many of Leslie Gore's then-recent hits, though also with a hint of some of the pre-Beatles teen-pop stars like Bobby Vee whose star had faded over the previous year or two. A pleasant enough pop trifle, this was released as a single but didn't chart. This is easily the highlight of the album, though given the rest of the album that's rather damning with faint praise.

Baby It's Me

Writer: Mark Anthony

"Mark Anthony" is actually a pseudonym for Tony Hatch, who wrote this song for Petula Clark. It was an unsuccessful single for her in 1963, but after her 1964 hit with "Downtown" it was included on the 1965 album of that name. Jones' version replicates Clark's version closely, so if you've ever wanted to hear Davy Jones sing a bouncy bit of froth that was a flop for Petula Clark, this track is the one for you. Otherwise it's better than some of the first few tracks on the album, but that's about all you can say about it.

My Dad

Writers: Barry Mann and Cynthia Weil

Mann and Weil have written some of the greatest songs ever, but this isn't one of them. Musically, it's a $\frac{12}{8}$ ballad, very much in the style of "Unchained Melody" or "Ebb Tide", both of which had been hits for the Righteous Brothers shortly before the recording of this album. As Mann and Weil wrote several songs for the Righteous Brothers (including their number ones "You've Lost That Lovin' Feelin'" and "(You're My) Soul and Inspiration"), it's possible that the song was originally intended for them. However, it's hard to see them deciding to sing schlock like this, with its lyrics about how special the singer's father was.

This Bouquet

Writers: Hank Levine, Murray MacLeod, and Smokey Roberds

And we end with the best of Hank Levine's three songwriting contributions to the album, although "best" is a relative term here. A bouncy piece of nothing, which one could easily imagine Neil Sedaka performing, but which has absolutely no distinguishing features, again except for Jones' Manc vowels slipping through an otherwise Mockney performance. A dull, uninspiring ending to a dull, uninspiring album.

Bonus tracks:

Take Me to Paradise

Writers: Toni Wine and Steve Venet

Co-written by Toni Wine, who would go on to sing in Don Kirshner's next manufactured group, the Archies, this was the B-side to "Dream Girl" single. This is an inoffensive pop ballad, with few distinguishing features, apart from some really tortured vowels from Jones.

The Girl From Chelsea

Writers: Gerry Goffin and Carole King

This is a non-album single, produced by David Gates, who would later write "Saturday's Child" for the Monkees (and later still would go on to fame as the leader of Bread). This is an interesting attempt to split the difference between the plinky-plonk music hall style of much of the *David Jones* album and current pop sounds – and of all the songs here, it's the one that's closest to sounding like Jones' Monkees work. The combination of Gates, Goffin, and King is a much more sympathetic one for Jones, and this is recognisably the same performer, appealing to the same audience, that we would later hear on "Daydream Believer" or "Forget That Girl".

Michael Nesmith and Micky Dolenz Singles

Michael Nesmith

Wanderin'

Writer: Michael Nesmith

A little country-folk ballad, performed solo by Nesmith on guitar (with what sounds like a second guitar overdubbed), which
he doesn't play very well. It's an early song, and he's not quite
got the hang of songwriting yet – there are some awkward moments where the lyric doesn't quite fit the melody – but there's
a certain endearing charm to it.

Well Well

Writer: Michael Nesmith

An attempt at a singalong folk song in the style of Pete Seeger,
who is a very strong influence on the song. Nesmith is multi-
tracked here on vocals, and the backing (acoustic guitar, banjo,

and some sort of thumped percussion) is presumably also him. This and the preceding track were released as a very limited run of singles, by what amounted to a vanity label.

Mike and John and Bill

How Can You Kiss Me?

Writer: Michael Nesmith

This is recognisably the same man who would make the early Monkees records. A folk-rock song in the style of the Byrds, with harmonised vocals, jangly guitars, and a drum break for a hook, this is very much in the same style as "You Told Me" or "Mary Mary", although not as polished. This is far from a great record, but it's a pleasant, listenable, one.

This and the following two tracks were produced by Chance Halladay.

Just a Little Love

Writer: Michael Nesmith

The B-side to "How Can You Kiss Me", later also released as an A-side in its own right, this seems to be an attempt to write in the style of John Lennon's songs on *Beatles For Sale*, with a similar poppified-Dylan feel to it. The middle eight, with its rising melody towards the end, is structured very similarly to several of Nesmith's Monkees-era middle eights, notably "The Girl I Knew Somewhere".

Curson Terrace

Writer: C. H. Whitman

An instrumental released as the B-side to a reissue of "Just A Little Love" put out under Nesmith's name after the Monkees became successful, this was credited to "Mike and Tony", and Nesmith has confirmed that it was definitely him, though not who "Tony" was.

It's quite surprising that it is Nesmith, though, because the main guitar riff here is very similar to "Last Train to Clarksville", which would otherwise suggest that it was put together by a producer to sound a little bit Monkees-ish. It's a stomping blues-inflected garage rocker with a Bo Diddley beat, and undistinguished but not unlistenable.

Michael Blessing

The New Recruit

Writers: Trad arr. Sam Ashe and Bob Krasnow

A recording of an old folk song more usually known as "The Willing Conscript", this was the first of the "Michael Blessing" singles, and was ColPix's attempt to "enter the protest field", at least according to their announcement to Billboard, in which they said the single would be released "by Lauren St. Davis". One must assume that that was a stage name for Nesmith, and was changed when the label realised what the initials spelled. Incidentally, that same Billboard announcement mentioned that ColPix were on the lookout for songs for two other signings, Hoyt Axton and David Jones...

I've been able to find out little about Sam Ashe, the co-producer of the Blessing sessions, but Bob Krasnow later went on to found Buddah and Blue Thumb, and to produce Captain Beefheart and Love among many others.

The track itself is the kind of thing a lot of labels were releasing in the early-mid sixties – a bit of genial anti-war singalong folk, with Nesmith singing from the point of view of a draftee who is pretending to be eager to learn to kill, and is asking ingenuous questions. The backing is very much in the same folk-rock vein as tracks like "Eve of Destruction", and Nesmith does a rather funny "well gol-lee" hick voice, but it's easy to see why the single wasn't a success.

As well as the deluxe box set version of *The Monkees*, this is also available on *Infinite Tuesday*, a compilation put together as a soundtrack for Nesmith's autobiography of the same name.

A Journey with Michael Blessing

Writers: Sam Ashe and Bob Krasnow

A $\frac{12}{8}$ bluesy guitar instrumental, with four or five separate guitar lines going on, presumably played by the session musicians who played on "The New Recruit", this was the B-side to that single, and it's unsure if Nesmith played on this at all (it was common practice at the time to put out instrumental filler by session musicians as the B-side to singles, to ensure that DJs would only play the A side).

Until it's Time for You to Go

Writer: Buffy Saint-Marie

A rather lovely recording of a song which singer/songwriter Buffy Saint-Marie had recorded earlier that year, and which later became a hit for, among others, Elvis Presley and Neil Diamond.

Backed by a harpsichord-driven arrangement (by Shorty Rogers, a great jazz musician who would later work as arranger on several Monkees sessions) played by the Wrecking Crew, Nesmith sings this song, from the perspective of a lover who knows the object of their affection won't be with them forever, but is accepting of it, in a much higher, more vulnerable, voice than he would normally use. One of the interesting things about these Blessing singles is just how varied Nesmith's vocal style is – he's clearly experimenting and finding his voice, but he also sounds remarkably good in each of the different voices he chooses to use. In this case, there's some hesitation in his phrasing that perhaps weakens the song, but his voice sounds beautiful.

What Seems to be the Trouble, Officer?

Writers: Bob Krasnow and "Michael Blessing"

And this is a case in point – Nesmith doing a dead-on impersonation of Bob Dylan, good enough that one might easily believe it was him. And this isn't an impression of the nasal Dylan most people think they can do, but rather of the husky-voiced Dylan of his eponymous first album. In particular, this is a parody of the spoken opening of "Baby Let Me Follow You Down", with Nesmith replacing Dylan's "I first heard this from Ric von Schmidt" with "I first heard this song from Andy Segovia... Andy never made it as a blues guitar player..."

Unfortunately, while Nesmith's impersonation is uncanny (and this is a far more cutting imitation of Dylan than similar songs like Simon and Garfunkel's "A Simple Desultory Philippic"), the humour of the song – a spoken monologue over acoustic guitar – is somewhat mean-spirited and sixth-form. Mockery of Dylan's pseudo-Bohemian image as being commercial and phoney might have sounded better coming from someone who hadn't been signed in a calculated move to get a piece of the same market. But still, it really is a spookily good imitation of Dylan.

Who Do You Love?

Writer: Elias McDaniel

And this is really, *really*, good. Unreleased until the deluxe box set version of *The Monkees*, this is a stomping cover of the Bo Diddley R&B classic, with Nesmith singing in the low end of his range, all the hesitance of "Until It's Time For You to Go" gone. There's a swagger and confidence here that's missing from everything he'd done previously, and it's utterly infectious – and Bob Krasnow (who would later produce Captain Beefheart, Ike and Tina Turner, and Earl Hooker) is far more suitable as a producer of blues-rock than the commercial folk-rock of the Blessing singles.

Much of Bo Diddley's original lyric is removed, in favour of instrumental psychedelic blues freakouts, and... honestly, and I say this as a connoisseur of 50s blues and R&B, this may be better than the original. The instrumental arrangement is more inventive, Nesmith's voice has more character... this deserves to be known as a garage-blues/psych classic, not hidden away as a bonus track on a limited edition box set.

Get Out Of My Life, Woman

Writer: Allen Toussaint

The other unreleased Blessing track is a cover of Lee Dorsey's then-recent soul hit. This track is spookily ahead of its time – it sounds a *lot* like the music the Monkees would be making a few years later, in their R&B period; but more than that, the particular combination of slick LA session musicians (presumably Wrecking Crew members, though they're not credited) playing a soul groove, with a deep, masculine, Southern country-inflected vocal sounds spookily like the sound Elvis Presley hit on in 1968, with records like "A Little Less Conversation" or "Guitar Man".

This isn't quite up to the standard of "Who Do You Love?", but it's head and shoulders ahead of the early Nesmith singles that actually got released.

Micky Dolenz

Don't Do It

Writer: Micky Dolenz

An insanely fun Dolenz track, recorded just before he was signed to be part of the Monkees, this is a 12-bar blues garage pop dance track that could easily have been a Boyce/Hart song from the first couple of Monkees albums – it's very much in the same vein as material like "Let's Dance On". The lyric is mostly based around a double entendre – asking the subject of the song "you do it with everybody you see, why won't you do it with me?", but with the "it" in question later revealed to be dancing, rather than anything else you might be imagining it to be.

Dolenz's vocal is excellent here – less restrained and more hysterical than anything he would do on the first few Monkees albums, and with an astonishing self-assurance to it.

Huff Puff

Writer: Gary Pipkin

Gary Pipkin, who wrote this song, had previously co-written "Puddin 'n' Tain (Ask Me Again and I'll Tell You the Same)" for the Alley Cats, and this is much the same kind of thing, a twelve-bar blues somewhat modelled on the Coasters' hits, with Dolenz singing "I'm gonna huff and puff and blow your house down/If you don't let me in I'm gonna get mad..." and with a middle eight based on "this little piggy went to market".

Dolenz's vocal is in a ridiculous cartoon voice which is probably all the song deserves. There's little of value here.

Odd Non-Album Tracks

There are three tracks that feature several of the Monkees but which have not yet been made available on any Monkees-related album. Two are from a Christmas single from 1976, released in the wake of the Dolenz, Jones, Boyce, and Hart album, while another is from a Peter Tork solo album, on which he got his former bandmates to guest.

Christmas is My Time of Year

Writers: Chip Douglas and Howard Kaylan

Lead vocalists: Micky Dolenz and Davy Jones

Other Monkees present: Peter Tork (vocals, other instruments?)

After the release of the *Dolenz, Jones, Boyce, and Hart* LP, Dolenz and Jones reunited with Peter Tork, and with the band's old producer Chip Douglas, for a single for Christmas 1976. Tork had guested at a handful of Dolenz, Jones, Boyce, and Hart shows and was just starting to get back into making music himself after several years out of the business (the next year he would make a solo appearance at CBGB's, which has been widely bootlegged).

The single was initially only released to fan club members, and was credited to the band members as individuals rather than to the group, but ten years later a limited public release (credited to "We Three Monkees") came out. The 1986 version was remixed by Chip Douglas (as was its B-side) and had the addition of fairly awful synth drums. That version appears on the 1988 compilation *Cool Yule vol 2*.

The track itself is a passable piece of Christmas pop, a remake of a song Douglas had originally produced for "Christmas Spirit", a band featuring Douglas, Volman and Kaylan of the Turtles, Linda Ronstadt, and Gram and Gene Parsons and Clarence White of the Byrds. Interpolating bits of "Joy to the World" and "Hark the Herald Angels Sing", and with sleighbells and other Christmasey sounds, it does a perfectly reasonable job of being a Christmas novelty single, though it's not a patch on the original.

Dolenz sings the first half of each verse, Jones the second half, and everyone joins in for the chorus. It's not what one would hope for from a reunion of four-fifths of the team that made *Headquarters* and *Pisces*, but it's pleasant enough for what it is.

White Christmas

Writer: Irving Berlin

Lead vocalist: Davy Jones

Other Monkees present: Unknown (none audible)

The B-side to the Christmas single, this is a pleasant enough country-flavoured run through of the Irving Berlin classic, with Jones on vocal backed by a strummed acoustic guitar, pedal steel, and (at the beginning and end of the song only) sleigh bells. Again, an unexceptional track, but not unpleasant.

Milkshake

Writer: Martin Briley

Lead vocalist: Peter Tork

Other Monkees present: Micky Dolenz and Michael Nesmith (vocals)

This track is from Tork's 1994 solo album *Stranger Things Have Happened*, and featured backing vocals from Dolenz and Nesmith – making this the first time that Nesmith had contributed to a Monkees-related recording since *The Monkees Present* and the first time that Nesmith and Tork had worked on the same track together since the *33 1/3 Revolutions Per Monkee* TV special.

A fun, funny, bit of New Wave pop written by session musician/songwriter Martin Briley, this is very much of a piece with Tork's contributions to *Pool It!* and *Justus* musically, while lyrically it's a comic story about a waitress seducing the protagonist (using the novel means of dropping gumbo onto his lap and cleaning it off) before her husband, the chef at the diner, comes out and attacks him, and he has to make a getaway.

Stranger Things Have Happened is, as a whole, probably Tork's best solo work (though a little bit dated with its early 90s production), and this is one of the better tracks on the album – it's certainly much more enjoyable than the vast majority of either *Pool It!* or *Justus*, and listening to it one finds oneself wishing that Tork had ever been put in charge of a Monkees album project in the way Jones and Nesmith were. This isn't the best record ever made or anything like that, but it's a nice, fun, track.

Acknowledgements

This book would not exist without the wonderful work done by Andrew Sandoval in researching and releasing Rhino's reissues of the Monkees' music. Sandoval also wrote the single most important book on the Monkees - *The Monkees: The Day-By-Day Story Of The '60s TV Pop Sensation* (referred to throughout this text as Sandoval). Without Sandoval's work, there would be so little information available about the band that doing a book like this would be a fool's errand. Anyone with any interest at all in the Monkees should buy his book immediately.

The other principal resources I've used to help me write this are http://monkeessessionography.tripod.com/, which goes further than Sandoval by detailing the band's work in the 1980s and 1990s, and Davy Jones' autobiography *They Made A Monkee Out Of Me*, as well as a plethora of web-based resources used to check odd facts and dates. But wherever any two sources disagree, I've taken Sandoval as being the most accurate.

Comedy website Some Of The Corpses Are Amusing's analysis of *Head* at http://sotcaa.org/head was invaluable for that section.

For this second edition, I've also made use of several books that came out more recently, notably Melanie Mitchell's excellent guide to the TV series, *Monkee Magic*, Bobby Hart's autobiography *Psychedelic Bubblegum* and Michael Nesmith's frustrating but fascinating autobiography *Infinite Tuesday*.

Tilt Araiza, Holly Matthies and Rob McCabe checked the original version of this book and made a number of useful suggestions.

Chris Browning, Gavin Robinson, Trevor DeMont, 'borntorockandroll', S. Barrios, prankster36, Anton Gully, Marc Burkhardt and Bobsy all provided feedback and encouragement when I posted early drafts of some chapters to my blog.

Psycho Jello, the Monkees fan site (http://psychojello. tumblr.com) was kind enough to publicly praise the early drafts as well.

My comic-blogging friends the at mindlessones.com have always provided me with support and encouragement in my writing.

Jonathan Calder encouraged me in writing this - and I still owe him a guest post on his blog, http://liberalengland. blogspot.com

Thanks should also go to all those who have encouraged me in my writing in the past, including, but not limited to, Bill Ritchie, Steve Hickey, Lawrence Burton, Simon Bucher-Jones, Stuart Douglas, Philip Purser-Hallard, Andrew Ducker, Andrew Rilstone, Gavin Burrows, Alex Wilcock, Richard Flowers, Wesley Osam, Debi Linton, Jennie Rigg, Mat Bowles, Dave Page, Sarah Lawrence, Susan Lang, Wendy Taylor, Damon Howell, Leighann Howell, Paul Magrs and my parents.

Since the first edition of the book, my love for the Monkees has been sustained in large part by some of the people I have come to know through the band's fandom, especially Meg Psycho Jello, the two bloggers who run the Naked Persimmon fan site, Omorka, Sarah Clarke, Melanie Mitchell, and Iain Lee.

This book would not exist without the support of my backers at http://patreon.com/andrewhickey, who at the time of writing are David Brown, James Brough, Aditya Bidakar, Ian Alexander-Barnes, Chad Nevett, the Wait What podcast, Chris Sawer, Robert Young, Scott McAllister, Andrew Ducker, DreadPikathulhu, Petri Kuivalainen, Reinder Dijkhuis, David H. Adler, Verity Allan, Phil Shaw, Richard Gadsden, Adam E, Al Ewing, Gavin Robinson, Emily Wright, socketwench, Jon Andrews, Shawn Kilburn, Dan Liebke, Milton, Richard Docherty, Niki Kools, Scurra, Laurie Penny, James, Evan Zuk, Matthew Rossi, Jo Coleman, Anonymouse, Tom Healey, Lawrence Radley, Omorka, Adam Prosser, Alexander Thomas, Richard, dm, HE Cavanagh, Peter Rice, Evan Harrison Cass, and Andrew Rilstone. I am grateful to each and every one of them.

This book was written and typeset in the Free Software text editing program LyX (http://lyx.org), so thanks go to the creators of that software, as well as to the creators of LATEX, and, ultimately, Donald Knuth, whose typesetting language TEX is the ultimate basis of all those programs. It was created on a machine running the Debian GNU/Linux distribution, so thanks to all the many thousands of people who gave their work freely to that system.

And finally, of course, thanks to Micky, David, Peter and Michael, without whom there would be nothing for this book to be about.

Index

Song Index

Made in the USA
Las Vegas, NV
11 April 2022

47293884R00217